IMPACTS AND RISK ASSESSMENT OF TECHNOLOGY FOR INTERNET SECURITY
Enabled Information Small-Medium Enterprises (TEISMES)

T0189235

Advances in Information Security

Sushil Jajodia

Consulting Editor
Center for Secure Information Systems
George Mason University
Fairfax, VA 22030-4444
email: jajodia@gmu.edu

The goals of the Springer International Series on ADVANCES IN INFORMATION SECURITY are, one, to establish the state of the art of, and set the course for future research in information security and, two, to serve as a central reference source for advanced and timely topics in information security research and development. The scope of this series includes all aspects of computer and network security and related areas such as fault tolerance and software assurance.

ADVANCES IN INFORMATION SECURITY aims to publish thorough and cohesive overviews of specific topics in information security, as well as works that are larger in scope or that contain more detailed background information than can be accommodated in shorter survey articles. The series also serves as a forum for topics that may not have reached a level of maturity to warrant a comprehensive textbook treatment.

Researchers, as well as developers, are encouraged to contact Professor Sushil Jajodia with ideas for books under this series.

Additional information about this series can be obtained from
http://www.springeronline.com

IMPACTS AND RISK ASSESSMENT OF TECHNOLOGY FOR INTERNET SECURITY
Enabled Information Small-Medium Enterprises (TEISMES)

by

Charles A. Shoniregun
University of East London, UK

 Springer

Charles A. Shoniregun
University of East London
School of Computing & Technology
Dagenham, Essex
RM8 2AS, UK

A C.I.P. Catalogue record for this book is available
from the Library of Congress.

**IMPACTS AND RISK ASSESSMENT OF TECHNOLOGY FOR
INTERNET SECURITY**
Enabled Information Small-Medium Enterprises (TEISMES)
by Charles A. Shoniregun

Advances in Information Security   Volume 17

ISBN 1-4614-9891-0   ISBN-10: 0-387-26334-9 (eBook)
ISBN 978-1-4614-9891-9   ISBN-13: 978-0-387-26334-2 (eBook)

9 8 7 6 5 4 3 2 1   SPIN 11363569, 11500285

springeronline.com

DEDICATIONS

To my Beauty Queen and my Angels

TABLE OF CONTENTS

LIST OF FIGURES

LIST OF TABLES

LIST OF CONTRIBUTORS AND ORGANISATIONS

Alex Logvynovskiy   e-Centre for Infonomics; London South Bank University
Sonny Nwankwo   University of East London, UK
Kasim Charhabagi   University of East London, UK
Harvey Freeman   Booz Allen Hamilton Inc.
Paul Smith   University of East London, UK
Mohammad Saad   University of the West of England
Ken Ife   The Technology Centre, UK
Jen-Yao   IBM T.J. Watson Research Center, USA
Liang-Jie Zhang   IBM T.J. Watson Research Center, USA
Vyacheslav Grebenyuk   Ukrainian Association for Distant Education, Ukraine
Patrick Hung   University of Ontario Institute of Technology, Canada
Ioannis Chochliouros   Hellenic Telecommunications Organisation SA, Greece
Max Stempfhuber   GESIS, Social Science Information Centre, Germany
Ziyang Duan   Reuters America, USA
Subhra Bose   Reuters America, USA
AT&T
Dell
Hewlett-Packard Labs
UK Department of Trade and Industry (DTI)
Microsoft Research
AOL
British Telecommunication
eBay
Lucent Technologies
Intrusion.com
Counterpane Internet Security Inc.
University of Massachusetts
CERT Coordination Centre
Computer Virus Consulting Ltd.
National Institutes of Standards and Technology
National Security Agency
Ernst & Young
Sun Microsystems, Inc.
Honeywell
Pricewatercooperhouse
VeriSign Inc.

PREFACE

This study investigates the impacts and risk assessment of technology-enabled information (TEI), which are engaged in the process of discovering the opportunities and challenges presented by TEI to the new form of small medium enterprises (SME) business transactions: Technology Enable Information Small Medium Enterprises (TEISME). Within the UK economy, the notion of TEISMEs is one that forms the focus for this research. Other technologies that enabled information are also discussed. For example electronic mail (e-mail), voice mail, facsimile machines (fax), teleconferencing, data conferencing, video conferencing, electronic data interchange (EDI), and mobile phone (WAP), which are geared towards ease of transferring information are investigated. The electronic marketplace itself can be described as an on-line location for buyers and sellers to meet and conduct their business and complete transactions.

This study identified ways of minimising the risk liability of TEISME business operations as a result of their dependences on TEI (Internet-eC). The rapid evolution and spread of information technology (IT) during the last few years is challenging SMEs, governments and the Internet security professionals to rethink the very nature of risk exposure. Parallel to this notion is the task of identifying: the technologies for Internet Security, the generic problems with network protocol layers, and key elements or threads that might be common to all TEISMEs business operations.

However, the study has revealed that there is an urgent need for a risk assessment model that can be applied to TEISME business operational risks. It has also been found that it is necessary for all TEISME to identify the products' (goods or services) suitability for Internet-eC. The suitability of any products that may be sold on the Internet-eC is just one factor that needs to be taken into account by TEISME. Many TEISMEs launch Internet-eC websites without thinking through what it will take and how the website will impact on their business operations. Without a solid business plan, regardless of whether the business has an 'e' in front of it or not, the TEISME have already prescribed their own downfall. Nevertheless, a trend is apparently beginning to emerge regarding which commodities sell well electronically and which do not. It appears that the sectors of travel, technology, literature and music are reaping the benefits of online retailing, whilst other sectors are missing out.

Furthermore, the success of the Internet-eC will also depend on a variety of factors independent of the Predictive Model of Internet-eC suitability, such as security and risk assessment of TEISME business operations. It has also been established that the weaknesses in the existing security risk assessment approaches have many delimiting factors, which are problematic in nature.

ACKNOWLEDGEMENTS

Many authors and researchers have produced an inordinately long list of acknowledgements. The list sometimes includes all their family names and friends, other authors, researchers, bookmaker and the milkman. I now know how they felt but only brevity prevents me from imitating these great people.

Thanks to my editor Susan Lagerstrom-Fife, publishing director Jennifer Evans and Rudiger Gebauer for their support. Indeed, those kind reminders and useful comments from Susan and Sharon are all appreciated.

A special thank you to a dear friend, Dr Alex Logvynovskiy of e-Center for Infonomics and London South Bank University, for his ever-ending contribution '—never mind, life always gives a chance'.

My sincere thanks to Professor Sonny Nwankwo '—It's a club', Professor Kasim Charhabagi '—You should be OK', Richard Bottoms '— I know the feelings' (East London Business School, University of East London), Dr Paul Smith '—Well done Charles', Dr Fadi Safieddine '— This is very good contribution' (School of Computing and Technology, University of East London), Dr Mohammad Saad (School of Operational Management, University of the West of England) and Dr Ken Ife (The Technology Centre).

I would also like to acknowledge my appreciation to the following organisations: AT&T, Dell, e-Center for Infonomics, HP, IBM, Microsoft Corp, AOL, British Telecommunications, UK Department of Trade and Industry (DTI), eBay, and Lucent Technologies.

And also special thank you, to all the TEISMEs who voluntarily participated in the survey questionnaire and the TEISMEs directors/managing directors who gave their time to be interviewed and participated in the case study observations. The results of all the survey questionnaire, interviews and case study observations became the cornerstone on which chapter 5 'Results' is based.

Undoubtedly, my reflection to past experiences both in the commercial sector and academia has help to bridge the gap in my understanding of the technology for Internet security and the nature of the problems encountered by TEISME within their business operations.

The time spent in writing this book has been particularly difficult on my family. My absence, irritability and frustration to carry on have often reached uncharted personal heights. Tangential thanks go to my beauty queen and my angels for all their support, of which even the most carefully chosen words cannot adequately represent.

My special appreciation to my mother, this book is a testimony of your lifetime belief, and to the memory of my father, sister, and grandmothers.

Chapter 1

RESEARCH OVERVIEW AND TECHNOLOGIES FOR INTERNET SECURITY

1.   INTRODUCTION

The purpose of this study is to identify the key impacts and risk assessment within the context of technology-enabled information (*TEI*), which are engaged in the process of discovering the opportunities and challenges presented by electronic data or information transfer to small medium enterprises (*SMEs*) business operations. The SMEs are facing dramatic changes brought about by 'information technology (IT) revolution'. Its magnitude does not seem to be any less than the industrial revolution at the start of twentieth century. The advances in information and communication technologies are the main drivers behind this evolution. Explosive popularity of the Internet as a business tool has created a new type of economy, which may be called 'TEI economy'. This emerging economy is bringing with it new forms of TEI inter-mediation, on-line businesses, virtual supply chains, rapidly changing *Internet-eC* technologies, increasing knowledge intensity, and unprecedented sensitivity of time-to-market by customers (Shoniregun, 2002b). Kalakota and Whinston (2001) argue that soon every business will be an electronic business. Customers are increasingly demanding more value, goods customised to their exact needs at less cost and as quickly as possible. To meet these demands, the new form of SMEs need to innovate and adopt new ways of creating value. This will require different enterprise architectures, different IT infrastructures and different ways of thinking about doing business. The transformation of business from old SMEs to a new, agile, electronic market and global business is not easy and requires a lot of thinking, planning and investment. Furthermore, there are some hidden factors that are slowing down the popularity of Internet-eC among consumers and the immediate progression of TEI implementation by other SMEs. Indeed, trust and risks in the Internet-eC will require time to evolve. A good example of history repeating itself is the example of ATM machines in the UK. These ubiquitous machines were implemented in the 1960's, but did not gain popularity until the 1980's (KPMG and EIM, 2000). So, too, will it take time for commerce over the Internet to be a normal everyday occurrence taking into account the publicity of all identified risk encountered by those SMEs who rely on TEI?

2.   RESEARCH RATIONALE

Why this focus? —The radical shift in the way people do business and the electronic transmission of sensitive data or information is essentially caused by the convergence of two technologies: computers and telecommunications. The work of Shannon and Weaver (1949) lay the groundwork for a variety of further research both in the communication theory and communication technology. The fact that one can use the Internet search browsers to explore and view, or for receiving and transmitting information is, by itself, an immense leap in the technology of information transmission that Shannon and Weaver were interested in since the late 40's (Ettlie, 2000; Shannon and Weaver, 1949). The era that we live in is being characterised as the Information Age. Since the 1940s the industrial manufacturing age has declined in importance and has been replaced by the Information Age where the majority of the workforce is involved in some form of information handling, processing and dissemination. The Information Age is often referred to as the post-industrial society (Elliot and Starkey, 2001). No technology symbolises our age better than the Internet. The resulting effect on SMEs is referred to as *MetaCapitalism* (Means and Schneider, 2000). With commercialisation of the Internet in the early 1990's and its rapid growth, Internet-eC has suddenly exploded into the scene. The Internet not only supports application-to-application (A2A) eC similar to the already known *EDI*, but also and especially, person-to-person (P2P), business to-business (B2B), and person-to-application (P2A) forms of Internet-eC. Through the Internet-eC, a wider market was opened to the new form of SMEs with worldwide reach and enormous commercial opportunities.

In 1996 Dan Farmer, one of the leading members of the Internet security community, analysed the number of Internet sites using a tool known as SATAN which reports on security vulnerabilities. He discovered that out of 2200 sites he accessed, 1700 were relatively easy to attack (77 per cent of the sites). This is a staggering figure; however, what makes it more staggering is the fact that Farmer chose sites which should have been neurotic about security, for example, sites owned by banks, government agencies, insurance companies and credit card companies (Ghosh and Swaminatha, 2001). It is not only a question of whether a site is technologically safe from fraudsters (Pinheiro, 2002), but also whether technology can protect us from fraudulent websites. To quantify and characterise the need for an Internet-eC assurance service, POLLARA, a research company, conducted a nation wide survey designed to assess the opinions, perceptions and concerns about commerce over the Internet. About 57% of Internet users who have been held back from conducting Internet-eC transaction say that they would be more likely to conduct online transactions if they were given some assurance about the security and privacy of their personal information and delivery of the right product. Nearly 70% of Internet users under the age of 35 responded that their Internet purchase would increase with these assurances (Tayler, 2001). Given the past record of information technology and its aversion to open discourse, it might take many decades of failure, deceit, and dishonesty, although few people will recognise or admit it 'for fear of being contradicted', or worse.

3. RESEARCH HYPOTHESIS

To identify ways of minimising the risk liability on the new form of SME business operations which depend only on TEI (Internet-eC). The following leading research questions have emerged and yet remain unanswered:

- What precisely constitutes TEI and SMEs?
- Is classification and taxonomy of TEISMEs possible?
- What are the Impacts of TEI on SME's business operations?
- What are the technologies for Internet security?
- What constitute the failure of the technologies for Internet security
- Is security an issue for TEISMEs business operations?
- Is there any Risk Assessment Model that can be use to assess the possible risk incurred by TEISMEs on their reliance on TEI?

The hypotheses have been formulated based on the above questions and literature review (which includes ongoing access to on-line resources). Special consideration has been given to the null hypothesis (see Table 5–19). A null hypothesis may be either accepted or rejected. If rejected, it does not give conclusive prove that the null hypothesis is valid but rather there is no enough evidence to reject the emerging hypothesis.

Hypothesis 1:
- Null hypothesis (H_0^1): *TEISMEs* are complementary to, but not in direct competition with SME;

- Alternative (H_A^1): TEISMEs are complementary to and in direct competition with SME.

Hypothesis 2:
- Null hypothesis (H_0^2): Absolute security is unattainable on TEISMEs business operations;
- Alternative (H_A^2): Absolute security is attainable on TEISMEs business operations.

Hypothesis 3:
- Null hypothesis (H_0^3): Risk assessment is unattainable on TEISMEs business operations;
- Alternative (H_A^3): Risk assessment is attainable on TEISMEs business operations.

As the popularity of the Internet-eC grows, security issues become one of the most challenging topics for all Technology-Enabled Information Small Medium Enterprises (TEISMEs) and also users. Many SMEs wish to conduct cost effective on-line business through Internet-eC, despite the risk of system corruption, fraud, theft and viruses. This fact points to the need for enhancing security. The legal and privacy issues remain unsettled and are hotly debated in many forums. The Electronic Communications Privacy Act of 1986 is the main law governing privacy on the Internet today. Of course, this law was enacted before the general public began its wide use of the Internet. Ethical issues are significant in the area of on-line privacy because laws have not kept pace with the growth of the Internet-eC and the Web. The privacy of personal behaviour that may be revealed by websites collecting information about visitors' page-viewing habits, product selections, and demographic information is significant. Differences in culture throughout the world have resulted in different expectations about privacy in Internet-eC.

In Europe, most people expect that information they provide to a commercial website will be used only for the purpose for which it was collected. Many European countries have laws that prohibit companies from exchanging consumer data without the express consent of the consumer. In 1998, the European Union adopted a Directive on the Protection of Personal Data. This directive codifies the constitutional rights to privacy that exist in most European countries and applies it to all Internet activities. In addition, it prevents businesses from exporting personal data outside the European Union unless the data will continue to be protected in accordance with the directive. Although Kalakota and Whinston (2001) argue that customers are increasingly demanding more value, goods customised to their exact needs, at less cost, and as quickly as possible. To meet these demands, enterprises need to innovate new ways of creating value and will require different enterprise architectures, different IT infrastructures and different way of thinking about doing business. However, the research has proved that the consumers are still very much concerned about transaction integrity, control, authorisation and confidentiality of online shopping. Indeed, trust needs to be preceded by strong and effective interpersonal skills which constitute the pivotal foundations for effective relationships (Saad *et al.*, 1999), but the concern over security has resulted in many UK TEISMEs offering their electronic services over private, dial-up propriety networks, which are perceived as more secure and trustworthy than the open nature of the Internet; still problems do arise which will trigger needs to protect the TEISMEs business operations risk. Many businesses admitted that security was a major concern during the development of their Internet service(s). In turn the society is adopting digital certificates to verify third party, together with two passwords, but what if things do go wrong, who is going to carry the 'vicarious liability' of the TEISMEs business operational risks.

4. CONCEPTUAL RESEARCH CONTEXT

The past decade has seen an explosion in the use of Information and Communication Technologies (ICT) – ICT are being used more than ever to position businesses within their market place in order to outperform their rivals and achieve competitive success. The evolution of technology, our understanding of how to use it, and the comfort with doing business on electronic channels using TEI have changed the rules for business success developed by early pioneers. There is no single uniformly acceptable definition of SMEs, but within this research the EU definition has been adopted (by and large, the definition of TEISME will be within the context of existing definition of SME).

The Internet is a worldwide collection of connected computer networks that are accessible by individual variety of ways using a particular set of communication protocol to communicate, know as Transmission Control Protocol/ Internet Protocol (TCP/IP). Today millions of end systems use the Internet regardless of national or geographic boundaries or time (Isern, 2002). However, along all its advantages the Internet is not fee from risks and cyber criminalities as in the real world. The main goods on the Internet are valuable information which can be lost eavesdropped, manipulated or misuse and the computer systems which can be corrupted. The Internet is in general an adversary environment where attacks can be quick easy, inexpensive and may be hard to pervert, detect or trace. The consequences are however, drastic in terms of time and money. In general, it is difficult to ensure the main security goals regarding confidentiality, integrity and availability. There are many reason for today security risks in the Internet, the Internet was designed to be an open and distributed environment without any central instance controlling the communication among the users and mutual mistrust was not primary concern. The Internet is a complex and dynamic environment in terms of both topology and emerging technology. Security measures applied to small well-defined networks cannot work effectively. The lack of adequate knowledge and understanding of software and security engineering leads to security vulnerabilities, e.g. by inappropriate programming, getting even worse under deadline pressure and rush-to-market issues. Some solution may be effective today, but as technology changes, new risks and challenges appear. Moreover, different solutions must be combined to be effective against, different types of attacks, and the security of the system must be constantly monitored (Larochelle, 2001). The development and expansion of the Internet has created innumerable new opportunities for personal interaction and entrepreneurial ventures. Not only have the costs of communication fallen considerably, but also perhaps even more importantly, the sphere of potential trading partners has expanded dramatically creating immense new gains from exchange. Critical to advances in ICT is the existence and development of Internet security. With the risk of being a victim fraudulent act, information theft, and viruses and security is critical because it provides users an environment in which they can feel comfortable engaging in activities on the Internet.

4.1 Technology Enabled Information (TEI): What is TEI?

In the pursuance of what constitutes 'Technology-Enabled Information' (TEI), Dewan *et al.* (1998) studied a range of case studies and statistical analyses, which revealed that investment in ICT, where this is accompanied by appropriate changes in business processes, could bring high rates of return on TEI. The TEI within the context of this book refers to Internet-eC, but other TEI are briefly discussed as follows (Shoniregun, 2003b; Shoniregun *et al.*, 2004d):

- *E-mail:* The e-mail is one of the simplest and most widely used of the Internet and on-line services by Internet-eC businesses for sending and receiving messages. It provides a reliable, standard means of communication between different organisations. Many organisations and work groups depend on e-mail packages and their wide and local area networks for electronic mail. Similarly, many e-mail packages can route messages to multiple end users, based on pre-defined mailing lists, and provide password security, automatic message forwarding, and remote user access.
- *Voice mail:* The voice mail is for storing and forwarding voice messages. The technology is very valuable to companies for sending and receiving or-

ders outside office hours. This is an important tool for businesses to bridge the gap, where there is a time difference.

- *Facsimile machine (FAX):* The fax digitises and transmits documents, either by text or graphics, over telephone lines, which are transmitted over a network and reproduced in hard copy by a receiving fax within seconds/ minutes. The facsimile allows organisations to transmit important working documents between companies and individuals.
- *Teleconferencing:* Teleconferencing enables an electronic meeting system (EMS) to take place, which allows a group of people to hold meetings at the same time at different venues all over the world, or in the same building, utilising electronic mail group communication software such as video and audio systems. This facility saves businesses a lot of money in travelling costs and time for staff attending meetings away from their normal work locations.
- *Data conferencing:* The data conferencing users at distant locations are able to edit and modify data files such as word-processed documents and spread sheets.
- *Video conferencing:* The video conferencing allows participant at different locations to speak with each other and exchange information with the aid of a video screen.
- *Electronic Data Interchange (EDI):* EDI provides a standardised system for coding trade transactions so that different computer systems can communicate directly with one another without the need for printed orders and invoices, thereby eliminating all the delays and errors associated with paper handling. Large supermarket chains, for transactions, commonly use this technology with their suppliers and it is reported to reduce Internet-eC transaction costs. Transactions are automatically transmitted from one information system to another via a telecommunication network, thus eliminating the printing and handling of papers at one end and inputting of data at the other end. According to Loudon and Loudon (1999), EDI as enabling technology provides networked-based capabilities for communication, coordination, and speed for the flow of purchase and sale transactions.
- *Mobile phone and Wireless Application Protocol (WAP):* The WAP designed is specifically to deliver web information to mobile phones, which enabled users to access, the Internet. This is done by translating Internet information in to a format which can be displayed within the constraints of a mobile device (Shoniregun, 2002a). However, the mobile phone is not only appealing, but also necessary for m-commerce. In the meantime, there are too many systems within a system, and the mobile phone is increasingly enhancing other technologies, with huge competition among network providers and mobile phone manufacturers (Shoniregun *et al.*, 2004a).

All the above technologies are geared towards ease of transferring information and possible long-term cost effective SMEs business operations. The definition of TEI is proposed as follows:

'TEI is the combination of theoretical and practical knowledge, skills and artefacts that can be used to develop products and services as well as their production and the deliverability of services using any forms of communication technologies based on the fundamental principle of EDI (electronic data interchange), which includes software and hardware that embody "SMEs" business operations'.

4.2 The impact of SME definition on the 'Micro' or 'Dot com': Why SMEs?

The Bolton Committee (1971) definition will be appropriate to identify the size, structure and the likely turnover of SME businesses. The definition used by the Bolton Committee is shown in Table 1–1. Since the Bolton classification of SME does not include the 'Self-employed' or 'Sole Traders', and the 'Micro' or 'Dot com' small businesses that spring out to take advantage of the Internet-eC and popularity. It is very important now, rather than later, to include Self-employed/Sole traders, and the 'Dot com' businesses into the definition of small businesses.

The European Commission has adopted a recommendation concerning the definition of Self-employed or Sole-traders and the 'Micro' or 'Dot com' businesses, which now provides a clear global framework for all the measures directed towards small enterprises. A Self-employed or Sole traders consist of one employee, who is likely to be the business owner(s) with a turnover of £5,000 to £100,000. The adopted definition of 'Dot com' or 'Micro' businesses states that 1 to 9 employees, which may include the owner(s) and maximum turnover of £100, 000 or more.

The Section 248 of the UK Companies Act of 1985 states that a company is "small" if it satisfies at least two of the following criteria: has turnover of not more than £2.8 million; has a balance sheet total of not more than £1.4 million; has not more than 250 employees. On the other hand a medium sized company must satisfy at least two of the following criteria: has a turnover of not more than £11.2 million; has a balance sheet total of not more than £5.6 million; is made up of not more than 250 employees. The definition by both the Bolton Committee and the Companies Act of 1985 has been overruled by European Union defined small and medium enterprises. The European Union defined small and medium enterprises as a 'legally independent company with no more than 500 employees'. SME is a convenient term for segmenting businesses and other organisations that are between '*small office-home office*'

Table 1–1. Bolton Committee classification of small firm or SME

Sector	Definition
Manufacturing	200 employees or less
Construction	25 employees or less
Mining and quarrying	
Retailing	
Miscellaneous	Turnover of £50, 000 or less
Services	
Motor trades	Turnover of £100, 000 or less
Wholesale trades	Turnover of £200, 000 or less
Road transport	Five vehicles or less
Catering	All excluding multiples and Brewery-managed houses

(*SOHO*) size and the larger enterprise. European Union recognised that it may be more appropriate to define size by the number of employees in some sectors, but more appropriate to use turnover in others (see Table 1–2 for detailed definition of SMEs), (DTI, 2002a).

According to the European Commission, SMEs are the cornerstone of Europe's competitive position and job creation. They form a dynamic and heterogeneous community, which is confronted by many challenges. These include increased competition resulting from the completion of the European internal market and the growing demands of larger companies for which they often work as sub-contractors. To meet those challenges and to remain competitive, SMEs need constantly to innovate. Among other things, this means developing new technologies in-house or gaining access to them. Besides this, many SMEs try to internationalise in search of new markets and business opportunities (Ettlie, 2000). SMEs are developed in a context where search and selection of information is affected by time and resource limitations and the risk-bearing capacity of such firms are also limited (La Rovere *et al.,* 2004). The following are facts and figures of current state of SMEs in the UK (MacInnes, 2003):

- The number of business enterprises in the UK at the start of 2002 was estimated 3.8m, an increase of 1.4 per cent on the start of 2001.
- Almost all of these enterprises (99.1 per cent) were small (0 to 49 employees). Only 27,000 were medium-sized (50 to 249 employees) and 7,000 were large (250 or more employees).
- At the start of 2002, SMEs accounted for more than half of the business turnover and employment in the UK.
- The estimated combined turnover of the 3.8m business enterprises was £2.2trn. Small enterprises accounted for 37 per cent and medium-sized enterprises accounted for 15 per cent.

Table 1–2. EU Definition of SME

Criterion	Micro	Small	Medium
Max number of employees	9	49	249
Max annual turnover	–	€7m	€40m
Max annual balance sheet total	–	€5m	€27m
Max % owned by one, jointly by several enterprise(s) not satisfying the same criteria	–	25%	25%

*   IDC estimates size of the total IT spending in the UK SME market (for companies with 1–999 employees) is approximately $33bn (£20.6bn) in 2003.
*   DataMonitor estimates IT spending by UK firms of less than 500 employees will amount to around $19bn in 2003.

The SMEs, and especially those in the more traditional sectors, are generally unaware of the possibilities that innovation offers in terms of enhanced performance and enhanced prospects for survival (Warwick, 2000). This lack of awareness about the potential benefits of innovation is not the only obstacle to the diffusion of innovation among SMEs (Lahorgue and Cunha, 2004). Several authors suggest that SMEs have a new role in capitalism, now that productivity gains are no longer based only on scale and specialisation economies. However, isolated SMEs may not have the necessary capabilities to compete in the new global economy (La Rovere *et al.*, 2004).

4.3   What is TEISME?

TEISMEs are SMEs that provides services based on 80% electronic business operation which involves the transferring of sensitive and non sensitive data or information and 20% of human interaction, within their normal course of business operations. By the definition, the amalgamation of TEI and SMEs has given birth to TEISMEs (see Figure 1–1).

However, there is no doubt that the trends of TEISMEs are everywhere, and their combined share of the economy is growing. Since 1998, awareness of the importance of harnessing information and communications technologies in business has increased dramatically. The number of smaller businesses in the UK that are connected to the Internet has grown significantly, and evidence from many studies suggests that penetration of digital technologies into businesses in the UK is increasing, and many SMEs with less than 100 employees, are now adopting TEI in their business operations. According to a recently published report from the UK Office of Telecommunications (Oftel), 92% of medium businesses and 62% of small businesses had Internet access. Oftel also reports that most small businesses (78%) were accessing the Internet with

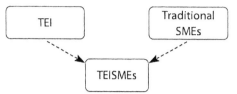

Figure 1–1. Amalgamation of TEI and SMEs

Public Switch Telephone Networks (PSTN) or dial-up services. The method of Internet connectivity was not as concentrated in one format among medium businesses—Integrated Services Digital Network (ISDN) connections were used by 43%, and 37% used PSTN or dial-up services (Oftel, 2002). Oracle's 2becom.com, which went live in March 2000, claims to be the first full-service for the on-line marketplace in European Internet-eC start-ups and aims to help SMEs progress more quickly from idea to an initial public offering, or sale. 2becom.com offer links to venture capitalists, legal counsel, accountancy, recruitment, and marketing – all for free (Da Costa, 2000; DTI, 2001).

> "The Internet changes everything"
> —Bill Gates (President Microsoft, 1999)

According to Pegasus Research International survey March 2003, revealed that the Internet access will take Europe by storm, Internet usage is quickly ramping up. From an estimated 32 million users last year, Internet users are expected to grow fourfold over the next four years. By the end of 2003, roughly 130 million people will eSurfing the web in Europe. Furthermore, with an estimated 390 million people living in Europe, this translates to a penetration of roughly 32% and the e-Envoy estimated 1 billion users would have access to the Internet by 2004.

A survey of SMEs businesses with fewer than 100 employees, carried out by the Cyber Dialogue in June 2001, revealed the following benefits accruing to SMEs with Internet-eC websites: 42% improved customer service, 42% expanded business territory, 41% kept up with the competition, 35% increased sales leads, 29% lowered marketing costs, 25% increased off-line sales, and 20% increased on-line sales (PRI, 2003; E-Enovy, 2000; Ofcom, 2004). The SMEs business operations has changed so much in terms of overall Internet usage (see Figure 1–2 and chapter 2). There are a number of benefits that promote the use of Internet among TEISMEs and also there are huge implications for the TEISME in that it opens businesses up to the worldwide market. Using the Internet-eC allows business operations to be 24 hours a day. Also there are many benefits in terms of costs, compared with a retail outlet or a new office, setting up Internet-eC will be integrated straight into the infrastructure with

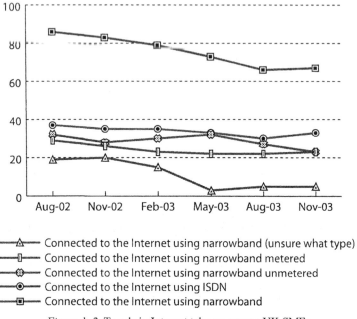

Figure 1–2. Trends in Internet take-up among UK SMEs

very little overheads or outlay. The TEISMEs business processes are less reliant on printed materials, customer service, and communication is fast and also the pricing and the contents of material published online is flexible. Despite all the advantages using the Internet-eC there also have been many concerns, which have stemmed from this new form of business and many incidents where security has failed and to assessed the risk occurrences has been a major problem, not to think of assessing the insurance claims.

5.   TEISMES BUSINESS OPERATIONAL RISKS

A preliminary interview, which was conducted within 3 large UK Insurance Brokers, shows clear indication that the risks involved in TEISMEs business operations are not currently insured. As with any other area of risk management, businesses can choose to accept IT security risk, mitigate them or transfer them using insurance cover. Unfortunately, for all UK TEISMEs business operations, risk transfer is no longer an option. Increasingly, insurance companies are tightening their general policies to exclude the rising cost of insurance payouts in the light of high profile IT-related incidents (DTI, 2002b).

Although some long for the days when the Internet was used strictly for research and collaboration, the Internet must be recognised for its critical role in business today. As in any other means of business, it cannot be assumed all the players will abide by a code of moral conduct. The mere fact that business is being performed online over an insecure medium is enough to entice criminal activity to the Internet. Security solutions are available to businesses that are not afraid to invest in the security of their networks, deploying potential solutions can prove to be an expensive task and result in tighter control of the network and reduced flexibility.

The rapid evolution and the spread of TEI during the last few years is challenging both SMEs and insurance companies to rethink the very nature of risk —and how TEISMEs business operations can be insured at present time. However, no insurance companies are willing to insure such business operations in the UK, due to in availability of dynamic risk assessment model. One painful aspect of this has been that yesterday's strategic coup may be today's high-overhead, inefficient liability —outperformed by those 'fast followers' that improved on the original design and took advantage of the latest technologies. The advances in information and communication technologies (ICTs) are among the defining technological transformations of the 21st century TEISMEs set-up.

However, despite all the hype of getting their products and services online, TEISMEs have been faced with an even bigger problem, 'the threat of Internet security', which is one of the main barriers to Internet-eC. The original Internet was designed for research not Internet-eC. As such, it operated in a single domain of 'trust'. While provisions were made to allow remote users to globally access critical files on computers worldwide, security generally relied on users' mutual respect and honour, as well as their knowledge of conduct considered appropriate for interacting on the network. Like any other distribution channel, the TEISMEs business operations pose a unique set of security issues, which must be addressed at the outset to minimise risk. Since TEISMEs business operations have been growing over the Internet, the security of information and monetary transactions has been a major point of uneasiness for many who are considering joining this new modality of buying and selling. The Internet-eC lacks security and reliability arising from the issues of a 'completely trustworthy relationship', among trading partners. Customers will submit information via the web only if they are confident that their personal information, e.g. credit card numbers, financial data is secure. They are vulnerable to not knowing what the receiver might do with the information they have access to. They know there is a possibility that information could be used in many ways, which take advantage of them or the TEISME (Shoniregun, 2003a).

6.   TECHNOLOGY FOR INTERNET SECURITY

The Internet is basically insecure channel for sending messages. When a message is sent from one Internet site to another, the message (or packet) is routed to the through a number of intermediates sites before reaching its destination. And unlikely the voice circuits that carry out conversations, it fixed path is not established for all messages passed between the message on originator and it recipients. Dynamic routing algorithms can alter the flow of the packets through the Internet depending on the traffic conditions between the many links that route the message to its destination. The intermediaries that transfer packets from link to link are generally unknown to the source and sink in a transmission (though they can be traced). Any surreptitious intermediary can intercept, read, destroy, or modify an Internet packet that is passed through its interface. Whether absolute security is unattainable or not, the major initiative is to ensure that each of the following is addressed adequately:

*   *Authentication*;
*   *Access control*;
*   *Integrity*; and
*   *Confidentiality*.

The Internet uses simple mail transfer protocol (SMTP) to transmit electronic mail and most business transactions. These have as much privacy as a postcard and travel over insecure, 'untrusted' networks. Anyone anywhere can intercept and access the information. Therefore, it is easy to forge e-mail or use another person's name. Theft of identity is becoming the nation's leading incidence of fraud (Desmarais, 2000). The first objective in improving security is to control physical access by limiting it to authorised individuals. Most applications nowadays rely on passwords, cards, personal identification numbers and keys to access restricted information or confidential files. The aims of providing security are to protect all aspects of the computer systems: hardware, software, data, confidentiality, computer environment and the Internet. To produce a secure system, the threats must be classified first. The following categories of security threats are encountered by TEISMEs:

*   *Physical threats* (theft, vandalism, fire, war, earthquakes)
*   *Accidental error* (programmer error, user/operator error)
*   *Unauthorised access* (breaking into the system remotely/directly, access to data and output)
*   *Malicious misuse* (virus programs, file infectors, system and master boot-record infectors, macro viruses, worms, Trojan horses)
*   *Users* (destroying files, data corruption) and

• *Computer fraud* (modification of programs).

All of the above categories of security threat are of major concern to financial institutions business communities, the designers of networks and to society in general. A review of security control measures suggests that although the argument that 'absolute security is unattainable' is not disputed, security risks can be minimised by putting in place appropriate security control measures. The threats for both internal and external can be addressed through a powerful combination of security technologies, including encryption is, authentication, firewalls, and intrusion detection systems. The security of business transactions includes authenticating business transactions, controlling access to resources such as web pages for registered or selected users, encrypt in publications, and ensuring the privacy and effectiveness of transactions. The following are among the most widely used technologies for Internet security, which are currently used by TEISMEs as a measure for securing their business operations:

6.1   Cryptography

The study of encryption and decryption is called cryptography. The enormous advances in network technology have resulted in an amazing potential for changing the way people communicate and do business over the Internet. However, for transmitting confidential data, the cost effectiveness and globalisim provided by the Internet are dismissed by the main advantage of public networks; security risks, the significantly increasing growth in confidential data traffic over the Internet makes the security issue a fundamental problem. Consequently applications such as electronic banking, electronic commerce, and vital private networks require an efficient and cost effective way to address the security threats over public networks. Cryptography is the fundamental component for securing the Internet transactions. There are three basic cryptography methods:

i. *Symmetric key* encryption is created when their power at the least to users who want to send message in a secure communication. All the users have the same secret key to encode, and decode the message.
ii. *Asymmetric key* encryption is a public key, which have two keys is values namely private and public keys. These keys are used to encrypt or the crypt in message, which is sent from a sender to a recipient. This method enabled TEISMEs to resolve problems of in secure transmission, but not always guarantee.
iii. *One-way hash function* changes message of text of any length into a fixed string of digits. The message is used as an import to a hash function for producing a hash message, message fingerprint or message digest. In other

words, there would be more than one input message that could produce a given hash value.

Furthermore, cryptographic algorithms impose tremendous processing power demands that can be a bottleneck in the high-speed networks. The implementation of cryptographic algorithms must achieve high processing rate to fully utilise the available network bandwidth. To follow the rapid changes in algorithms and standards, a cryptographic implementation must also support different algorithms and be upgraded in field. Otherwise, interoperability among different systems is prohibited and upgrades results in excessive cost. The ultimate solutions for problem would be an adaptive Digital Certificates that can provide flexibility with hardware performance.

6.1.1   Digital certificates

The digital certificates are electronic identification cards that establish an individual's credentials when doing business on the Internet. They are similar to a watermark on a bank note. They are used to verify that the author of a message is both authentic and that the message has not been tampered with. Anyone can send an encrypted message or verify a signed message, but only someone in possession of the correct private key can decrypt or sign a message (Hawkins, *et al.*, 2000). Financial transactions over the Internet normally use Secure Sockets Layer (SSL) and Secure Electronic Transactions (SET). SSL defines an interface in which a client and a server can perform data encryption, assure message integrity, validate user authentication and support digital certification. RSA Data Security have developed SSLv3 protocol for Java applications for use in banking, financial services, web publishing and customer Internet-eC. While SSL provides encryption for transmitting credit-card numbers on the Internet, SET goes further using digital certificates to verify the identities of both the customer and the merchant. The customer selects the credit card he/she wants to use from an on-screen 'wallet'. The wallet resides on their PC hard drive, which has a graphic representation of each type of card. After selection, the order information goes to the merchant, BUT the credit card data will go to the participating financial institution for verification. The merchant does not receive actual credit card numbers, only authorisation, so that credit card numbers are not floating around on 'untrusted' networks like the Internet. The Bank of America and Lawrence Livermore National Laboratory discovered that by using Financial EDI, that they could transmit sensitive information securely and reliably over the Internet. Their results confirm that the Internet has the capability of transmitting crucial data, e.g. payment instructions accurately, even with current security measures. The Open Financial Exchange (OFX) is also working on developing online financial standards and solutions. It is focusing on the integration of XML into the client and server, enabling anyone with a PC and web browser to engage in Internet-eC. The Financial Services Technology Consortium is also creating an electronic messaging format. It is focusing on XML and intends to make it the standard for electronic cheque processing via the Internet (Desmarais, 2000). Similarly a decryption requires a decryption key. A key is a seemingly random string of bits. The key length as a number of bits depends on the particular cryptosystem. An obvious use of cryptosystem is to provide confidentiality. The plain text represents unprotected sensitive data. The corresponding cipher text may be transmitted in untrusted environments because, if the cryptosystem is a good one, it will be infeasible for anyone to reduce the plain text from the cipher text without knowing the decryption key. Cryptosystems also have uses other than confidentiality. There are two basic types of cryptosystems; symmetric systems, which are sometimes called private keys or secret key systems and public key system, which are sometimes called asymmetric systems. These have distinct characteristics and are used in different and are used in different ways to provide security services (Net Figures, 2001).

The cryptographic techniques such as Key Management and Digital Signatures are important building blocks in the implementation of all the security services. The most basic building block is called a cryptosystem or encryption algorithm. A cryptosystem defines a pair of data transformation called encryption and decryption. Encryption is applied to data, known as plain text that directly represents information such as the words or numbers constituting a message. Encryption transforms the plain text data into unintelligent data called cipher text, results in the regeneration of the original plain text. An encryption transformation has two inputs:

$$\text{plain text} \otimes \text{independent data value} = \text{encryption key}$$

The data encryption scrambles plain text using an encryption algorithm into an incomprehensible cipher text which is decrypted and transferred into a plain text. It is the most basic form of e-Security implementation, and it is applicable mainly for low value information transactions, such as e-mail inquiries.

6.1.2   Key management

The key management acts as a 'key' to access encrypted data. The sender and receiver of a message know and use the same secret key: the sender uses the key to encrypt the message and the receiver uses the same secret key to decrypt the message, known as secret-key or symmetric cryptography. Public Key Infrastructure (PKI) has been around since 1976 when Whitfield Diffie and Martin Hellman first introduced it in order to solve the key management problem. Individual users are issued digital certificates that accompany transactions. Businesses use this as confirmation of the user activity on their websites. The Diffie and Hellman's (1976) system gives each person a public key and a private key. The public key is published and the private key is kept secret, therefore the need for the sender and the receiver to share secret information is eliminated; all communication involves only the public keys, and no private key is transmitted or shared. Messages can be sent using the public information, but only decrypted with the private key. It can also be used for authentication (digital signatures) and other techniques. The secret key cryptography is referred to as symmetric cryptography. It is a 56-bit key, made up of 0's and 1's, dealing with encryption and authentication. Banks tend to use this method of encryption (Desmarais, 2000; Kelly, 2001).

6.1.3 Digital signature

The digital signature is used to check the integrity and authentication of message. This technique was developed to ensure that online businesses know their customers via the use of third-party agents whose role is to issue and manage digital signatures. A message digest is generated using a one-way harsh function. The message digest is unique to a practical message or transaction. The digest is encrypted with the sender's private key, and appended to the original message. On reception of the message with the digital signature, the receiver knows who send the message if the digital signature can be successfully decrypted using the sender's key. However, impersonation is a big concern for TEISMEs business operations.

6.1.4   Weaknesses of cryptography

The cryptography limitations are less recognised, and it is often oversold as the solution to all Internet security problems or to threats that it does not address. For example, back in 1995 the headline of Jim Warren's op-ed piece in the San Jose Mercury News 'encryption could stop computer hackers'. Unfortunately, encryption offers no such thing. It does not protect against many common methods of attack, such as attacks on hardware, and those that exploit bad default settings or vulnerabilities in network protocols or software. Moreover, the protection provided by encryption can be illusory. If the system where encryption is performed can be penetrated, then the intruder may be able to access plain text directly from the stored files or the contents. The intruder may even modify network protocol, application software, or encryption programs in order to get access to encryption key files or plain text data or to subvert the encryption process. For example, Pretty Good Privacy (PGP), could be replaced with a Trojan Horse that appears to behave like PGP, bought creates a secret file of the users key for later transmission to the program's owner. Information security requires much more than just encryption. For example, Internet Protocol Security (IPSec), key management, secure electronic transaction (SET), SSL, firewall, vulnerability scanning or intrusion and detection, address verification system, card security code (CNC) and 'chip and pin', Kerberos, and Biometrics are other technology for Internet security.

6.2   Internet Protocol Security (IPSec)

The predecessor to IPSec was known as swIPe, an experimental protocol designed in 1993. In 1994, identifying the need to build security into IP communications, the Internet Engineering Task Force (IETF) defined IPSec as a mandatory protocol for IP v6. The base architecture for IPSec compliant systems is defined in RFC 2401 (Security Architecture for the Internet Protocol) by the Network Working Group of the IETF. The RFC 2401 defines IPSec as *'a framework that provides security services at the IP layer by enabling a system to select required security protocols, determine the algorithm(s) to use for the service(s), and put in place any cryptographic keys required to provide the requested services'*. Roland and Newcomb (2003) clarify this further by defining IPSec as *'a collection of open standards that work together to establish data confidentiality, data integrity, and data authentication between peer devices'*. The IPSec works at the Network layer and can protect multiple data flows between peers, in both the IPv4 and IPv6 environments. The IPSec uses the Internet Key Exchange (IKE) protocol to negotiate protocols between peers and generate encryption and authentication keys. The IPSec can be implemented between, two hosts, two security gateways (e.g. routers or firewalls) or between a host and a gateway by using the Key management.

The IPSec has been implemented by a large number of vendors, and interoperability between multi-vendor devices makes IPSec an ideal option for building Virtual Private Networks (VPNs). The GNU/Linux FreeS/WAN project is an implementation of IPSec and IKE for GNU/Linux systems. Several companies are co-operating in the Secure Wide Area Network (S/WAN) project to ensure that products will interoperate. There is also 'a VPN Consortium fostering widespread of IPSec by providing source code that is freely available and runs on a range of machines. IPSec is defined in a number of Requests for Comments (RFC) that defines the various security protocols, algorithms and mechanisms that comprise IPSec. The initial IPSec standards were defined in RFCs 1825-29 and have since been made obsolete by the current standards. The current RFCs addressing IP security issues include RFC 2401 – Security Architecture for the Internet Protocol (IPSec), RFC 2402 – IP Authentication

Header (AH), RFC 2406 – IP Encapsulating Payload (ESP) and RFC 2409
The Internet Key Exchange (IKE).

The latest efforts by the IETF include looking into providing a more flexible and unified policy mechanism for IPSec. It is also hoped that support for
common Application Program Interface (API) will be integrated, allowing end
applications to request security services from IPSec. This will result in end
user applications, such as e-mail and instant messaging being able to take advantage of IPSec. Efforts are also underway to provide complete integration of
IPSec with the IPv6 stack.

6.2.1   Weaknesses of IPSec

There is old adage that, 'if your most familiar tool is a hammer, the whole
world starts to look like a nail'. Unfortunately, there is a tendency to regard
IPSec as an all-inclusive security solution. As a result of this misconception,
IPSec is considered as a solution to all security concerns. This is clearly the
result of a lack of understanding of the IPSec standard. In a network with hundreds of IPSec Peer or Key Management, all wishing to establish IPSec VPNs
with each other, each peer needs to be configured individually. IPSec does not
provide any mechanism for automating the configuration process. The implementation and maintenance of a large IPSec network is very resource intensive, large businesses are often forced to employ dedicated IT staff to manage
the network.

In a normal IPSec operation, it is the destination peer that chooses the SPI.
However, in multicast communications, there is no single destination for a
given address. This clearly poses implementation issues. The IPSec also poses
some problems with streaming multimedia. In normal IPSec operation, the
selection of outgoing IPSec policy parameters is based on the examination of
IP addresses, the upper layer protocol ID and port numbers. This works well
with protocols that use stable port numbers. However, some application using
streaming multimedia utilise UDP and RTP (Shoniregun *et al.,* 2004b). The
source and destination port numbers used for RTP are dynamically assigned,
making it very difficult to define IPSec policies to select the appropriate UDP
streams to protect.

Due to the end-to-end encryption performed by IPSec, it is not possible for
any intermediary routing devices to check and process flags contained within
the original IP headers. The ability to look up certain fields such as the Type
of Service (ToS) and IP Precedence fields within IP packet headers is essential
to the operation of Quality of Service (QoS) mechanisms. As a result of the
restriction posed by IPSec encryption it is not possible to secure communications such as IP Telephony data that rely heavily on QoS. No mechanism in
place to secure the communication endpoints, such as the end user machines

or applications. This is rather unfortunate, as the original goal of IPSec was to enable the protection of all types of IP communications.

The RFC 3715 describes known incompatibilities between Network Address Translation (NAT) and IPSec. IPSec does not interoperate with most firewalls and gateways that implement NAT. This is one of the major limitations of IPSec. The NAT routers typically sit on the border between private and public networks and translate private addresses in each IP packet into registered public addresses.

6.3   Secure Electronic Transaction (SET)

The Secure Electronic Transaction (SET) is a protocol that is theoretically perfect. The SET was developed by Visa & MasterCard in 1997. This protocol serves many security requirements, but has been slow in gaining acceptance due to the ease of using SSL and the costly infrastructure required. This has resulted in SET being used in larger businesses for consumer transactions.

The SET registers ensures both vendor and buyer are valid through digital certificates. SET's components are similar to SSL where SET provides the security and privacy services of SSL and more additions. The merchant is provided with only enough information for one purchase, therefore ruling out risks of security attacks. This is a non-repeatable unique transaction where unique identifiers and the date and time of purchase are included in the verification of purchase, which rules out a dishonest merchant or staff member from making a repeat transaction, as this would have a different time and a different unique transaction identifier.

The SET also provides a 'dual signature' as it hides credit card numbers from the merchants, and purchase details from the bank, thereby ensuring increased security and privacy. Merchants cannot keep a record of credit card numbers on servers, nor are able to provide valuable market research information. It can be used with or without digital certificates, though for more security and privacy digital certificates are used. When digital certificates are used an electronic wallet will be held within. The wallet can either be stored on a PC or an integrated circuit (IC) chip within a smart card. ICs provide an advantage, as they are mobile, though integration with the PC and other forms of electronic payment, e.g. e-cash, has proved difficult.

Although SET sets out some benefits as stated above, there are however some drawbacks of SET. This is because certificates are needed with infrastructure, and as yet the transfer of certificates has not proved to be sufficient enough.

6.3.1   Weaknesses of SET

The SET implementation is a very costly technology. It use a delay mode so when a site uses SET protocol, it takes between 50 secs for processing transaction. The asset table download time for a site is 15 secs and if it is above 30 secs then the customer move over to another site. While looking on those facts, 52 secs is hardly acceptable for customer to wait. To use the SET protocol from a computer, cardholder needs software to be installed in that particular machine and also need certificate for every credit card. Although the SET has proved to be one of the secured system systems for implementing transaction security boards on the user end if the cardholder system remains open or have not password protected then there is no guarantee of protection.

6.4   Secure Socket Layer (SSL)

Netscape developed SSL in 1986. The Version 3 of the SSL was designed with public review and it was published as an Internet draft document. SSL is making use of the TCP/IP protocol in order to provide a reliable end-to-end secure service. The TCP/IP is responsible for the reliable transport and routing of data over the Internet, but it does not ensure security during the transmission of packets. There are some other protocols, such as, Hypertext Transport Protocol (HTTP), Lightweight Directory Access Protocol (LDAP), or Internet Messaging Access Protocol (IMAP), that run on top of TCP/IP, meaning that they use TCP/IP to fulfil some applications, such as displaying of web pages or running e-mail servers.

The Secure Sockets layer provides secure communications, authentication of the server and data integrity of the message packet. In the following figure, which depicts the protocol stack for Internet communications, SSL lies underneath the application layer. It makes use of a combination of public key and symmetric key encryption. The symmetric key encryption is much faster than public key encryption, but public key encryption provides better authentication mechanisms. More specifically, SSL secures the communications channel by providing end-to-end encryption that is sent between a Web client and a Web server.

The SSL is placed on top of TCP/IP layer and below the application layer. In order to understand the popularity of SSL it is essential to understand the relationship between SSL and other web protocols. SSL provides confidentiality, server authentication, integrity and optional client authentication for a TCP/IP connection, but replay attack and man-in-the middle attacks still threaten its use. SSL is a standalone solution because it is built into an application and it can support many other application protocols. Also, it does not need to be updated like other application protocols. Besides, it is quite flexible, and it also supported by all web browsers and servers making it reliable and proven protocol.

6.4.1 Weaknesses of SSL

The TEISMEs business transactions are typically protected using SSL. However, there exit risks in the use of SSL, clients trust the certificate of authority (CA) to certify the identity of a server. These include the information being stored at the end point of the communication link. Although SSL does the latter, the security service is optional and usually omitted. This is because of the fact that users typically do not have the necessary asymmetric key pair. Since SSL protects data only while it is being transmitted, the merchant has access to sensitive information such as the debit/credit card number. The storage of unencrypted debit/credit card information at the merchant server therefore represents a risk that is not currently addressed by the use of SSL to secure electronic payment transactions. One reason for these vulnerabilities is that SSL does not obligate client authentication. As a result, it is not easy to verify if the person who is making a payment is the legitimate cardholder. A malicious user, who may have obtained card details by some means, may then be able to use them to make payments over the Internet at the expense of the legitimate cardholder. Using SSL to protect an Internet-eC transaction poses another threat. SSL was designed to secure the communications link with one-to-one transactions, in contrast with SET, which handles multi-transactions. Moreover, there are some security risks associated with the traditional implementation of SSL. This has to do with the server's private key, that is critical to the encryption of transactions reside on an unsecured hard drive and are copied to the processor when needed. Both the processor and the hard drive are vulnerable to threat. As a result, merchant servers have become a target for attackers who wish to obtain card details. All these problems could be avoided by use of the SET protocol, a scheme devised jointly by Master Card and Visa to protect entire Internet-eC transactions. Unfortunately, however, SET has not been fully implemented, apparently for a variety of reasons. Foremost among these reasons are the major initialisation and implementation overheads it imposes on both e-consumers and merchants. Secure Electronic Transaction (SET), in spite of the backing of the major credit card companies as a payment scheme that closely resembles the current method for real world credit card transactions, there are some areas in the implementation of SET that remains unclear, but MasterCard and VISA could push this to the front of online payment protocols. Another possible problem with SSL is that no version of SSL protects against traffic analysis. A cryptoanalyst can watch the number of message sent to and from a particular Internet address. Thus alternative ways of enhancing the level of security provided by SSL, which do not impose major overheads, are urgently needed. If client authentication is to be provided by SSL, then the user must establish a public key pair. A secure place will also be needed to store the private part of the key. Usually the key is stored in the user PC and hence the user has to use the particular machine every time a payment is to be made. Although a smart card could be employed to store the key and enhance mobility, not many user PCs are equipped with smart card readers. The current Web infrastructure provides secure

6.5   Firewall

A firewall is the front line defence mechanism against intruders. It is a system designed to prevent unauthorised access to or from a private network. Firewalls can be implemented in both hardware and software, or a combination of both. Firewalls are the first line of defence against external threats and act like a security guard for the company's internal trusted network, filtering all incoming traffic from the Internet (untrusted network). These generally implement one of two basic design policies: permit any service unless it is expressly denied; or deny any service unless it is expressly permitted. The first policy is less desirable, as it offers more avenues for getting around it. Depending on security and flexibility requirements within the organisation, certain types of firewalls are more appropriate (Hawkins *et al.*, 2000).

There are basically two different types of firewalls – packet filters and proxies. Packet filtering firewalls are those designed to filter IP addresses, MAC addresses, TCP or UDP ports, and subnets, among others. A packet filter is, in principle, a router with the ability to filter or block traffic to and from a network. Packets to a specific service can also be blocked. IP packets to a computer on an internal network with certain options turned on or off could also be screened. Information on the TCP/IP level is used to decide whether to allow or disallow a particular type of traffic. The packet filtering firewalls look at each packet header entering or leaving the network and accept or reject a particular packet based on specific rules defined by the user/network administrator. The packet filtering is fairly effective and transparent to users, but it is difficult to configure and also susceptible to IP spoofing—a technique used to gain unauthorised access to computers, whereby the intruder sends messages to a computer with an IP address indicating that the message is coming from a trusted host. The proxy servers, on the other hand, intercept all the messages entering and leaving the network. The proxy hides IP addresses of the clients in the internal network and acts as a mediator for the traffic passing through them. The proxy separates internal networks from the external networks (e.g. the Internet), so that it operates as a server for outsiders and as a client for the insiders. A stateful-inspection firewall has the capability of tracking connections and to make decisions based on the dynamic connection state of packets. For example, if an internal client establishes a connection to the Internet through a specific port, the firewall will maintain state information about the connection pertaining to that specific port. Thus, an ICMP packet is checked if it is related to that TCP/UDP connection. Any TCP/UDP packets are checked against the state table to find if the packet matches with the established port of that connection. An application firewall is a software-based firewall (e.g. McAffee personal firewall) in which a user can control (in real time) to allow or deny connections to it. These different firewall implementations can be used alone or as a combination of several of them (Zwicky, 2000).

Nowadays, most firewalls use packet-screening methods such as Transmission Controls Protocol (TCP) and User Datagram Protocol (UDP) that are based on pre-defined rules. The application gateways are more sophisticated and secure types of firewalls. These use services such as HTTP and Telnet that, run on a server with two network connections, acting as a server to the application client and vice versa. The firewalls prevent internal IP (Internet Protocol) addresses from appearing to users outside the trusted network. Additional firewalls are used internally by organisations, e.g. to cordon off servers in different departments (Madden, 2001). The 'IPv6' was designed by the IETF, which includes a new expanded IP address, part of which has a unique serial number record of each computer's network-connection hardware. Every data packet sent will carry a user's electronic fingerprint.

6.5.1   Weakness of Firewalls

The firewall is an integral part of any security program, but it is not a security program, for instance, it lacks the ability to backtrack an attacker to IP address. The firewalls only address the issues of data integrity, confidentiality and authentication of data that is behind the firewall. Any data that transits outside the firewall is subject to external factors control. The firewall can effectively control the traffic that passes through it but it dose not protect against back doors into the site. For example, if unrestricted modem access is still permitted into a site protected by a firewall, attackers could effectively again access.

The firewalls do not provide protection from insider threats it is designed to prevent outsiders from obtaining sensitive data. Thus, it is faulty to assume that the existence of a firewall provides protection from insider attacks. It is perhaps unwise to invest significant resources in a firewall if other avenues for stealing data or attacking systems are neglected.

Moreover, the firewall cannot protect against users downloading virus-infected personal computer programs from Internet archives or transferring such programs in attachments to e-mail. There are too many ways of encoding binary files for transfer over networks, and too many different architectures and viruses to try to search for them all. In general, a firewall cannot protect against a data-driven attack–attacks, which is something mailed or copied to an internal host where it is then executed.

6.6 Vulnerability Scanning

The vulnerability scanning is a new category of software that has been founded by ex-hackers! The 'turned-good' hackers maintain an extensive database of all known vulnerabilities in systems and the vulnerability software that explores websites from the outside, to try and detect any susceptible areas. The software generates a report of these weaknesses and the group will make suggestions to business on how to resolve them. An example of an ex-hacker group is 'VigilantE' (Computer Weekly, 2000). Vulnerability scanning cannot really be described as a tool or technology for security; however, it is a method of detecting flaws in business systems. The perfect way to catch a thief is to use a thief. These vigilant ex-hackers have put their skills to good use by forming consultancies as a means of making an 'honest living', doing what they like to do, but then also having the challenge of making the systems 'un-hackable'.

6.6.1   Weaknesses of vulnerability scanning

The main functions of vulnerability scanning, is to log data. Too much useless data can hide the important bits of information about deadly attacks. A consistent attack by a determined intruder can be hidden in mountains of data from script kiddies who do not know any better and are just port scanning at random.

Another failure of vulnerability scanning is their inability to learn of new attacks. The new attacks come out on a daily basis. If the firewall that is in use is not versatile enough, a new attack can bypass the filter rules of vulnerability scanning without recognising it as a new form of attack. For example, many Web attacks use port 80 (http). If the vulnerability scanning, cannot distinguish between normal Web surfing traffic and an attack against the operating system through port 80, then the Web server can be under attack at any time.

6.7 Address Verification System (AVS)

The address verification system (AVS) is the most effective and the latest system to prevent the online frauds. The main objective of address verification system is checking address of the person who is paying by card, because the bank or issuer of credit cards keeps the record of account holder address. When that card is used for purchasing than cardholder is being asked about the address, apartments number, street name, and postcode or zip code.

6.7.1 Weakness of address verification systems

The AVS can reduce the crime but still it is neither as effective or reliable. When a customer's provide address online AVS matches that billing address provided by the customer with the address in the file of issuing bank. But it still need much investigation because if customer change its address or force information has been giving then goods will be delivered to address giving by the criminal. The AVS does not work for most of the international address, so if the criminals use numbers from other countries, which they usually do, then the address verification will not be able to restrict them and online merchants will deliver the products to those countries. In the USA only zip code and the numeric part of the billing address is verified. However, if the financial institution do not have the right address or it is entered wrongly then the legitimate customer transaction will be refused and any other subsequent transactions will be abort.

6.8 Card Security Code (CNC) and 'Chip and Pin' Number

To make the credit card secured, a four digits security code called card security code (CNC) is asked from the person presenting the card for transaction. This code is printed on the back of the card on the signature bar.

The chip and pin number is a smart card, which contains microprocessor and memory that can store information. It is more than a simple magnetic swipe type credit card as the memory and process allows it to continually update and store new information at the same time, preventing access the information as only the user knows the pin number to use the card. The microchip is embedded in the plastic card.

6.8.1 Weakness of CNC and 'chip and pin'

It is hard to remember the pin numbers, and some online shoppers are concerned about the privacy, that they have to enter pin numbers on all the time when using the different computers, it would make it easy for criminals to catch the pin numbers. Relying on network to perform chip and card transaction between client and server. These cards can be used for fraudulent activities for example if the pin numbers were stolen, then the card can be used without the consent of the legitimate cardholder. This type of card information can also be altered the well-organised criminals are so well equipped with encoding machine that can altered the information. It requires more hardware and software, which needs past and future considerations.

6.9 User Authentication

User authentication hardware and software is coming into use to verify the identity of the user. Systems that rely on IP (Internet Protocol) address verification limit access to users with a specific domain name or Internet address. Authentication services should be fully integrated into the TEISME security policy, and can be centrally managed through a graphical user interface, tracked through a log viewer (White, 2001). The most popular authentication method used by TEISMEs is Kerberos, while biometrics is an up-coming method that will eventually be widely accepted if the cost of implementation and the ethical issue can be addressed.

6.9.1 Kerberos

The Kerberos protocol was created by Massachusetts Institute of Technology (MIT) as a solution to network security problems, which is used by many commercial systems. Kerberos is freely available from MIT, under copyright permission. It is designed to provide strong authentication for client/server applications by using secret-key cryptography. The secret-key enabled a user to prove his or her identity to a server (and vice versa) across unsecured network connection. Through the use of encryption the key can only be decrypted if the client knows the secret key. The Kerberos knowledge of the secret key is considered sufficient as a proof of identity, and the server can be trusted to authenticate any client to any other client. In the case of servers or software systems, a random key is generated. The secret-key information (ticket) is a time stamp to prevent replay attacks. The Windows® 2000 operating system implements the Kerberos version 5 as the default with extensions for public key authentication.

6.9.2 Weaknesses of Kerberos

The Kerberos is vulnerable to password-attacks because user-generated passwords are easy-to-remember and can be easily guessed. The CERT Advisory CA-2000-11 reports of several potential buffer overflow vulnerabilities in the Kerberos authentication software, and it allows remote intruders to disrupt normal operations of the Key Distribution Centre (KDC) (MIT Kerberos Team, 2000). For example, a remote attacker can cause the KDC to issue invalid tickets, generate a 'Server unknown' error or can cause the KDC process to crash. Due to these vulnerabilities, the security of Kerberos is questionable as a single security measure.

6.9.3 Biometrics

Computer manufacturers are now building systems that incorporate fingerprint and eye scanner software into their machines so that TEISMEs can authenticate their customers by verification of finger, thumb, palm, hand geometry, wrist vein, face, eye, voice prints, key stroke dynamics or hand written signatures. Biometrics could be a major security system for the future in the battle against online crime. It is basically concerned with digitally encoding physical attributes of the users voice, eye, face or hand to a unique ID. Such an ID is now used for clearance into buildings. The biometrics identification could be used in the future to secure online transaction(s) (Chen, 2000).

Research into biometrics is currently being carried out to see if it could become a viable option to be used by TEISMEs. The foolproof way of authenticating someone is by physical identification, therefore, making it impossible for fraud to occur (unless of course, the hackers turned to kidnapping!). Despite the fact that it would be an expensive process to scan every customer with a biometric scanner, many companies, especially the financial ones, will probably adopt this strategy anyway. Overall, the cost of biometrically scanning customers may be less expensive than the costs incurred by fraud in the long term.

The Infineon Technologies AG and Veridicom Inc. have produced finger-scanning chips that can be embedded into a computer keyboard or mouse to verify authentication of the user by fingerprint ID. As technology becomes cheaper, it is not impractical to think that people may have chips implanted into computer keyboards 'as standard'. Keyware Technologies Inc and Proton World International have in turn produced a Smart Card that can identify the authenticity of the user. When validity is confirmed, the smart card then allows release of credit card and user details to the website (Chen, 2000).

This technology is really not as 'sci-fi' as one can imagine. Already ING Direct, Canada, has issued fingerprint biometric security systems to their online banking customers. ING Direct has distributed computer mice to a selected group of customers with embedded fingerprint chips. Results from trials will determine whether Biometrics is a viable security option. However, initially this type of technology will be very difficult to install due to the systems required for it and the expense of it. In the longer term, the costs should decrease and one day it may be possible for everyone owning a computer to have the technology for trouble free purchasing on the web.

The UK's Barclays Bank has been using finger scan technology for employee access to buildings since 1996 and is also currently involved in a pilot program for PC log-ins to the corporate networks. In 1998, Nationwide Building Society became the first organisation in the world to trial iris recognition technology supplied by ATM manufacturer NCR. 91% of their customers said

Table 1–3. Table of biometric technologies

Technology	Applications	Benefits/Barriers
Face Scan	Cheque cashing kiosk, time and attendance verification, ATM access	Facial hair can cause false rejection and this is highly dependent on lighting conditions. In addition, people generally do not like to have their picture taken, which could create resistance by consumers.
Finger Scan	Authentication for bank teller ID, customer ID	An inexpensive technology, although it can be difficult to read some population's fingerprints.
Iris Scan	ATM access	Very accurate under normal circumstances, though there is a high false rejection rate for individuals who wear designer contact lenses. Also iris scanning is quite costly to implement.
Hand Scan (Hand Geometry)	Physical security, time and attendance verification	Easy to use and easily accepted by users as this is not viewed as intrusive. Quite expensive to implement, and physiological changes in the hands can cause false rejection.
Keystroke Dynamics	In beta testing	Can be used with any device that uses a keyboard
Retina Scan	Network access, PCLogin	Extremely accurate and resistant to fraud, but requires the user to stand within six inches of the scanner. Also very expensive to implement.
Signature Scan (Dynamic Signature Verification)	Mortgage pooling application	Not very accurate because handwriting can change over the years.
Voice Scan (Speaker Verification)	Voicemail access, telephone banking	A logical choice for the mobile arena, though the false rejection rate is high

they would chose iris identification over PIN's or signatures in the future (see Table 1–3 and Table 1–4), (Desmarais, 2000; White, 2001).

6.9.4   Weaknesses of biometrics

The barrier in growth of biometrics is the cost of implementation, cost of connectivity, speed of services, and speed of authentication. For finger scanning, as people become older they loose the fat in their skin, so the fingerprints worn out, which can make difficult for scanner to image it. Research has proved that some biometrics features are expensive and less accurate in result such as hand scan. There could be some false rejection because of external environment like in face scanning lightening can effects the result. External noise can effect the authentication of voice recognition. However, voice changes with the passage of time. The factors such as flu, soar throat, or emotional conditions can also affect the voice recognition.

Table 1–4. Table of the financial institutions currently using biometrics

Financial Institutions	Technology used	Application
BACOB (Belgium)	Voice Scan	Telephone account access
Bank of Central Asia (Indonesia)	Finger Scan	Physical security
Bank United	Iris Scan	ATM transactions
Barclaycard	Finger Scan	Physical security and network logging
Chase (New York)	Hand Scan	Network login
Citibank (New York)	Hand Scan	Physical security
Charles Schwab (California)	Voice Scan	Telephone account access
ING Direct (Canada)	Finger Scan	Online banking
Perdue Federal Credit Union	Finger Scan	Standalone banking kiosks
Royal Bank of Canada	Hand Scan	Physical security
Wells Fargo	Face Scan	ATM transaction

7. SUMMARY OF CHAPTER ONE

This chapter has set the scene for understanding TEI. The direction to which this book is going has been made clear and the hypothesis postulated. The historical background of the concept of SME has been set and provides a springboard for a better understanding of TEISMEs business operations and technologies for Internet security, and in particular their weaknesses. Although biometrics is still relatively expensive and immature, the integrated multiple biometrics features, such as fingerprints, palm prints, facial features and voice patterns to authenticate a person's identity and verify his or her eligibility to access the Internet, are in the development stage. The current content protecting techniques only permits different roles operating on file (such as read-only, write-only and read-write), (Shoniregun *et al.,* 2004c), which does not meet the needs of TEISMEs transaction risks. Because everyone has unique physical attributes, in theory a computer can be programmed to recognise person. Passwords, cards, pin numbers and keys can be forgotten, stolen, forged, lost or given away, so the way forward is to integrate biometrics into existing Internet security technologies which however does not guarantee security of TEISMEs business transactions. The next chapter will exploits the impacts of TEI on SMEs and the generic problems with network protocol layers that affect TEISMEs business operations.

REFERENCES

Bolton, J., 1971, *Small firms report of the committee of inquiry on small firms*, Bolton Committee: London, HMSO.

Chen, A., 2000, 'Biometrics – the end of online fraud?', *eWEEK* (27 February 27, 2002); www.zdnet.com/filters/printerfriendly/0,6061,2444322-2,00.html.

Computer Weekly, 2000, 'Is poor security worse than no security at all?', *Computer Weekly* (September 12. 2000); www.computerweekly.com.

Da Costa, E., 2000, *Global E-commerce Strategies for Small Businesses*. The MIT Press.

Dewan, S. and Kraemer, K.., 1998, 'International dimension of the productivity paradox', *Communication of the ACM*, 41(8):56–62.

Department of Trade and Industry (DTI), 2001, *The small business research initiative*; www.dti.gov.uk/support/rndguide.htm (July 23, 2003).

Department of Trade and Industry (DTI), 2002a, 'RSA Security, Symantec Genuity, Country wide-Porter Novelli and Price Water House Cooper', *Report on Information Systems Breaches Survey*, London, DTI URN02/319.

Department of Trade and Industry (DTI), 2002b, *Information Security Breaches Survey*, p. 20; ukonlineforbusiness.gov.uk/cms/template/infor-security.jsp?id=213097 (January 8, 2003).

Desmarais, N., 2000, 'Body language, security and E-commerce', *Library Hi Tech*, 18(1):61–74.

Diffie and Hellman, 1976, 'New directions in cryptography', *IEEE: Transactions on Information Theory*, June.

E-Enovy, 2000, *Mapping E-commerce: Statistic on National Internet Usage*; www.e-envoy.gov.uk/2000/strategy/estatmap/estatmap.htm.

Elliot, G. and Starkey, S., 2001, *Business Information Technology*, Addison Wesley Longman.

Ettlie, J. E., 2000, *Managing Technology Innovation*, John Wiley and Sons.

Ghosh, A. K. and Swaminatha, T. M., 2001, 'Software security and privacy risks in mobile e-commerce', *Communications of the ACM*, 44(2):51–57.

Hawkins, S., Yen, D., and Chou, D.C., 2000, 'Awareness and challenges of Internet security', *Information Management and Computer Security*, 8(3):131–143.

Isern, G., 2002, 'Internet Security Attacks at the Basic Levels', *ACM SIGOPS Operating Systems Review*, 32(2): 4–15.

Kalakota, R. and Whinston, A. B., 2001, *Electronic Commerce: A Manager's Guide*, Addison Wesley.

Kelly, R., 2001, *Secure Procurement*, Finance On Windows.

KPMG Consulting and EIM Small Business Research and Consultancy, 2000, *The European Observatory for SMEs: Sixth Report*, EIM Business & Policy Research: Zoetermeer, Netherlands.

La Rovere, R.L., Hasenclever, L., and Erber, F., 2004, 'Industrial and technology policy for regional development', *International Journal of Technology Management & Sustainable Development*, 2(3):205–217.

Lahorgue, M.A., Da Cunha, N., 2004, 'Introduction of innovation in the industrial structure of a developing region. The case of the Port Alegre Technopole "HomeBrokers" Project', *International Journal of Technology Management & Sustainable Development*, 2(3):191–204.

Larochelle, D., 2001, 'Statically detecting likely buffer overflow vulnerabilities', in *Proceedings of the 10th USENIX Security Symposium*, August.

Loudon, K. C. and Loudon, J. P., 1999, *Essentials of Management Information System*, 3rd ed., Prentice Hall, Inc.

MacInnes, B., 2003, *IT Management SMEs: small talk*, (February 6, 2004); www.computerweekly.com/Article126984.htm.

Madden, L., 2001, *Great Walls of Fire*, Finance on Windows.

Means, G. and Schneider, D., 2000, *MetaCapitalism: the e-Business Revolution and the Design of 21st-century Companies and Markets*. John Wiley and Sons.

MIT Kerberos Team, 2000, *CERT Advisory CA-2000-11: MIT Kerberos Vulnerable to Denial-of-Service Attacks*, 14 September 2001; www.cert.org/advisories/CA-2000-11.html (31st October).

Net Figures, 2001, 'E-Business at a glance', *Financial Times – Connecties*, 9 March.

Ofcom, 2004, *The Ofcom Internet and broadband update*; www.ofcom.org.uk/research/consumer_audience_research/139330/InternetandBroadband.pdf (February 6, 2004).

Oftel, The Office of Telecommunication, 2000, *Internet use among Small and Medium Enterprises (SMEs): summary of Oftel SME surveys*, June; www.oftel.gov.uk/publications/research/bint 0800.htm (October 7, 2002).

Pinheiro, R., 2002, *Strong user authentication for electronic and mobile commerce*, www. giac.org/practical/Robert_Pinheiro_ GSEC. doc (December 3, 2003).

Pegasus Research International LLC (PRI), 2003, *European Web Users*; www.pegasusresearch. net/metrics/growtheu.htm (December 12, 2003).

Roland, J.F., and Newcomb, M.J., 2003, *CSVPN Certification Guide*, CISCO Press.

Saad, M., Rowe, K. and James, P., 1999, 'Developing and sustaining effective partnerships through a high level of trust', *Public And Private Partnerships: Furthering Development*, Cork, Ireland, 26–29 May.

Shannon C. E., and Weaver W., 1949, *The Mathematical Theory Of Communication*, University of Illinois Press.

Shoniregun, C. A., Grebenyuk, V. and Logvynovskiy, O., 2004a, 'The impact of next generation mobile phone on the society', in *Proceedings of the 31st International Conference: Information Technologies in Science, Education, Telecommunications and Business*. Crimea, Ukraine.

Shoniregun, C. A., Nwankwo, S., and Imafidon, C., Wynarczyk, P., 2004b, 'Information security challenges facing by TEISMEs', *International Journal for Infonomics*, e-Centre for Infonomics: London, 1:65–77.

Shoniregun, C.A, Logvynovskiy, O., Duan, Z., Bose, S., 2004c, 'Streaming and security of art works on the web', in the *Proceeding of the IEEE Sixth International Symposium on Multimedia Software Engineering (ISMSE'04)*, December 13–15, Miami, Florida, pp. 344–351.

Shoniregun, C.A.., Chochliouros, I.P., Laperche, B., Logvynovskiy, O. and Spiliopoulou-Chochliourou, A., 2004d, *Questioning the Boundary Issues of Internet Security*, e-Center for Infonomics: London.

Shoniregun, C.A., 2002a 'Is M-commerce really the future or is it another E-commerce with many bubbles waiting to be burst', *EC NL*, June, pp. 4–6.

Shoniregun, C.A., 2002b, 'To ignore E-commerce is to allow competitors to steal a lead'. *EC NL*, June, pp. 8–9.

Shoniregun, C.A., 2003a, 'Are existing Internet security measures guaranteed to protect user identity in the financial services industry?', *International Journal of Services, Technology and Management (IJSTM)*, 4:194–215.

Shoniregun, C.A., 2003b, *MSc eC Lecture Handbook*, University of East London: London.

Tayler, K. W. H., 2001, *Information Technology: A Philosophical Inquiry into the Mechanisation and Ownership of Intelligence*, PhD thesis, University of East London (unpublished).

Warwick F., Baum M.S., 2000, *Secure Electronic Commerce: Building the Infrastructure for Digital Signatures and Encryption*, 2nd ed, Prentice Hall.

White, M., 2001, *Networking in a Networked Economy*, Finance on Windows, pp. 82–83.

Zwicky, E, 2000, *Internet and Web Security: Building Internet Firewalls*, O'Reilly, Beijing, p. 869.

Chapter 2

IMPACTS OF TEI ON SMEs

1.   INTRODUCTION

One of the major challenges facing the technologically advanced world is how businesses can function through vast interrelated and complex networks, without sacrificing human creativity and individuality. Against a backcloth of psychedelic change, the TEISMEs must create plan and control their business operations to achieve high goals.

> '...Opportunities out there are enormous as are the risks.'
> —Nwankwo, S., and Aiyeku, J.F., (2002) Dynamic of Marketing in
> Africa Nations

The TEISMEs business operation relies exceptionally and heavily on information transfer via the Internet. This chapter is based on the impacts of TEI on SMEs, disintermediation and reintermediation, electronic payment systems, and the generic problems with network protocol layers that affect TEISMEs business operational network.

2.   IMPACTS OF TEI ON SMES IN THE UK

The economic impacts of TEI on SMEs are pervasive, both on SMEs business operations and on the society as a whole. For those small businesses that fully exploit its potential, TEI offers the possibility of breakpoint changes – changes that so radically alter customer expectations and re-define the market or create entirely new markets. Businesses can often conduct payment among

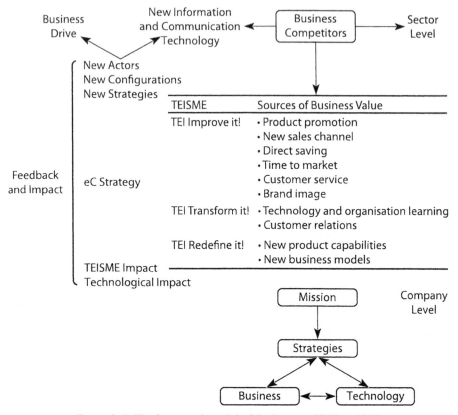

Figure 2–1. The framework model of the impact of TEI on SMEs

themselves electronically through private network or by using EDI, which is a generic term to describe processes in which commercial data is exchanged between different businesses computer systems.

The electronic transactions in 1993 amounted up to 33 billion, and are expected to exceed 118 billion by the end of 2001. Paper transactions, however, are expected to grow from 117 billion to 135 billion. The banks and retailers are seeking to decrease paper transactions in favour of electronic as the processing overheads for transactions are both labour intensive and costly (Kosiur, 1997).

'There is no doubt that electronic commerce is going to have a profound effect on business, government and consumers and on the way people live and work. e-Commerce presents enormous challenges.'
—Rt. Hon, Tony Blair (British Prime Minister, 1998)

All other businesses, including those that try to ignore the TEI, will then be impacted by these changes in markets and customer expectations (Shoniregun, 2002). Equally, individual members of society will be presented with entirely new ways of purchasing goods, accessing information and services, and interacting with branches of government. Choice will be greatly extended, and restrictions of geography and time eliminated. The overall impact on lifestyle could well be comparable to say that of the growth in car ownership or the spread of mobile telephone.

The discussion in this section is based primarily on experts' opinions, logic, and some actual data. The Figure 2–1 presented the author's modified framework proposed by Block and Seger (1998), their original framework approach shows the impact of Internet-eC from a value-added point of view. This framework has been adopted to position the understanding of TEI. The Block and Seger model is adopted to show the impact of TEI on SMEs, which divides into three major categories: TEI improves direct marketing, TEI transforms SMEs, and TEI redefines small businesses; these categories are discussed below.

2.1 TEI Improves Direct Marketing

The traditional direct marketing is done by mail order (catalogues) and telephone (telemarketing). Block and Seger (1998) suggest the following product promotion, new sales channels, direct savings, reduced cycle time, customer service, and brand which comprehend TEI impacts:

- *Product promotion*: TEI enhances promotion of products and services through direct, information-rich, and interactive contact with customers.
- *New sales channels*: TEI creates a new distribution channel existing products, thanks to its direct reach of customer and the bi-directional nature of communication.
- *Direct savings*: The cost of delivering information to customers over the Internet results in substantial savings to senders (when compared with non-electronic delivery or delivery via VAN systems). Major savings are also realised in delivering digitised products (such as music and software) versus physical delivery.
- *Reduced cycle time*: The delivery of digitised products and services can be reduced to seconds. Also the administrative work related to physical delivery, especially across international borders, can be reduced significantly, cutting the cycle time by more than 90 percent. One example is TradeNet in Singapore, which reduces the administrative time of port-related transactions from days to minutes.

- *Customer service*: Customer service can be greatly enhanced by enabling customers to find detailed information online. Also, intelligent agents can answer standard e-mail questions in seconds. Finally, human experts' services can be expedited using help-desk software.
- *Brand or TEISME image*: On the Web, newcomers can establish corporate images very quickly. What TEISME need to do is to try and achieve some trust via on-line customers and TEISME image means trust, which is necessary for direct sales.

Other marketing-related impacts are customisation, advertisement, ordering systems and traditional markets.

2.2   TEI Transforms SMEs

TEISMEs will have to immediately learn the new technologies. Learning may be followed by strategic structural changes. These changes may transform the way in which business is done:

- *Technology and requirement learning*: Rapid progress in TEI will force TEISMEs to adapt quickly to the new technology and offer them an opportunity to experiment with new products, services, and processes.
- *Changing nature of work*: The nature of work and employment will be transformed in the Digital Age; it is already happening before our eyes. Driven by increased competition in the global marketplace, businesses are reducing the number of employees down to a core of essential staff and outsourcing jobs to countries where wages are significantly less expensive.

2.3   TEI Redefines SMEs

Changes may redefine the missions of TEISME business operations, and the manner in which they operate:

- *New product capabilities*: TEI allow new products to be created and/or for existing products to be customised in innovative ways.
- *New business models*: These changes affect not only individual TEISMEs and their services, but the entire industries. This will lead to the use of new business models, based on the wide availability of information and its direct distribution to consumers.

Table 2–1. An Increase importance of Intermediation Services

	Sample	Aggregation	Trust	Facilitation	Matching
		Provision of one-stop shopping	Provision of authentication and secure communications	Exchange of messages between customers and suppliers	Provision of marketing information to suppliers
Retail Business to business	2	Yes	Yes	Yes	Yes
Retail Business to consumer	3	Maybe	Yes	Yes	Yes
Automotive Business to business	2	Yes	Yes	Yes	No
Automotive Business to consumer	3	No	Yes	Yes	No
Information goods Business to consumer	3	No	Yes	Yes	Yes

Kalakota and Whinston (1998) argued that SMEs are under continuing pressure to reduce costs in order to stay competitive. TEI offers efficiencies and cost savings at many levels/processes to SMEs:

- *Supply/demand level*: low cost electronic transactions with suppliers, with high accuracy.
- *Marketing/management level*: low cost global information sharing and advertising.
- *Post sale/maintenance level*: low cost customer service alternatives to telephone call centres.
- *IS Infrastructure level*: low cost technological infrastructure that reduces the burden of technology obsolesces and upgrading.

The TEI allows the integration of internal and external operations. Externally TEI moulds the vast network of supplies, government agencies and contractors to a single community with the ability to communicate across boundaries and deferring computer platforms. Just in time manufacturing can reach new levels of efficiency with this type of external integration. However, the integration of TEI into SMEs has yielded even greater economic efficiency than ever before The internal process such as re-distribution of data within differing businesses can be made much more efficient using TEI solutions. The availability of TEI to TEISMEs has led the disintermediation to be reintermediation; this will be the focus of the next section.

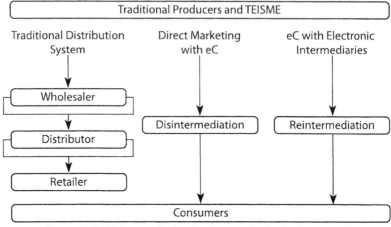

Figure 2–2. Disintermediation is reintermediation by Internet-eC

3.   DISINTERMEDIATION AND REINTERMEDIATION

The key impacts of TEI on TEISMEs business operations are disintermediation of traditional distribution channels and Internet-eC reintermediation. Bailey and Bakos (1997) explore thirteen case studies of firms participating in electronic commerce and find that, for the majority, new roles arise for electronic intermediaries that seem to outweigh any trends towards disintermediation. Although the sample is too small for formal empirical analysis, but it indicates that there is a general perceived increase in the role of intermediation services (see Table 2–1).

Disintermediation is a new term that refers to the removal of business process layers responsible for certain intermediary steps in a given value chain. In the traditional distribution channel, there are intermediating layers such as wholesaler, distributor, and retailer, between the manufacturer and consumer as depicted in Figure 2–2 (Shoniregun *et al.*, 2004b). A logical alternative to disintermediation is reintermediation, which actually points to the shifting or transfer of the intermediary functions.

Furthermore, it is clear that the nature of Internet-eC and the change in relative costs it generates will cause a restructuring of the intermediation function, with some services gaining while others lose. In many cases, these new intermediary services will address the issues of trust and risk sharing that plague Internet-eC (Shoniregun *et al.*, 2004a). New entrants may often provide the solutions, but because of the need to engender confidence, established intermediaries are able to adapt to the new environment and perhaps well positioned. The demand for intermediaries will vary considerably by sector, but in nearly all cases, TEISMEs will be information-intensive and will exploit the information infrastructure to deliver the service. In addition, TEI capabilities are giving birth to entirely new classes of business intermediaries. Forrester Research groups identified business activities under three headings: aggregators, auctions, and exchanges. These new activities attack different inefficiencies sectors, and provide different opportunity such as (Lief, 1999):

- *Aggregators*: The aggregators create a business community. Aggregators pool supplier content to create a searchable one-stop shopping mall with predefined prices for buyers within a business community. For example, Chemdex serves this function for the buyer community of research scientists. These cyber-stores help geographically dispersed buyers and sellers find each other fast.
- *Auctions*: The auctions create markets and reduce sellers' losses. Auctions pit buyers against each other to purchase seller surplus. On the Web, sellers and buyers can participate in multiple, real-time auctions simultaneously–without accruing physical-world search and travel costs.
- *Exchanges*: The exchanges create stable online trading markets. Like stock exchanges, online exchanges provide vetted players with a trading venue defined by clear rules, industry-wide pricing, and open market information. An online industry spot market can operate at a fraction of physical-world cost.

4. PROMOTE PRODUCTS TO SUIT EACH INDIVIDUAL CUSTOMER

It has become clear that TEISMEs are much more customer focused. An electronic transaction is essentially a one-to-one transaction, and information about each individual customer's buying habits and preferences can be stored. This allows TEISMEs to promote products to suit each individual customer and allows the companies to gain a closer link with each customer removing the traditional 'faceless' image that big companies have nowadays. It is equally important for customer service representatives to be able to access and manipulate all the information involved in a customer's order. Current thinking is that TEISMEs will thrive, because many of the cost of conventional or traditional SMEs can be eliminated. There will also be economies of scale, thanks to the huge numbers involved. IT is reshaping the basics of business. Customer service, operations, product and marketing strategies, and distribution are heavily, or sometimes even entirely, dependent on IT. The computers that support these functions have become an everyday part of business life (Keen, 1991).

The online sales are expected to grow tenfold in the next four years. The act of shopping will be made so easy that barrier to purchasing, and in particular, to impulse buying will be lowered. The great number of advantages and huge competitive edge that TEI has to offer SMEs and the wealth of information available to both consumers, and businesses all at the click of a button will ensure the success of this new found star. To further fuel the growth of the TEI the de-regulation of the telecommunications industry, hence the competition this creates will ensure that Internet charges are kept to a minimum, but the risk facing TEISMEs business operations will continue despite the de-regulation of the telecommunications industry. So, with all the disintermediation that has been reintermidiated the next question to ask is that *'how is payment for goods or services sold by TEISMEs made'*. This is the focus of the next section.

5.   ELECTRONIC PAYMENT

The electronic payment (e-Payment) is another impact on TEISMEs business operations. By the nature of their business, goods are paid for in a number of ways, either by credit cards, smart cards, digital cash electronic wallets (e–Wallets), 1-Pay.com™ and PayPal™. TEISMEs can often conduct payment among themselves also electronically through private network or by using EDI, which is a 'generic term to describe processes in which commercial data is exchanged between different businesses computer systems'. The e-Payment implementations are one of the recognised growth areas in TEI and vendors have been rapidly developing their systems to ensure competitive edge.

5.1   Credit Card Payments over the Web

Most companies collecting payment over the web accept payments using credit cards. The simplest approach is for the merchant to collect the credit card information via a separate phone call or fax and then to check the card through a call to the credit card Company in the normal way. Credit card companies charge a larger commission on these 'customer-not-present' transactions. Merchants are required to repay fraudulent or non-authorised use of credit cards through charge backs. It is important therefore that every effort is made to minimise these charge backs, possibly by refusing business from high-risk locations, or by requiring a valid e-mail or physical address. The cardholder's liability is limited to the first £50 of a fraudulent transaction, and nothing else, once the card issuer has been informed of loss or fraud. Section 75 of UK Consumer Credit Act offers valuable extra protection to consumers who pay by credit card. The online consumers can claim against the card issuer as well as against the supplier if something goes wrong, but the risk facing TEISME business operations remains uninsured. More recently, TEISMEs have multiple pain points due to online fraud:

1. Discount rates for card-not-present transactions are typically higher than in-store rates. On average, online TEISMEs pay their acquiring bank the value of each online transaction, plus a small transaction fee. TEISMEs that outsource their Web-based payment processing also pay additional fees to Internet payment gateways. With razor-thin sales margins, many TEISMEs are loath to pay the higher card-not-present rates.
2. TEISMEs receive no payment for fraudulent purchases, and incur shipping costs for delivery of physical goods.
3. While screening for fraud, TEISMEs may reject valid sales due to suspicious transaction characteristics.
4. Charge-back penalties for fraudulent transactions are typically within the £9 to £18 range. Internal investigation and charge-back management costs are additional.
5. TEISMEs can lose their accounts for consistently high fraud and charge-back rates, and this can effectively drive TEISMEs out of business.

Fraud transaction rate have increased steadily since 2000, despite significant efforts by merchants, card issuers and law enforcement to curb fraud. In 2000, online fraud losses were 1.13% of $44.2 billion in annual online sales. In 2001, some $700 million was lost, representing 1.14% of $61.8 billion in online sales (Kerr and Latin, 2002). If all other things are been equal, it can be assumed that network protocol layers have no generic problems regarding TEISMEs business operations. The answer to this question is the focus of the next section.

6. GENERIC PROBLEMS WITH NETWORK PROTOCOL LAYERS

The way security is realised has a great impacts on both TEISME and online shoppers. It may be a precondition for trust, when the online shopper believes that their interests are maintained and the transactions are secured. The essence of security is finding the right balance between protecting the business interests and resources, and letting people get their work done (Harrison, 2003). Network security is best implemented as part of a comprehensive business policy and will quite often involve the deployment of a variety of security solutions. Although security hardware and software is robust and versatile for securing TEISME transactions, it is not a complete solution for all transactions.

6.1   Security Problems with TCP/IP

Passing information through the layers—the information moves through the layers successively layer by layer of the TCP/IP communications software when it is being transmitted from one computer to another via the Internet. As the information passes through the layers each layer performs specific functions that enabled the information (or message) to pass from one host through a network to another host on the same, or another network within the Internet boundaries. In the event that the packet (information file) must be routed through an intervening host, in order to be transmitted to a server on another, then only the data-link layer (Network Interface) and possibly the Network Layer of the TCP/IP will be involved. Each layer of the TCP/IP suite in the sending host will add data or information to the packet and each layer of the protocol suite in the receiving host will remove data or information from the packet. This process is commonly known as encapsulation. Hence, the application layer will generate the data or information and pass that data or information to the transport layer. The transport layer will then add data or information to the front of the data or information, which it will then pass onto the network layer. The message or packet will become longer as each successive layer adds data or information to the packet. Once the packet is received at the receiving host, each corresponding layer in the receiving host will use and remove the data or information added by the corresponding layer from the sending host and pass it onto the next corresponding layer, and via-versa. The risk of virus infection, and the hacker's intrusion on servers within the Internet boundaries are greater than ever before with the later process.

According to Stalling (2001), the attacks that often occur on the networks fall into two classes namely 'passive' and 'active'. The passive attacks have to do with eavesdropping on, or monitoring, transmissions, for example electronic mail, file transfers, and client/server exchanges are examples of transmission that can be monitored. The active attacks includes modification of transmitted data or information and attempts to gain unauthorised access to computer systems or the service providers server or the TEISMEs business operation server. The magnitudes of attacks on TEISMEs business operation servers by intruders are a real and growing problem, which prompt for a dynamic risk assessment model (see chapter 3 for further discussion). The reasons for the trend include the following:

i.   *Globalisation*: The pressures of international competition have spawned a number of recent cases of industrial espionage. There is also evidence that a number of the 'hacker clubs' are beginning to sell their services for this purpose.

ii. *The move to client/server architecture*: Many TEISMEs have traditionally kept most of their data or information either on mainframes, which can be guarded with sophisticated security software, or on stand-alone PCs, which usually have not been accessible remotely. But as client/server architectures become increasingly popular, both barriers are removed. Many servers run UNIX, which is notorious for its lack of mainframe-style security features and a particular favourite of hackers.

iii. *Hackers' steep learning curve*: Hackers love to share information. Underground bulletin boards are used to exchange dial-in port phone number compromised passwords, security holes in systems, and intrusion techniques. Furthermore, when security personnel do exchange information about vulnerabilities, attackers can often eavesdrop and exploit these vulnerabilities before the holes are plugged on all affected systems.

However, no technology has ever existed to make the Internet 100 percent secure (Shoniregun, 2003), this open the argument in support of (H_0^2): Absolute security, and risk assessment is unattainable on TEISME business operations.

The TCP/IP is so widely used and forms the basis of the Internet, it has therefore been extensively studied, hence the strengths and weaknesses of TCP/IP are well known. Another point to consider is that TCP/IP is over 20 years old and it remains largely unchanged, whilst hardware and software has advanced considerably and thus the resources at the disposal of the attacker are far greater and with greatly advanced techniques also being available. The problems with security with regards to TCP/IP are generic problems, which are detailed below:

i. *Data Link Layer Security (DLLS)*: The DLLS consists of the Address Resolution Protocol (ARP), which performs the task of translating hardware or Ethernet addresses on a Local Area Network (LAN) or a Wide Area Network (WAN) into IP addresses. This protocol is vulnerable to manipulation. Not all systems will determine or check incoming ARPs for any possible outstanding requests associated with the ARP packet. An example of such a system is the UNIX system. The lack of checking of the ARP packets could result in malicious responses being sent to ARP requests in addition to which, it also makes the ARP table open to unauthorised or invalid updates. The most common or likely effect would be the denial of service. This form of attack will have the attacker manipulating addresses so that traffic routed between two hosts is transmitted through a compromised machine that masquerades as each host to the other.

ii. *Network-Layer Security (NLS)*: No matter how reliable the NLS architecture and the sound IP implementation, it can however still be manipulated.

The routing of data packets is fairly open, which as a result can lead to data or information not conforming to configured routing. Packets from the IP protocol can be injected directly onto the network as well. The Internet control message protocol (ICMP) protocol has no authentication, which could permit manipulation of routing (Landwehr, and Goldschlag, 1998). The Internet protocol allows source routing. Source routing specifies the path a packet must take to its destination. Accordingly, an attacker can use source routing to force a device to pass a packet to an intended target. For this reason, source routing must be turned off in firewall routers attached to an Internet. Furthermore, the ICMP is installed with every IP implementation. By its nature, ICMP is inherently insecure. For instance, ICMP redirect messages can tell a host to send its packet to a different router. Falsifying such messages can cause packets to take a path to the attacker's machine, is to limit the scope of change that may be dictated by ICMP. However, old ICMP versions do not use the extra information. Upon arrival of such messages, all connections between same pair of hosts will be affected. For example, if no destination unreachable message is received, stating that some packet was unable to reach the target host, all connections to that host will be turned down. This presents a weakness in ICMP, which is exploited by hackers programs, however exploiting this weakness can be captured. Hackers have used ICMP weaknesses to create new paths to a destination. The hacker can tamper with the knowledge of the proper route to a destination, and is capable of penetrating that host. For example, a user with malicious intent will be able to subvert local routing tables, or ICMP could permit unsolicited mask reply packets. In the event that an incorrect routing table is broadcast to major Internet backbone providers by the Internet Service Provider (ISP), it would result in huge amounts of traffic to be routed to itself, denying large groups of users or communities of their service, as a result, the 'black hole' will be created. The protocols managing the network routers are vulnerable enough to cause a further compromise of network security. Poor authentication is provided by Simple network management protocol (SNMP), and unless routers are correctly configured, they remain open to malicious attackers who may reconfigure them with relative ease (Bellowin, 1989).

iii. *IP Security Labels:* The IP security option is one of the security features of IP, it was primarily used by military sites, with commercial variants currently being defined. The data packet is labelled with the level of sensitivity of data or information. The labels used include a hierarchical component, which will state the level of sensitivity (secret, top secret, etc.), and also an optional category such as nuclear weapons, cryptography, hammer, and procurements. Within the networks, the main purpose of security labels is to constrain routing decisions. A packet marked 'top secret' may not be transmitted over an insecure link cleared only for 'bottom secret' traffic.

iv. *IP Origin Forgery:* The forgery of the origin of IP messages does not pose a serious security problem in itself, even though an IP message origin can be forged with relative ease. The seriousness of this problem, however, comes to the forefront when taking into account the fact that most of the high level protocols use the IP origin as a mode of identification. One such example of the use of IP origin as an identification tools, is the example of the 'r' commands (r login, rsh). These commands enable access between UNIX systems without the use of authentication, as the IP source is used as the primary authentication method in these instances, opening a doorway for the hacker who may use IP origin forgery (see chapter 4).

v. *Transport-Layer Security (TLS):* The mechanism for ensuring the consistent use of port numbers is weak within TCP, UNIX systems assume that only privileged processes initiate connections from port numbers less than 1024, however there is no reason to assume that such processes are trustworthy (Landwehr and Goldschlag, 1998). However, each IP packet must specify the kind of header that follows either a TCP or UDP herder. Since some applications use TCP (such as File Transfer Protocol) and others employ UDP (such as the Simple Network Management Protocol), an attacker can instantly learn the type of the message in the packet. Once the type of packet is known the attacker can look in the TCP or UDP header and discover the exact application to which this packet pertains. This is possible because many applications in the TCP/IP suite are assigned port number. The first 1023 port numbers are assigned by Internet assigned numbers authority (IANA) and are available to anyone who cares to look. Therefore, figuring out the source, destination, and contents of the packet is relatively easy. The TCP segments that follow the IP header also contain sequence numbers. Sequence numbers allow receiving TCP software to detect missing, duplicated, or out-of-order segments. It is possible for a 'spoofer' to guess some of these sequence numbers pretty easily as the numbers often follow a predictable sequence in some UNIX implementations. Using a combination of predictable sequence and knowledge of the target's IP address, it is possible to prosecute an IP spoofing attack against a target. In addition the TCP check summing of IP packets that are not very strong, which can lead to a potential for forgery, injection of information and tailgating of packets. The randomness of TCP initial sequence numbers varies across the UNIX system, resulting in a potential to inject the packets into a connection between two users.

The next section will focus on application security and the current vulnerability that affects TEISME's business operations.

7.   APPLICATION SECURITY PROBLEMS

Generally speaking any network connected to the Internet is open to global attack, the attacker trying to infiltrate an organisation's network may exploit a number of higher level protocols in the TCP/IP protocol suite. An attacker has the capability to obtain root privileges in a short space of time, due to much vulnerability, such as in the 'send mail' applications. The root privileges enable the hacker to delete any audits of their actions, stop any further audits of their actions from being carried out, install malicious software, delete, read, or modify TEISME and customer's applications, or information belonging to TEISME and customers. A large number of other software components / applications and protocols also contain similar bugs and vulnerabilities found in the 'send mail' system. The majority of the bugs found in the protocols are results of errors in the code, which may result from failures to check array bounds. The application layer also has several vulnerabilities that must be taken into consideration, the following vulnerabilities generally occur above the application layer:

i. *Security in the application-layer*: The system password file is vulnerable in all systems connected to the Internet, allowing the system password file to become compromised would leave the system open to hostile attacks of different kinds. For example, a recent study of Windows XP exposed a

```
proc virus() {

        goto main
        main:        // virus signature (guard) 12345678901234567

        loop:                                        //infection routine

        file := select_random_executable

        if file contains 12345678901234567
                then goto loop
                else prepend virus to file

        if trigger_condition = true            //trigger condition
                then remove all the files        //malicious function

    }
```

Figure 2–3. Generic program structure of a virus

Table 2–2. Classification of Internet viruses

Types of Virus	Infectors
File infectors	File infector viruses infect files on the victim's computer by inserting themselves into a file. Usually the file is an executable file, such as .EXE or .COM in Windows.
System and master boot-record infectors	A very common type of virus that infect system areas of a computer such as the Master Boot Record (MBR) on hard disks and the DOS boot record on floppy disks. More attractive in propagating the Internet within a short time.
Macro viruses	Macro viruses are simply macros generated by the Microsoft Word. Melissa is considered to be a mass-mailing worm with a viral payload.
i. Multi-partite viruses	Multi-partite virus is hybrid virus that infects the files, and system boot-records. This means that multi-partite viruses have the potential to be more damaging, and resistant, which makes them type of blended attack.
ii. Stealth virus	A stealth virus is one that attempts to hide its presence. This may involve attaching itself to files that are not usually seen by the user.
iii. Polymorphic viruses	The polymorphic viruses use encryption and decrypt it to run. Polymorphic viruses are difficult to eradicate than other types of viruses as the bulk of the virus is encrypted, it is harder to detect and analyse.
Worms	The worm virus is a self-replicating program that propagates over a network.
i. Mass-mailing worms	The mass-mailing worm is a worm that spreads through email. Once the email has reached its target it may have a payload in the form of a virus or Trojan.
ii. Network-aware worms	The network-aware worm such as SQL Slammer has shown that a well-written worm can degrade the Internet operation. The type of infection may include loading Trojans onto the target host, creating back doors or modifying files. Once infection is complete, the target host is now compromised and can be used by the worm to continue propagation
Trojans	Trojans virus carries some payload such as remote access methods, viruses and data destruction. The Trojan virus can be propagated through the Back Orifice 2000 (BO2K), used by network administrators to manage computers on their network remotely. However, it can be used maliciously because it provides a back door for the malicious attacker during the following operations: Session logging, Keystroke logging, File transfer, Program installation, Remote rebooting, Registry editing, Process management. BO2K has the ability to install itself silently so that the user is unaware that BO2K has been installed.

Table 2–3. Number of unique phishing attacks

	December 2003	January 2004	February 2004	March 2004	April 2004	May 2004	June 2004
Citibank	17	34	58	98	475	370	492
eBay	33	51	104	110	221	293	285
US Bank	0	2	0	4	62	167	251
Paypal	16	10	42	63	135	149	163
Fleet	1	2	9	23	28	33	55
Lloyds	1	1	0	4	15	17	24
Barclays	1	1	6	11	31	15	19
AOL	4	35	10	10	9	17	14
Halifax	0	10	0	1	6	9	11
Westpac	1	3	0	10	17	12	11
FirstUsa	0	0	0	0	0	0	10
VISA	4	2	8	7	0	21	9
Earthlink	6	9	8	5	18	6	7
e-gold	2	0	2	2	5	3	6
Bank One	1	0	0	5	4	6	5
Bendigo	0	0	0	0	0	1	5
HSBS	0	1	0	4	3	3	5
MBNA	0	0	2	0	2	1	4
Suntrust	0	0	0	1	5	1	4
Verizon	0	0	0	0	0	2	4

vulnerability that allowed a hostile web page to unobtrusively to extract a user's password and transmit it to the page's author. Meanwhile, Microsoft sends forth a stream of patches intending to correct what it designates as 'critical' security flaws in it systems, applications, and even its own previous patches. Microsoft certainly is not alone when it comes to software flaws, but as the massively dominant desktop system vendor, its software and support decisions tend to have much more influence on most consumers, and businesses (Weinstein and Neumann, 2003).

ii. *Malicious software*: Software of a malicious nature, which executed on the Internet-connected machine will have Internet protocols and facilities to propagate itself, or it may be used by the author for password sniffing, whereby on an Internet-connected machine it will mail copies of password files to its author. Malicious software can be a problem at many levels. A virus could be a set of macro commands for word processors (i.e. Microsoft Word), the macros will copy themselves into all document, which

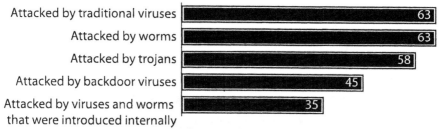

Attacked by traditional viruses — 63
Attacked by worms — 63
Attacked by trojans — 58
Attacked by backdoor viruses — 45
Attacked by viruses and worms that were introduced internally — 35

Figure 2–4. Network security problems according to US enterprises security proffesional

are created using the word processor on the machine where the virus was executed. Therefore, virus can disguise as an object code, which will copy itself into other executable files when it is executed. Just as viruses can affect humans, in the same way a computer virus can cripple a computer. Infected computers would typically experience degradation in performance, files becoming corrupt, hard drives being over-written or deleted and in some cases even the BIOS being altered. In a worst case scenario a virus can totally destroy a business organisation within a matter of hours. Computers are most vulnerable to contracting computer viruses via the Internet. A computer can also contract computer viruses by receiving documents over the network, installing software on a machine and copying files from another hard drive or disk. In 1998, the Melissa virus, Chernobyl virus and the Happy99 virus made headlines, causing damage to personal and corporate computers around the world. On March 27, 1999 the Melissa virus began spreading via e-mail attachments. When attachments were opened in Word 97 or Word 2000 with macros enabled, the virus infected the normal template causing documents referencing that template to become corrupt. If the infected document was opened on another computer, the document would propagate, this resulted in mail servers experiencing performance slowdowns and eventually shutting down completely. On January 20, 1999, the Happy99 hit the Internet. The Happy99 virus is an executable file that displays fireworks and the words 'Happy99' on users screen. During its run cycle, the virus modifies files on the system. Further attack was lunched in April 26, 1999, a virus called Chernobyl (CH1) started spreading. This infected executable files and then spread by executing an infected file. Eventually when then CH1 virus activated, the virus began deleting information from hard drives and overwrote each system BIOS. Indeed, it is equally important to remember the damages caused by the 'Love bug' or 'I LOVE YOU' in May 2000. The viruses are self-replicating programs that infect and propagate through files, which will cause them to be run when the file is opened. The Table 2–2 presents the types of viruses that have been identified in this research.

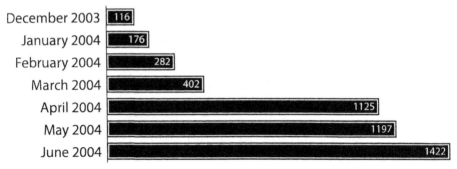

Figure 2–5. Number of unique phishing attacks per month (December 2003–June 2004)

The replication function of viruses exploits specific features of the host system using binary formats, scripting languages, specific directories where other executable programs can be found, which are tightly bound to a specific platform. The generic program structure of a virus is presented in Figure 2–3.

The IT department of Amplitude Research surveyed 103 enterprise security decision-makers and network administrators in the US, which was based on the virus activity experienced by enterprises during normal business operations. The outcome of their survey is presented in Figure 2–4 (eMarketer, 2005b). Further details and comprehensive list of past and current viruses are available in the Norton Anti-virus Software© website. The virus attacks are becoming more frequent, damaging and widespread, despite the effort of anti-virus product development. Viruses are the hardest security breach to deal with and the hardest to apportion blame for.

iii. *Phishing Attacks*: The new 'Phishing Attack Trends Report', published by the Anti-Phishing Working Group (APWG), which monitors these scams, the unsettling growth rate of this insidious type of online fraud continues to climb. The phishing attacks use 'spoofed' e-mails and fraudulent websites designed to fool recipients into divulging personal financial data i.e. credit card numbers, account user names and passwords. The number of unique phishing attacks reported in June was 1,422, and the organisation most targeted by phishing attacks during the month was Citibank, with 492; eBay, US Bank, PayPal and Fleet also ranked high on the list of companies being spoofed (see Table 2–3 for phishing comparison with other businesses), (APWG, 2004). In June 2004, APG reported 1,422 new cases of phishing attacks, which represented a 19% increase over the number of attacks reported in May (1,197). The average number of phishing attacks per day in June was 47.4, up significantly from the per day count for May (38.6). On a weekly basis, every week in June averaged over 300 attacks. However, the trend for the year is what is most unsettling (see Figure 2–5). In addi-

Figure 2-6. Threats that US IT professionals feel their networks are least protected against

tion, eMarketer research in collaboration with VeriSign©, Gartner©, and APWG found that (eMarketer, 2004):

- The majority of phishing attacks were launched between 9:00 pm and 4:00 am, when helpline staff are off duty or few in number.
- Phishing has accounted for $2.4 billion in fraud worldwide.
- The APWG report claims the average lifespan of a phishing site is only 2 1/4 days.
- The best protection against phishing is for TEISME to be educated on what to do in order to avoid any attack.

However, phishing is a concern to TEISME business operations and banks that acted as merchants to enabled the synchronisation of business transaction payment possible. It is also equally important to mention that PayPal is the most popular means of payment for goods and services sold by TEISMEs. The figures in Table 2-3 show that PayPal is among the targeted companies, this again calls for rethinking of how to sustain TEISMEs business operations among all the abundance of vulnerabilities (eMarketer, 2004). Furthermore, phishing also makes it possible to prove that absolute security is unattainable on TEISME business operations (see chapter 5 for further discussion). A considerable amount of information may be stored in a file by an application, which may not be visible when a file is opened by the application. An example would be the very popular fast save option used in Microsoft's Word processor application. Deleting the text in this application does not necessarily mean the information is removed. When deleting the text and saving the document again, the text is not deleted by MS Word, instead MS Word inserts a note instructing itself not to display the deleted data or information. It is possible to retrieve the deleted text using a program, which disregards MS Word instruction. It is often more or less impossible to fully review the contents of a computer file or an Internet file, thus causing concern that sensitive information may inadvertently be exported from the service provider's server and the TEISME servers. As an example of vulnerabilities in newer protocols, one may consider the 'World Wide Web' (WWW) or web (Shoniregun and Logvynovskiy, 2004). The web servers provide information in response to requests from the web browsers. If a request exploits a bug in the web server, the web server's security mechanism may be bypassed. The information accessible from the web varies widely, ranging from 'Plaintext' to forms of executable content. Some like Postscript can alter the behaviour of a printer, others like Java or ActiveX, may allow access to resources and data on the computer that should be inaccessible. Although Java's basic model is secure, the different levels in the model may introduce bugs. The security policy may not be correctly specified. The Java Virtual Machine (JVM) assumes that the byte code verifier finds certain classes of errors, so bugs in the verifier may admit hostile programs. The interpreter may not detect every possible attack, and if Java is opened to ease access by Java programs to other parts of the operating system, Java security may be bypassed (McGraw and Felton, 1997).

iv. *Spyware*: Spyware is now the biggest concern of Internet security and on TEISMEs business operations. The WatchGuard Technologies, study revealed that spyware accounts for the highest threats, which the US IT professionals feel their networks are least protected against, December 2004 – January 2005, as a percentage of respondents (see Figure 2–6) (eMarketer, 2005b). It is malicious software that installs on a computer without the user's knowledge and it can secretly gather information about a person or organisation. The WatchGuard Technologies Inc., which provides network security solutions for small and medium-sized businesses, surveyed 686 security administrators and IT managers in the US during December 2004 and January 2005 on what the biggest threats are to their network, and how aware other employees are of the threat. The out come of the survey findings shows that more than two-thirds of respondents pick it as the greatest security threat, compared to 23% who say viruses and 10% who say phishing. Unfortunately, respondents also feel least protected from this serious threat—66% felt least protected against spyware, compared to 27% who feel the same about phishing and 7% who feel the least protected against viruses. The survey also stated that executives are less concerned about spyware and more concerned about viruses. More than 50% of executives are concerned about the viruses, while 40% believed that spyware constitutes the biggest threat and 7% choose phishing. The result was not surprising because viruses have been a threat for a number of years the threats from spyware are a relatively new development (Euretig and Whitcomb, 2005; eMarketer, 2005a).

v. *Malware*: The malware attacks on TEISME's business operations are occurring very frequently, its crashes systems, erases data, send confidential documents of customers to unauthorised viewers, and installs software that makes PCs redundant in performing the normal business operations. In 2002, malware attacks rendered the Microsoft Internets Explorer browser inactive for a longer period of time, which led to Microsoft, making several changes to its browser as a result of this attack. In the future, malware will take two-step virus approach: users will first received a harmless code string and later receive another code that will combine with the first code to cause major problems. The TEISMEs need to be at alert not to compromise, such inevitable malware code for granted.

8. SUMMARY OF CHAPTER TWO

On a serious note, TEI has a number of impacts on TEISME, such impacts include the following:

- Shrinking the production
- Reducing intermediation and changing its nature
- The e-Payments implementation
- Generic problems with network protocol layers

The reason why the Internet is vulnerable to malicious programs, and other fraudulent transactions can be associated with its generic architecture. The Internet security demands attention at multiple levels. The Internet cannot be controlled, but it can be pro-actively monitored. Antivirus specialists have tended to explain the success of social engineering viruses, in part, by casting aspersions on the intelligence of the victims, calling them 'ignorant' or suggesting that they needed to apply 'common sense'. The variants of 'MyLife' virus were spreading because the tricks used by the virus to fool people into double clicking on the attachment, and becoming infected, were crude. It is hardly controversial to claim that the end of February and beginning of March 2004 was the worst period ever, regarding the sheer number of new malicious programs threatening the Internet community. New variants of Bagle, My-Doom and Netsky were spread daily – sometimes even more than once per day. The ability of attackers to rapidly gain control of vast numbers of Internet hosts poses an immense risk to the overall security of the Internet. Once subverted, these hosts can not only be used to launch massive denial of service floods, but also to steal or corrupt great quantities of sensitive information, and confuse and disrupt use of the network in more subtle ways. However, anti-virus software is often inadequately used. If the software is not set to automatically scan files or there are not regular updates to the software, it is not effective. In some cases, updates cannot be created and disseminated fast enough to prevent infection.

Predicting the future in any technological field is a difficult task. This is even more so when talking about the impact of TEI on SMEs. Therefore, SMEs that are thinking of implementing TEI or TEISMEs that are starting online business need to make a critical decision, which must be supported by an understanding of the hidden impacts of TEI on business operations. The next chapter focuses on the fundamental concepts of risk and detailed analysis of available risk assessment models, and their weaknesses.

REFERENCES

APWG (Anti-Phishing Working Group), 2004, *'Proposed solutions to address the threat of email spoofing scams'*; www.antiphishing.org (February 11, 2004).

Bailey and Bakos, 1997, *The impacts of eC on the efficiency of the economy: OEDC*, white paper, London, Stationery Office.

Bellowin, S. M., 1989, 'Security problems in the TCP/IP protocol suite', *Computer Communications Review*.

Block and Seger, 1998, 'Leveraging eC for competitive advantage: a business val framework', *Proceedings of the 9th International Conference on EDI-IOS*, Bled, Slovenia.

eMarketer, 2004, *'Phishing for sucker'*; www.emarketer.com/Article. aspx?1002975Aug (5 July 2004).

eMarketer, 2005a, *'Spyware Awareness Varied among Execs'*; www.emarketer.com/Article. aspx?1003232 (February 7, 2005)

eMarketer, 2005b, *'Security and Privacy report: What, IT Worry?'*; www.emarketer.com/Article.aspx?1003258 (February 20, 2005)

Euretig, K.R., and Whitcomb, S., 2005, *'WatchGuard Survey Indicates IT Managers View Spyware as Top Network Security Threat in 2005'*; www.watchguard.com/press/releases/wg299. asp (January 27, 2005).

Harrison, J., 2003, *'VPN Technologies – A Comparison'*; vnu.bitpipe.com/detail/ RES/1046358922_393.html (February 12, 2005).

Kalakota R. and Whinston, A. B., 1998, *Electronic Commerce: A Manager's Guide*. Addison Wesley.

Keen, P., 1991, *Shaping The Future: Business Design Through IT*. Harvard Business Press.

Kerr, K., and Litan, A., 2002, *'Online Transaction Fraud and Prevention Get More Sophisticated: Companies, Markets, Forces'*, Gartnerg online; www.gartnerg2.com/research/rpt-0102-0013.asp (November 6, 2003).

Kosiur, D., 1997, *Understanding eC*. Microsoft Press.

Landwehr, C. E. and Goldschlag, D. M., 1998, 'Security issues with Internet access', in the *Proceedings of the IEEE*, 85(12):2034–2051.

Lief, V., 1999, *'Anatomy of new market models'*, Forrester Research; www.forrester.com. (February 27, 2004)

McGraw, G. and Felton, E., 1997, *Java Security: Hostile Applets: Holes and Antidotes*. New York, John Wiley & Son.

Shoniregun, C.A. and Logvynovskiy, O., 2004, 'Securing XML documents', *the Australian Journal of Information Systems*, September 2004, pp.18–28.

Shoniregun, C. A., Omoegun, A., Brown-West, P. and Logvynovskiy, O., 2004a, 'Can eCRM and trust improve eC customer base?', in the *Proceedings of the IEEE conference on E-Commerce technology*, San Diego, California, USA, pp. 303–310.

Shoniregun, C.A., Chochliouros, I.P., Laperche, B., Logvynovskiy, O. and Spiliopoulou-Chochliourou, A., 2004b, *Questioning the Boundary Issues of Internet Security*, e-Center for Infonomics: London.

Shoniregun, C.A., 2002, 'To ignore E-commerce is to allow competitors to steal a lead'. *EC NL*, June, pp. 8–9.

Shoniregun, C.A., 2003, 'Are existing Internet security measures guaranteed to protect user identity in the financial services industry?', *International Journal of Services, Technology and Management (IJSTM)*, 4:194–215.

Stalling, W., 2001, *Business Data Communication*, 4th edition, Prentice Hall.

Weinstein, L. and Neumann, P., 2003, 'Risks of content filtering', *Communication of the ACM*, November.

Chapter 3

RISK ASSESSMENT OF TEI ON TEISME

1.   INTRODUCTION

Risk and the risk assessment are fundamental to the security of any business. The process of determining which security methods are appropriate and cost effective is very complex. One of the prime functions of security risk assessment is to put this process onto a more objective basis. Today many of the conventional methods used for performing security risk assessment are becoming more untenable in terms of usability, flexibility and also in terms of what they can produce for the enterprise.

> 'Enterprises share a universal risk from information security breaches. The impact on an enterprise's reputation can be much greater; more attention and deterrent measures needs to be taken'.
> —Yag Kanani (2003), Computer Weekly

It is essential for TEISMEs to ensure that risk assessment methodologies are in place to fully commensurate with the risk to which it is exposed, it does so with the view that should a weakness be exploited as a result of accepting that risk, the impact on the business operations will be such that the business will continue despite this impact. A negatively impacted, sometimes severely, should have been taken care off in advance by insuring against such risk, but no insurance companies in UK are willing to insure TEISMEs business operations *'Who will insure the safety of TEISME's business operations?'* and *'Who will be liable for stolen or fraudulent act during the transmission of data or information?'*. However, trying to answer these questions will require a risk assessment model that can project an accurate probability of the risk. This chapter is based on the fundamental concept of risk, implied definition of risk and detailed analysis of available risk assessment models (quantitative and qualitative risk assessments approaches) that are applicable to TEISME business operations and their weaknesses.

2.   CONCEPT OF RISK

The notion of the entrepreneur as a risk-bearer was recognised relatively early in the study of entrepreneurship by an Irishman, Richard Cantillon, a businessman and financier. Cantillon's 'Essay on the Nature of Commerce', was first published in 1755, 21 years after the author's death. His approach was the first important work in economics that gave the entrepreneur a central role in trade. Cantillon showed the entrepreneur to be a pivotal figure who operates within a set of economic markets. It views the entrepreneur as providing the right goods at the right place in order to satisfy given consumer wishes. Cantillon does not see the entrepreneur as creating demand through new production developments or by marketing techniques. Thus, although Cantillon's entrepreneurs must be forward-looking, entrepreneurs need not to be innovative in the sense of creating anything new. The entrepreneur must be alert to profit opportunities; however, these opportunities will occur when demand and supply do not match in a particular market.

> 'TEISME think that the profits to be won outweigh the risk to be incurred'
> —Shoniregun, C. (2004), Keynote speech at HIC'04 Hawaii

The modern view is that the entrepreneurs are basically risk-bearer, and that the profit is the reward for risk-bearing, stems from the work of an American economist Frank Knight, who first published his ideas in 'Risk, Uncertainty and Profit' in 1921. Knight's important contribution was to emphasise the distinction between insurable risk and non-insurable uncertainty and to develop a theory of profit that related to this non-insurable uncertainty. Knight (1921), argues that previous 'risk-theories' are ambiguous, because they did not distinguish sufficiently between two very different kinds of risk. On the one hand, risk means a quantity capable of being measured; in other words, the objective probability that an event will happen. However, because this kind of risk can be shifted from the entrepreneur to another party by an insurance contract, but this is not the case with TEISME, it is not an uncertainty in any meaningful sense. On the other hand, 'risk' is often taken to mean an un-measurable unknown, such as the inability to predict consumer demand. Knight termed the latter 'true' uncertainty and geared his theories of profit and entrepreneurship to its magnitude. Knight's work offered a new refinement to Cantillon's theory of entrepreneur as the bearer of uncertainty, because it isolated the concept of uncertainty and sharpened its meaning. Newbold (1991) suggested a different outlook to risk as applied to statistics for business and economics, which he refereed to as Utility Analysis of Risk. The expected value criterion provides a framework for decision-making that has wide practical applicability. Newbold presents the three types of utility functions of risk:

i.   The utility increases at a decreasing rate as payoff increases, reflecting an aversion to risk.

ii. The utility increases at an increasing rate as the payoffs (the ability to in-sure TEISMEs business operations *de facto*) become higher. This implies a taste for the highest payoffs that is more than commensurate with the monetary amounts involved, thus showing preference for risk.

iii. The utility increasing at a constant rate for all payoffs. In this case, the monetary values of the payoffs provide a true measure of utility and thus demonstrate indifference to risk. This is to say, in many instances, TEISME Director(s)/Managing Director(s) will believe that their presence and their business operations offers the highest expected monetary values are the preferred course. However, this is not invariably the case; there is always a need to consider the inevitable risks and the risks assessment of using TEI in business operations.

Mayer *et al.* (1995) states that risk is an essential component of trust one must take a risk in order to engage in trusting action. However, it is unclear whether risk is an antecedent of trust, or is an outcome of trust. One could argue that risk-taking behaviour and trust behaviour are really different sides of the coin. What really matters is that the connection between risk and trust depends on the situation and the context of a specific, identifiable relationship (Shoniregun *et al.*, 2004; Shoniregun, 2002).

Risk-tracking takes into account the profitability of the occurrence of an event between parties and the difference in the anticipated ratio of what Deutsch (1958) calls 'positive and negative emotional consequences' to the parties. The probability of negative consequences will depend on how risky the situation is and the existence of security measures that can avoid the risk from happening or reduce its impact. However, what level of security is adequate is difficult to establish as TEISMEs business operations vary considerably from one another in the degree of assurance they require before they will act in a situation that has the potentiality of danger or negative consequences. Modern science attacks the complex problems arising in the direction and management of large systems of men, machines, materials and money, in industry, business, government and defence. The distinctive approach is to develop a scientific model of the system incorporating measurements of factors such as change and risk, with which to predict and compare the outcome of alternative decision, strategies or controls from TEISMEs business operations and the insurance company's point of view.

According to Lucy (1995), probability can be defined as the quantification of uncertainty, while uncertainty may also be expressed as 'likelihood', 'chance' or 'risk'. Probability is represented by p, and can only take values ranging from 0, i.e. impossibility, to 1, i.e. certainty. For example it is impossible to buy an item from a TEISME's Internet-eC website without giving your credit card details if that is the only acceptable means of payment. It is certain that during the course of the transaction the data or information can be intercepted by the third party for fraudulent act i.e. Internet hackers. This is expressed as:

$$p(\text{buy an item from an SME Internet website}) = 0$$

$$\text{and } p(\text{intercepted}) = 1$$

Communication theory, which is nowadays refer to as information theory, also uses a mathematical measure of probability to quantify the properties of symbols to convey messages. It has important uses for the telecommunication engineer. Its primary value in studying management information lies in the key ideas of probability and the reduction of uncertainty and the notion of noise, lag and error in transmission. Knowledge of the risk and security processes behind TEI appears to be widespread. TEISME takes risk and security of information transfer for granted or assume there are known threats despite the lack of insurable risks. An example of the latter view is that 'nothing should be sent on the Internet which one would not send by postcard since the security levels are about the same'. Before examining the security requirements for TEISMEs, it is necessary to outline its major business and technological risks.

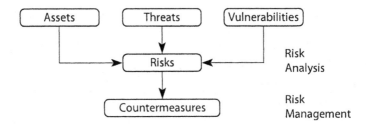

Figure 3–1. Three stages of GAMM method

It should be remembered that risks do not generally occur in isolation but tend to interact with each other.

The next sections take a closer look at the definition of risk and the risk assessment approaches.

3.   RISK AND THE RISK ASSESSMENT APPROACHES

The risk and risk assessment are popular in finance and investment problems, and compulsory for the design of potentially dangerous systems, such as nuclear and waste isolation plants (Helton *et al.*, 1997), and certain industrial activities, such as the chemical industry (Palle, 1994; Brehmer *et al.*, 1994).

> 'Risk is the potential realisation of undesirable consequences from hazards arising for a possible event.'
> —The McGraw-Hill Dictionary of Engineering

There is no standard definition of risk. From current knowledge it would seem that risk assessment has not been used to assess the type of risks TEISME encounter during their normal business operations. The term risk can be presented from four different perspectives:

i.   The general terminology: any chance of loss
ii. From the Insurance point of view: the insured, or the peril insured against.
iii. From management point of view: an approach of management concerned with the preservation of the assets and earning power of a business against risks of accidental loss.
iv. From consumers' perceptions: risk refers to the uncertainty and negative effective of engaging in an activity (Holak and Lehmann, 1990).

Furthermore, Carroll (1995) defined risk from the perspective of probability, which states that *'probability that a threat agent (cause) will exploit system vulnerability (weakness) and thereby create an effect detrimental to the system'*. Another definition of risk by Neumann (1995), considers risk as *'the adverse effects that can arise if vulnerability is exploited or if a threat is actualised'*. Smith (1993) further goes on to consider risk as *'asset value (the worth of the asset in danger), the sum of threats (those events which cause harm), and vulnerabilities (the openness of an enterprise to the threats)'*. The top level of the GAMM method suggested by Smith (1993) is depicted in Figure 3–1.

Figure 3–2. E-Risk radar

Waring and Glendon (1998), define risk as the *'probability or likelihood that (for a pure risk) a specified hazard will result in a specified undesired event or (for a speculative risk) a specified event or course of action will result in a specified gain or enhancement and/or specified loss or detriment'*. The authors went on to describe pure risk as the product of the potential severity of hazard consequences and the probability that the undesired event will occur.

According to Chapman and Ward (1999), *risk is the probability of a downside risk event multiplied by its impact*. The authors, however, warn that focusing on a 'downside' risk (i.e. on reducing threats or adverse outcomes) misses what they call 'upside risk', which they argue is the key part of the overall picture, because the purpose of 'improving performance implies a wide perspective which seeks to exploit opportunities or favourable possibilities'. Ould (1999) perceives risk as *'any threat to the achievement of one or more of the cardinal aims of the project'*. The Harvard Business Review (1999), classify 'uncertainty' into four levels:

- *Level 1:* is where there are clear trends (e.g. market demographics can be identified) that can help define potential demand for future products or services.
- *Level 2:* is uncertainty where there is a host of factors that are currently unknown, but that are in fact knowable (i.e. that could be known if the right analysis were done). For example, aspects such as competitors' capacity-expansion plans are often unknown, but not entirely unknowable.
- *Level 3:* is the residual uncertainty, that is, the uncertainty that remains after the best possible analysis has been done (e.g. outcome of an ongoing regulatory debate or performance attributes of a technology still in development.
- *Level 4:* is the uncertainty, which presents itself even though quite a bit could be known about the residual uncertainties.

In one of the previous studies by Horton *et al.*, (2000), defined risk was based on *the possibility of harm or loss* used to express uncertainty about events and outcomes that could have an undesirable effect on an organisation and its goals. The study points out that risk is inherent to every business and classified risks into two areas:

- *Voluntary risk:* These are 'opportunity risks, deliberately assumed by man-agement, which are often drivers of organisational activities'.
- *Involuntary risks:* These are 'threats and other dangers that are not vol-untarily sought out or assumed, but exist as necessary part of doing busi-ness'.

Deise *et al.* (2000) further identified three broader categories of electronic business risks as follows:

- *Strategic risks:* These include competitive environment, wrong strategic direction, dependence on others (suppliers, buyers), wrong corporate cul-ture, lack of reputation, regulatory changes, and governance.
- *Financial risks:* These include currency management and changes, unclear tax situations, and cash flow.
- *Operational risks:* These include technological changes and the use of poor technology; security; poor project management; business process controls; poor operations management; problems with employees, including a lack of skilled people.

This study falls within the operational risk identified by Deise *et al.* (2000), and embeds the strategic and financial risks into the proposed risk assessment model (see chapter 4). Pederson (2000), 'Electronic-Risk Radar or e-Risk Radar' created the broader risk categories as shown in Figure 3–2. The e-Risk Radar is used to plot risks into broad business risk categories but not to assess the risk faced by TEISME within their business operations.

The broader risk categories, which may require assessment and manage-ment consideration, include the following:

i. Identifying key people dependencies,
ii. Identifying the risks relating to key technological changes/obsolescence

Martin (2000b) contends that despite the many rewards of Internet-eC, an equal number of risks pose concern for management. She explains that in an Internet-eC environment, the actual paper trail is significantly reduced *vis-à-vis* the present paper-based trading environment. It is Martin's view that in order to appreciate the level of risk of Internet-eC applications, two factors must be considered:

i.   The number of people involved
ii. The value of the operations/transaction (payment or contract).

It is her contention that as a general rule, the more parties that are involved, the greater the risk and the higher the value of the transaction, the greater the risk. Indeed, the Internet-eC means global trading, the quantity and range of parties that can attempt to assess the systems creates new challenges in protecting critical activities. A compelling view is that in attempting to manage risk, it is important to come to grip with the fundamental elements of risk, just as it is vital to be aware of new threats, changes in, and challenges of, new TEI that often open up new vulnerabilities in information security. There is a general agreement that computer systems not only increase productivity and efficiency but also contain added risks. Researchers examine risks from different perspectives. Abu-Musa (2003) discussed risk relevant to ensuring the security and integrity of computerised accounting information systems. Peterson and Kim (2003), and Shoniregun (2004), explored similarities and differences in IS risk factors, various types of IS failure and the overall failure rate of IS projects. However, Pollard (2003) assessed risk as it relates to Internet-eC project with a focus on online banking, electronic funds transfer, and EDI. Kim and Eom's (2002) study of web retailers shows that online retailers should emphasise how they guarantee on time and risk-free delivery as well as hassle-free returns. Liebermann and Stashevsky (2000) developed a perceived risk map using a qualitative research paradigm. Frye (2000) attempted to address one of the most complex Internet-eC issues: transaction documentation. Frye states that documenting Internet-eC transactions falls into two categories: creating and capturing adequate records, and maintaining adequate records overtime.

The traditional, risk assessment methodologies are based upon a simplistic model of risk, which identifies threats and vulnerabilities they exploit to affect a security breach. Countermeasures are identified which mitigate the threat/vulnerability pairs. Loss due to a security breach is calculated based on the probability of the threat overcoming the countermeasure and creating the breach. The traditional model is discussed below and is assumed to be complete in its ability to model all of the countermeasures and represent all of the loss—*it was not found this to be the case*. Threat/vulnerability pairs are all crossed with the countermeasures and the assessor must decide, which are counter-intuitive. Risk assessment is fundamental to the security of any businesses and requires security in any system, commensurate with its risks. The process of determining which security methods are appropriate and cost effective is quite often a complex and sometimes a subjective matter. The Los Alamos Vulnerability/Risk Assessment (LAVA) system developed by Smith and Jalbert (1990) automates a mathematical model based on classical risk assessment, hierarchical multi-level system theory, decision theory, fuzzy possibility theory, expert system theory, utility theory, and cognitive science. Jaworski (1993) has developed a tandem threat scenario methodology that extends the traditional risk assessment methodology by analysing the perpetration of succession of threats at multiple vulnerability points. One of the prime functions of security risk assessment is to put this process onto a more objective basis. Risk assessment is a well-developed science that has been successfully applied to field other than security (Drake *et al.*, 1994). Risk assessment is defined by BS7799 as *'the assessment of threats to, impacts on and vulnerabilities of information and information processing facilities and the likelihood of their occurrence'*.

This rather unwieldy definition translates risk into being some function of threat, asset and vulnerability. This concept has been around for at least two decades. Twenty years ago the British Government first took a serious interest in computer security. Since then computer systems have evolved from being system-centric mainframes to user-centric, mobile, and web-based technologies. There has been a shift of philosophy from risk avoidance to risk management, and there has been a change of emphasis in consideration of the threat (GAMM, 2003b).

Today many of the conventional methods used for performing security risk assessment are becoming more untenable in terms of usability, flexibility and also in terms of what they can produce for the business in relation to current vulnerabilities facing TEISMEs business operations. It is essential for TEISMEs to ensure that current risk assessment methodologies are in place which are fully commensurate with the risks to which it is exposed. According to Smith (1993), there are two distinct approaches to risk assessment broken down into:

i. Quantitative approaches
ii. Qualitative approaches

Risk can be assessed quantitatively or qualitatively. The quantitative assessment of information security risk management is an important tool for measuring the value of assets against the significance of threats and the effectiveness of safeguards and controls. According to Horton *et al.* (2000), 'we cannot manage what we cannot measure and the process of quantitative risk assessment for information security begins by identifying significant assets, interdependencies, and vulnerabilities of information networks to accident, error, or attack'. The next step is developing and implementing realistic programs – improving the performance of the existing programs – to remedy the vulnerabilities while continuing to upgrade assessment and remediation. On the other hand, qualitative risk assessment is equally important in that through risk assessment, risk managers 'seek the right balance of details and indicators to report upward through their organisation to the board of directors'. However, the Critical Foundations report of the President's Commission on Critical Infrastructure Protection (PCCIP) encourages private industry to perform periodic, quantitative risk assessments of their information and telecommunication systems, to enhance awareness of new vulnerabilities. The PCCIP argues that the actual exposure emanates from the threat of an event that has the potential of becoming a risk (Hoyt *et al.*, 1995).

4.   QUANTITATIVE APPROACHES

A number of approaches for quantitative risk assessment have been proposed. This includes the annualised loss expectancy (ALE) value, Illinois approach of the economics of security, the Courtney approach, and the Security-Specific Eight Stage Risk Assessment model. Each of these is examined below.

4.1   Annualised Loss Expectancy (ALE) Model

The ALE value approach is determined by the following elements:

i.   Determine the *financial value* of the assets or resources at risk
ii. Determine the *exposure factor*—that is, the percentage of the asset value at risk
iii. Compute the *single loss expectancy*:

Table 3–1. Parameters for cost of impact and frequency of occurrences

Estimated cost of impact	i	Estimated frequency of occurrence	f
£10	1	Once in 300 years	1
£100	2	Once in 30 years	2
£1,000	3	Once in 3 years	3
£10,000	4	Once in 100 days	4
£100,000	5	Once in 10 days	5
£1,000,000	6	Once per day	6
£10,000,000	7	Ten times per day	7
£100,000,000	8	A hundred times per day	8

single loss expectancy = financial value × exposure factor

iv. Determine the *annualised rate of occurrence*—that is, the reciprocal of the average number of years between incidents of the risk
v. Determine the *annualised loss expectancy (ALE)*:

ALE = single loss expectancy ÷ annualised rate of occurrence

The ALE from information security breaches is worked out empirically from the business experience and intelligence regarding occurrences such as intrusions, viruses, denial of service attacks.

For example, given how much a single detrimental event would cost, it is possible estimate how many times it could happen in a year, then the multiplication of these two figures states the total loss that could happen in one year:

$$ALE = SLE \times ARO$$

ARO = Annualised Rate of Occurrence. (How often it happens per year)
SLE = Single Loss Expectancy. (How much a single-loss costs)
SLE may be calculated using EF (Exposure Factor)
To facilitate familiarity and ready comparison of figures, it is useful to quote in units of Loss-in-a-year no matter what the source data.

4.2 Illinois Method

The Illinois method is concerned with the enterprise making major assumptions in identifying and quantifying all possible access paths to assets and in estimating probabilities of failure of the protection mechanisms that block the paths (Smith, 1993). In this approach the total expected cost per annum to use the security system k is defined as:

$$C(\mathrm{k}) + L(\mathrm{k})$$

Where $C(\mathrm{k})$ is the cost (in £/year) to install and operate the system k, and

$L(\mathrm{k})$ is the expected loss (in £/year) due to exposure, or the cost of exposure,

when the security system k is in operation. The total loss $L(\mathrm{k})$ is found by considering all possible threats, where threats are access routes to the protected assets that is:

$$L(\mathrm{k}) = \sum[\text{exposed value} \times \text{probability of safeguard failure}]$$

4.3   Courtney Method

Unlike the Illinois method, the Courtney approach recommends and emphasis on relative magnitude of impacts and probability as indicated in the Table 3–1.

Lobel, (1980), describes two key elements of risk assessment in relation to information security, which is based on quantitative statement of possible loss event:

i.   Impact or cost if an exposure occurs, indicated by parameter i and
ii.   Frequency of occurrence, indicated by parameter f

The ranges of the parameters i, and f, are shown in Table 3–1. This parameters is used to calculate the annual loss expectancy L, where

$$L = 1/3 \times 10(i + f - 3)$$

For example, if an event with a potential loss of £1,000 per occurrence is likely to happen once every three years then the annual loss expectancy is

£16,667. If the above formula is used then the table gives $i = 5$ and $f = 3$, so that:

$$L = 1/3 \times 10(5 + 3 - 3) \times £100000 = 1/3 \times 50 \times £1000 = £16667.$$

4.4   The Security-Specific Eight Stage Risk Assessment Approach

Drake *et al.* (1994), proposed security-specific eight stages risk assessment model is based on the earlier work of Jaworski (1993). This risk assessment methodology was developed under contract F33657-93-C-2114 for the US Air Force Aeronautical Systems Centre. In this model, eight distinct stages are used to represent the activities that occur starting from the steps taken to prevent a threat to the system through to the resultant harm that can be caused. The eight stages of the model, with additional examples are detailed:

- *Stage 1. The obstruction of a threat occurrence:* A clear distinction is made between the existence of a threat, which is omnipresent, and threat occurrence.
- *Stage 2. The occurrence of a threat:* The occurrence of a threat is initiated. However, the occurrence of a threat does not imply that damage or harm to the system has occurred, only that the threat scenario has been initiated.
- *Stage 3. The detection of threat occurrence:* The threat detectors are smoke detectors, and password mechanisms that keep track of the number of times an incorrect password can be entered. In many cases there may not be a formal detection method beyond standard operating procedures. All detection mechanisms that are brought to bear against the threat occurrence are included in this stage.
- *Stage 4. The recovery from a threat occurrence:* In this stage, if totally successful, the threat occurrence is prevented from causing a security breach. All recovery mechanisms that are brought to bear against the threat occurrence are included in this stage.
- *Stage 5. The occurrence of a security breach:* A clear distinction was made between the security breaches, and the harm that the breach causes, which is modelled in stage eight. The three possible security breaches were idnetified as follows:

  i.   Compromise of classified, proprietary, or sensitive information
  ii. Loss of data or software integrity
  iii. Loss of system availability

  If backup systems are installed in a timely manner in stages six and seven, the resultant harm is minimised. This allows the ability to recover whatever possible, after a breach occurs, but before harm is brought to the system.
- *Stage 6. The detection of a security breach:* The security breach detectors are procedural hardware inspections for tampering, and period automated search of audit files to find a possible security violation. All detection mechanisms that are brought to bear against the security breach are included in this stage.
- *Stage 7. Eliminating the harm caused by a security breach:* In this stage, an attempt is made to limit or eliminate the harm caused by a security breach. All recovery mechanisms that are brought to bear against the security breach are also included.

- *Stage 8. Identifying five possible harms:* The term *'harm'* is used specifically for losses that are external to the system. This model identified five possible harms:

  i.   Failure of mission
  ii. Loss of personnel
  iii. Loss of resources
  iv. Loss of Dollars
  v.   Loss of time

For most types of security breaches, more than one of the harms can be the final result.

All the above eight stages are designed to allow the assessor to list all of the threat scenarios that are of interest to the system at hand. To depict from Drake *et al.*, (1994) eight stages of risk assessment approach, the security mechanisms for a system must have three opportunities to reduce the harm that could be caused by a threat: (i) detect the threat before it occurs, (ii) after the occurrence is detected, but before a security breach occurs, and (iii) after a security breach occurs and is detected.

The expected losses are calculated based on the risk level and the associated potential losses, but the driving principle of this approach is that not all of the losses caused by a security breach occur at the time of the security breach itself, therefore most of the losses occur later when the consequences of the breach are enacted.

5.   QUALITATIVE RISK ASSESSMENT MODEL

In contrast to the quantitative risk assessment model, the qualitative approach does not involve specific numbers and computation. Instead, the qualitative approach involves identifying situations, or scenarios involving one or more threats: CRAMM method, and Cobra Risk Consultant method. These two methods are discussed below. Most qualitative risk assessment methodologies make use of a number of interrelated elements some of which are:

- *Threats:* These are things that can go wrong or that can 'attack' the system; examples include fire or fraud. These threats are ever present for every system.
- *Vulnerability:* These make a system more prone to attack by a threat or make an attack more likely to have some success or impact. An example for fire vulnerability would be the presence of inflammable materials (e.g. paper).

- *Controls:* These are the countermeasures that are put in place for vulnerabilities. There are three types. They are firstly, that deterrent controls reduce the likelihood of a deliberate attack. Secondly, that preventative controls protect vulnerabilities and make an attack unsuccessful. Thirdly, that detective controls discover attacks and trigger preventative or corrective controls.

5.1   CRAMM Risk Assessment Model

The CRAMM (CCTA Risk Analysis and Management Method) method is owned, administered and maintained by the UK Security Service on behalf of the UK Government. The CRAMM method consists of three stages, each supported by questionnaires and guidelines. Each stage aims to answer one or two significant questions as follows:

- *Stage 1:* Is the value of assets (consisting of hardware, software and data) high enough to warrant security procedures more stringent than the use of a general 'code of good practice'? This stage identifies the system's assets by type, location and role. This knowledge will later drive the introduction of appropriate controls. Physical assets such as terminals, CPUs and printers are valued in replacement cost terms. Each data asset is valued according to the enterprise's perception of the likely damage to the enterprise. For example if the asset becomes:

  i.   Unavailable (over three variable time periods)
  ii. Destroyed
  iii. Disclosed (either to staff or outsiders)
  iv. Modified (accidentally or deliberately)

  The impacts described are then translated into quantitative measures drawn on predefined scales. Software assets are then identified and categorised as systems software or application software. They are divided into packages, utilities and programs. Where the software is unique and vital, its value to the enterprise can be defined in the same way used for assessing the value of data. After these initial assessments of value have been made, individual assets are then related together to identify their independence. For instance, CRAMM will try to determine the dependence of an application on the existence of a certain software utility. Such dependent assets, thereafter, take on the value of the data they support.
- *Stage 2:* What and where is the security need? The answers can be found by identifying the vulnerabilities of the system. This task can be supported by software, which identifies relevant threat types and can, when the oc-

casion demands it, group assets to simplify data collection. CRAMM recognises a total of 32 threat-types. These range from building fires and user error through to network failure. Questionnaires are used to interview the appropriate employees of the enterprise. These are comprehensive documents, which allow client-specific considerations to be included. Answers are used to calculate a score, which identifies low, medium or high states of risk. At the end of Stage Two, the asset values calculated during Stage One and these vulnerability scores are compared with a standard table. This supports the CRAMM enabler to identify 'security requirements' (more often known as measures of risk) which are expressed on an ascending scale from 1 to 5.

- *Stage 3:* How can the need be met? This stage contains a very large countermeasure library consisting of over 3000 detailed countermeasures organised into 70 logical groupings. CRAMM uses the measures of risks determined during the previous stage and compares them against the security level (a threshold level associated with each countermeasure) in order to identify if the risks are sufficiently great to justify the installation of a particular countermeasure.

CRAMM constructs a model, which the enterprise can interrogate to gain alternative approaches or to identify the impact of different scores. CRAMM also contains a range of documents (such as a recommended security policy and management report) that can be used to document a review and to formalise security. The accumulated CRAMM model can be used later on to assess the impact of changes and as an information resource for other reviews. At the end of Stage 3 one will know what modifications are required for the enterprise's system in terms of risk avoidance measures and the selection and implementation of specific countermeasures to reduce or minimise remaining risk levels.

5.2   The Cobra Risk Consultant

The Cobra Risk Consultant was originally launched in the nineties, and has continued to develop and move forward. It provides a unique 'next generation' paradigm to security risk assessment solution. It is a questionnaire based Windows PC tool, using 'expert' system principles and a set of bases. Cobra risk consultant can identify system threats vulnerabilities and exposure, measure the degree of actual risk for each area or aspect of a system, and directly link this to the potential business impact it can then offer detailed solutions and recommendations to reduce the risks and provide business as well as technical reports. The risk assessment process, using COBRA consists of three stages as follows:

- *Stage 1:* The first stage is carried out via module selection or generation, a base questionnaire is built to fit the environment and requirements of the enterprise. The questionnaire builder constructs an appropriate risk questionnaire for the environment/system under consideration. Individual 'Question Modules' are then specifically selected from the knowledge base. Each module embraces a particular area of risk or a specific threat class (e.g. Logical Access, Physical Access, Networks, Development, Operations, etc.). This questionnaire building process can be performed either manually or automatically. This process is further explained below.

  i. *Automatic Questionnaire Building:* With an automatic questionnaire build, the system creates a questionnaire that suits the enterprise's system/installation specifically. This is usually achieved through completion of the initial 'Business' or 'Impact' Questionnaire. Configuration, business function(s) and many other factors are taken into consideration, as well as the financial significance of each area of the system and its potential for loss (direct or indirect). The business/enterprise enabler can, therefore, be involved from the outset. The Business questionnaire covers each category in turn and upon completion generates a 'significance level' for each. This 'significant level' determines which question modules the Questionnaire Builder will select for inclusion in the detailed questionnaire.
  ii. *Manual Questionnaire Building:* This type of questionnaire is created by selection of the individual question module(s) from those defined to Risk Consultant. It may be selected for a number of reasons some of which includes:
     • Consideration of a specific aspect of security/risk
     • Performing risk analysis in various proposed scenarios
     • Analysis of all risk areas, even if some are not of real significance to the organisation.

- *Stage 2:* The second stage is the survey process. As Risk consultant questions are answered by an appropriate enterprise employee(s) and the information securely stored, Cobra Risk Surveyor manages the questionnaire completion process. Questions can be in various formats either mandatory single response, optional single response, mandatory multiple response, optional multiple response, text response, and numeric response. Most of these formats are a simple, multiple and a variety of choices. Full branching facilities are included, including the facility to branch to a secondary question module and return to the original. All input is validated and screens are of a standard format. Risk surveyor also provides the ability to skip one or more questions (for later completion), it comes along with a 'notepad' facility to enable additional comments and notes to be recorded. Different modules can also be completed at different times, enabling scheduling to be based around enterprise employee availability. The results generated are then brought together for the report generation stage.

- *Stage 3:* The third stage risk assessment is the report generator. The Report Generator is used to produce the results from the completed questionnaire from the second stage. The results are suitable for interpretation by both technical and non-technical management and are in the form of a professional business document. The content of the report are:

  i.   Recommended solutions and specific additional security control suggestions
  ii. A descriptive assessment and relative risk score for each 'risk category' in each area considered
  iii. A full impact analysis for the business or department
  iv. Direct linkage between areas of risk and the potential financial and business implications.

The report headings and the introductory text for each section can be changed and tailored to reflect enterprise requirements and culture. Output can alternatively be directed to a file. This enables import to word processing packages, if required.

6.   WEAKNESSES OF RISK ASSESSMENT MODELS

The weaknesses identified in the six selected model are presented in Table 3–2. These weaknesses have been incorporated into Shoniregun Risk Assessment Model presented in Chapter 4.

7.   WHY BS7799

The UK government is developing the standard known as *BS7799*—a code of practice for information security management, which looks like developing into a truly international standard. BS7799 allows compliant businesses to publicly demonstrate that they can safeguard the confidentiality, integrity and availability of their customer's information and is rapidly becoming an essential 'seal of approval' in the world Internet-eC. If a TEISME wants to trade securely over the Internet, it should ensure that both itself and its partners have this accreditation. As well as giving detailed security controls for computers and networks, BS7799 also provides guidance on security policies,

Table 3–2. Weaknesses of the selected models

Model	Weaknesses
Annualised Loss Expectancy (ALE) model	• ALE does not show clearly how all the elements in the model fit for purpose, and the steps required to fulfil expectations • ALE rolls up the contributions of all countermeasures into a single 'effectiveness' figure. However, no experimental methods for measuring rolled-up effectiveness have been found • The model is also flawed in that it assumes that all security breaches carry the same cost implications
Illinois method	• Minor variations in the values selected can contribute significantly to the time required to carry out the risk assessment • Averaging can cause countercyclical assessment behaviour, resulting in rising values when income is declining or vice versa • Illinois method uses actual farm-level data to estimate residual net income • The lack of detailed data needed to arrive at accurate income estimates is a common problem
Courtney method	• Courtney method does not provide a comprehensive bases for selecting risk reducing measures and for estimating the corresponding effect on annual loss expectancy
Security-specific eight stage risk assessment approach (SSESRA)	• SSESRA primarily addresses factors which are immutable: this implies that threat do not change without direct intervention and time is not a factor • SSESRA does not take into account dates, durations, and the cost of security breach occurrences. • The model lacks Tandem threat (where more than one threat is actively attempting to breach the system at a particular time), and cost/benefit analysis. • Information is only sensitive until when transactions are completed. Under these circumstances, the countermeasure to protect the information only needs to be effective for the period of sensitivity. The SSESRA does not take into account any other sensitive information that are stored in the systems.
CRAMM (CCTA Risk Analysis and Management Method)	• In CRAMM, each data asset is valued according to the enterprise's perception of the likely damage to the enterprise. • CRAMM recognises a total of 32 threat types so it will be difficult, if not totally impossible to accommodate new threats.
COBRA Risk Consultant	• COBRA asset valuation can proceed in advance of final development, a complete threat/vulnerability assessment cannot.

staff security awareness, business continuity planning and legal requirements. BS7799 is an essentially management standard intended to ensure that senior executives develop and then stick to approved methods of storing, processing and transmitting information and that they have adjusted these accordingly as commercial or technological conditional changes. The BS7799 standards are particularly pertinent to business governance in an Internet-eC context, where risk management not only has to contend with the usual risks of doing

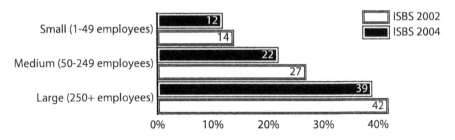

Figure 3–3. Proportion of UK businesses that are aware of the contents of BS7799

business, but also with rapidly changing IT/Internet risks and multiple legal jurisdictions. Thus the standards explain how to address the all-to-common and often devastating business impacts caused by viruses, website outages, improper disclosure of customer account details and incorrect pricing information, but not how assess or quantified the risks in terms of monetary value. This a failure in BS7799 because TEISME need to know the cost accrued from managing or prevent a particular risk occurrence from happening and if it does happened what does it cost TEISMEs' in relation to their business operations. In a survey conducted in 2004 by PricewaterhouseCoopers, about the proportion of UK businesses that are aware of the contents of BS7799 is shown below in Figure 3–3. The 2002 survey by PricewaterhouseCoopers found levels of awareness of BS7799 were disappointingly low. Two years on, this picture has not changed. Only 12% of people responsible for information security said they are aware of its contents, while 22% in the medium enterprises and 39% and in the large companies this raises to 39%, which is still very low (PricewaterhouseCoopers, 2004).

One of the key exercises that must be carried out in order to win and then keep BS7799 accreditation, is risk assessment or analysis. This process balances the particular planned safeguards against the risks (i.e. probability) of failing to meet business objectives. In this context, business objectives relate to exposure and the resulting regulatory penalties of financial losses. While the principles of Information Security can be complex to the uninitiated, this essentially boils down into an equation best represented by a cube drawn in a 3D space (see Figure 3–4) (GAMM, 2003c). The mitigating effect of a safeguard, for example, reduces the volume of the cube and helps TEISMEs to start reasoning about measuring risks. A number of risk analysis and management methods have been developed over the years and these are currently available either in the form of guidelines to apply manually or as interactive software packages, which does not directly address the risks that impact TEISME business operations. However, the nature of risk, to which TEISMEs are exposed, requires constant upgrading of their security software and vigilant observa-

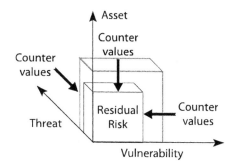

Figure 3–4. Threat, vulnerability and asset parameters

tions of transactions to and fro, as goods/services and money exchange hands in cyberspace. The possible solution that can ease these unstoppable threats will be to propose a model that will be user friendly to both TEISMEs and insurance companies for acceptance in calculating the possible risks/claims that might be incurred as a result of TEISME's reliance TEI.

8.   SUMMARY OF CHAPTER THREE

Within this chapter, a number of risk assessment models have been reviewed. None of the risk assessment models discussed so far are being used to assess or apply to the risk facing TEISMEs business operations at present, due to their inability to simulate the identified risk. There are substantial difficulties in attempting a quantitative or qualitative risk assessment approach. Not only that they are difficult to put precise monetary value to a threat, but to assign a monetary measure at all situations where threats have an impact on TEISMEs business operations. Estimating the frequency of attack or risk occurrence is usually problematic. The next chapter focuses on the methodology-adopted presents the Shoniregun's TEISME Risk Assessment Mode.

REFERENCES

Abu-Musa, A. A., 2003, 'The perceived threats to the security of computerized accounting information systems', *Journal of American Academy of Business*, Cambridge, Hollywood, September, vol. 3, no 1/2, p. 12.

Brehmer, B., Eriksson E. A. and Wulff, P., 1994, 'Risk management', *European Journal of Operational Research*, 75(3):477–566.

Carroll, J. M., 1995, *Computer Security*, 3rd edition, Butterworth Heineman.

Chapman, C. and Ward, S., 1997, *Project Risk Management*, John Wiley and Sons, USA.

Deise, M. V., Nowikow, C., King, P., and Wright, A., 2000, *Executive's Guide to E-business: From Tactics to Strategy*, John Wiley, New York.

Deutsch, M., 1958, 'Trust and suspicion', *Journal of Conflict Resolution*, 2(2):265–279.

Drake, D. L., Morse, K. L., 1994, 'The security-specific eight stage risk assessment methodology', in the *Proceedings of the 17th National Computer Security Conference*, San Diego.

Frye, E., 2000, 'Legal issues in documenting: e-commerce transactions', *Information Management Journal*, v. 35, no. 4, pp. 10–14.

GAMM (Gamma Secure Systems), 2003, *'Risk assessment models: IAAC workshop at Senate House'*, London, July; www.gammassl.co.uk/topics/IAAC.htm (March 2, 2003).

Glasman, S., Turn, R., and Gaines, R. S., 1977, 'Problem areas in computer security assessment', in the *AFIPS Conference Proceedings*, NCC, vol. 46, pp. 105–112.

Harvard Business Review, 1999, 'Managing Uncertainty', *Harvard Business Review*, Harvard Business School Press, USA.

Helton, J.C., Aderson, D.R., Marietta, M.G. and Rechard, R.P., 1997, 'Performance assessment for the waste isolation pilot plant: from regulation to calculation for 40 CFR 191.13', *Operations Research*, 45(2):157–177.

Holak, S.L., and Lehmann, D.R., 1990, 'Purchase intentions and the dimensions of innovation: An exploratory model', *Journal of product Innovation Management*, vol. 7, no. 1, pp.59–73

Horton, T.R., LeGrand, C.H., Murray, W. H., Ozier, W. J. and Parker, D. B., 2000, *'Managing information security risks'*; www.taudit.org/forum/riskmanagement/f319rm.htm (June 22, 2001).

Hoyt, D., Hutt, A., Bosworth, S., 1995, *Computer Security Handbook*, New York: John Wiley and Sons.

Jaworski, L., 1993, 'Tandem Threat Scenarios: A Risk Assessment Approach', in the *Proceedings of the 16th National Computer Security Conference*, Baltimore, MD: vol. 1, 1993. pp. 155–164.

Kim, E. B., and Eom, S. B., 2002, 'Designing effective cyber store user interface', *Industrial Management + Data Systems*, v. 102, no. 5/6, pp. 241–252.

Knight, F., 1921, *Uncertainty and Profit*, Boston, Schaffner & Marx Houghton Mifflin Company.

Liebermann, Y., and Stashevsky, S., 2000, 'Perceived risks as barriers to Internet and e-commerce usage', *Qualitative Market Research*, Bradford, v.5, no. 4, p. 291.

Lobel, J., 1980, 'Risk analysis in the 1980s', in the *AFIPS Conference proceedings*, NCC, v. 49, pp.831–836.

Lucy, T., 1995, Management Information Systems, DP Publications.

Martin, D., 2000, *'Risk assessment when auditing e-commerce activities'*; www.itaudit.org/fforum/riskmanagement/f303rm.htm (January 26, 2002).

Mayer, R. C., Davis, J. H. and Schoorman, F. D., 1995, 'An introduction of organisational trust', *Academy of Management Review*, 20(3):709–734.

Neumann, P. G., 1995, Computer Related Risks, Massachusetts, Addison Wesley.

Newbold, P., 1991, *Statistics For Business And Economics*, 3rd edition, Prentice Hall International Editions.

Ould, M. A., 1999, *Managing Software Quality And Business Risk*, John Wiley & Sons.

Palle, H., 1994, 'Overview of problems of risk management of accidents with dangerous chemical in Europe', *European Journal of Operational Research*, 75(3):488–498.

Pederson, L., 2000, *E-risk management*; www.gtnews.com/articles4/2262.html (March 23, 2002).

Peterson, D. K., and Kim, C., 2003, 'Perceptions on IS risks and failure types: A comparison of designers from the United States, Japan and Korea', *Journal of Global Information Management*, Hershey, July–September, v. 11, no. 3, pp. 24–32.

Pollard, C., 2003, 'E-service adoption and use in small firms in Australia: Lessons learned from a government sponsored program', *Journal of Global Information Technology Management*, v. 6, no. 2, pp. 45–66.

PricewaterhouseCoopers, 2004, *Information Security Breaches Survey 2004 Technical Report*, in association with Computer Associates, Entrust and Microsoft—DTIrecommendation; (www.pwc.com/images/gx/eng/about/svcs/grms/2004TechnicalReport.pdf (March 23, 2004).

Schweitzer, J. A., 1992, *Managing Information Security: a Program for the Electronic information Age*, Butterworth, London.

Shoniregun, C. A., 2004, 'An Investigation of Information systems project failure and its implication on organisations', *International Journal of Service Technology Management (IJSTM)*, v. 5, no. 1, pp.25–41.

Shoniregun, C. A., Omoegun, A., Brown-West, P. and Logvynovskiy, O., 2004, 'Can eCRM and trust improve eC customer base?', in the *Proceedings of the IEEE conference on E-Commerce technology*, San Diego, California, USA, pp. 303–310.

Shoniregun, C. A., 2002, 'To ignore E-commerce is to allow competitors to steal a lead'. EC NL, July, pp. 8–9.

Smith, M., 1993, *Commonsense computer security: your practical guide to information protection*, 2nd edition. McGraw Hill.

Smith, S. T., and Jalbert, M. L., 1990, 'LAVA/CIS Version 2.0: A Software for Vulnerability and Risk Assessment', in the *Proceeding of the 13th National Computer Security Conference*, October 1990, pp. 460–469.

Waring, A. and Glendon, A., 1998, *Managing Risk*. Thomson Learning.

Chapter 4

METHODOLOGY

1.   INTRODUCTION

To identify appropriate research methods for this research, the taxonomy of Information Systems research methods proposed by Galliers (1992) was adopted. In this taxonomy he adequately combined research methods. This chapter focuses on the methodology adopted in attaining the data and/or information required to prove or disprove the stated hypothesises in chapter. The Shoniregun Risk Assessment Model was proposed. The risk assessment model was implemented within 3 TEISMEs.

2.   METHOD

The methodology by any study must be appropriate for the objectives of that study. The scientific methodology is a system of explicit rules and procedures on which research is based and against which claims for knowledge are evaluated. The methodology used within the framework of this study are bound and based on a combination of the following:

i. *Formal theory* shows a theoretical structure of terms and relationships developed by inference from a set of axioms such as proving a theorem or designing a new solution process such as model.
ii. *Survey* indicates choice of sample and size, questionnaire design, target audience, analysis mechanism, hypothesis, methods of gathering data, and research strategy.

iii. *Case study observations* clearly show the methodologies used such as grounded theory, structured interviews, and case study observations.
iv. *Laboratory experiment* is a controlled research based on the lab experiment, which tested the reliability and validity of TEISME business transaction using sniffer packet.

This study opts for all of the above options, hence it is propounded that research without methodology is like a ship without a captain. The use of questionnaire surveys, a lab experiment, structured interviews, and case study observations are the primary methods of data collection and information gathering for the purpose of satisfying the hypothesis (see chapter 1).

2.1   Questionnaire

An interpretative epistemology was considered the most appropriate perspective from which to gather information about TEISMEs business operations, actions and experiences with regard to the use of TEI. An online survey questionnaire (the questionnaire was attached to an e-mail and visa versa) with 500 TEISMEs feedback out of 1800 within co.uk service provider, which the target audience were TEISMEs directors, and managing director(s) was performed. The result generates data used to identify the types of TEISMEs that can be classified under the proposed classification in this study (see chapter 5). It was possible to get this high feedback as a result of continuously chasing up the respondents. A follow-up of 400 TEISMEs were purposefully selected from three main sources at random: the Retail Directory of the UK, the Internet Webster directory, and the DTI directory, which directly aim at the TEISMEs directors, and managing directors. The rationale for this purposive selection was to ensure that different industrial sectors are included in the sample. This part of the research was to investigate the risks to which TEISMEs are exposed and how the risks are assessed. There was also the issue of security and privacy. It was felt that managing directors who formulate policies and strategies would be in a better position to fill in the questionnaire. It was hoped that their answers would enhance the validity of the research results (see chapter 5), and thus lend weight to the generalisation of the research findings and conclusions. There were 118 responses based on 5% responses by post and 95% online (the questionnaire was attached to an e-mail and visa versa). Furthermore, the author felt that the sample of 118 TEISMEs would be large enough for a research of this nature, given the time scale and the combination of research methods involved.

2.2   Interview

The questions outlined in the interview were aimed at TEISMEs directors, and managing director. The maximum number of questions for the interview was 9 and the time allocation for each interview was 30 minutes. The aim was to gather information on the type problems encountered by TEISME as a result of their reliance on TEI and what type of TEI business operations risk assessment are in place and/or currently in use. The structured interview is based on 'TEISMEs attitudes towards insuring the risk involve in their business operations. Face-to-face structured interviews were arranged among 6 different TEISMEs directors and/or managing directors, which were recorded by Dictaphone, with prior permission and type up for easy referencing. The maximum number of questions for the interview was 9 and time allocation for the each interview was 30 minutes; any more than this, it was felt, would put potential interviewees off. Structured interviews were adopted as a result of the following three aspects that distinguished the technique from any other data collection:

- Structured interviews are modifications or extensions of ordinary conversations, but with important distinctions.
- Interviewers are more interested in the understanding, knowledge, and insights of the interviewees than in categorising people or events in terms of academic theories.
- The content of the structured interview, as well as the flow and choice of topics, changes to match what the individual interviewee knows and feels (Rubin and Rubin, 1995).

The structured interviews follow a set schedule of questions pre-empted before the interview is commenced. Despite this degree of preparation it is not as rigid as a questionnaire and allows for probing and additional questioning to promote clarity, if necessary. The interview is designed to elaborate on the questions posed in the questionnaire survey to gain qualitative data. The information gathered allowed further insights into the feedback from the questionnaire survey conducted earlier in this research, and exploits the thoughts behind some of the answers given. However, the author was able to establish the risks to which TEISMEs business operations are exposed to, as a result of their dependencies on TEI.

2.3   Laboratory Experiment

A laboratory experiment was conducted among 50 existing TEISMEs that participated in the follow up questionnaire survey. The sniffer packet is used to test the reliability of the network security and also if security of TEISME business operation is attainable or not. A sniffer is a software program and/or device that monitors data travelling over a network. Sniffers can be used both for legitimate network management functions and for stealing information off a network. Sniffing is one of the most popular forms of attacks used by hackers. Sniffer as a product was originally created by Network General, which was acquired by Network Associates. Recently, Network Associates has decided to spin off the Sniffer product unit. The Sniffer unit has become a private company and has re-named itself as Network General.

The trial version of password sniffer has been adopted for the laboratory experiment based on the reviews from 15 hackers websites (digitalhackers.com, ehap.org, elitechathacker.homestead.com, sascha-jung.de, hackerwar2002.cjb. net, thenewbiesarea.f2s.com, attrition.org, 2600.com, onething.com, attrition. org, mgmua.com, hacked.net, onething.com, paybackproductions.com, turkeynews.net). The password sniffer has the following features:

- Displays the passwords as soon as it appears on network and supports various protocols.
- Fully supports application protocols of FTP, SMTP, POP3, and TELNET. That means user names and passwords used to send and receive e-mails, to log on a website, or to log on a server, can be fully captured and saved.
- Highlights syntax for application data in the format of HTML, HTTP and XML.
- Supports HTTP protocol, including proxy password, basic HTTP authenticate authorisation and most passwords submitted through HTML, no matter they are encoded by MIME or base64.
- Verifies whether the captured passwords are valid.
- It can tell whether the passwords captured are right. The replies from the server for the log-in are displayed, and it always keeps trying to get valid user name and password pairs.

Although there are over 100 sniffers available in the market today, the following are the most popular sniffers: ACE Password Sniffer, ICQ Sniffer, AIM Sniffer, EtherBoss MSN Monitor, Packet Sniffer, HTTP Sniffer, Password Sniffer, MSN Sniffer, RFC Viewer. The price of a sniffer, ranging from fifty pounds to tens of thousands of pounds, depends on who is the vendor. The trial versions of sniffer packets are available online for free download.

2.4   Case study

The term case study has multiple meanings. It can be used to describe a unit of analysis (e.g. a case study of particular business), or to describe a method. A case study approach is considered valid for this research. Yin (1984) and Ben-basat et al. (1987) discuss the merits of using multiple case studies to provide replication logic and rich descriptions of emergent research areas. Multiple case study analysis has been justified and validated by researchers such as Zik-mund (1997), who investigated inter organisation systems. For the purpose of brevity, three case studies representative of the different nature of TEISME's businesses within this study, are presented. The TEISMEs were firstly con-tacted by phone to get their consent (i.e. none of the TEISMEs' names or their website addresses will mentioned; they will otherwise be represented by the term 'TEISME A' etc.) for the facts gathering observations. However, the case study observations enabled us to determine, which type of risks are frequently encountered by TEISMEs in their business operations.

Finally, 3 TEISMEs were selected for case study observations. The se-lected TEISMEs were from two sources: retail directories of the UK, Internet Webster directory and the DTI Directory. The case study observations were used to identify any useful data and information that were subjective and rich. It highlighted variables, processes and relationships that aided in the endeav-ours of the research. The case study observations allow the collection of data and presenting of information in a way that provides more context, they are good for showing how something happens or works in a real life situation (Kane and O'Reilly-de, 2001). In 2003 to 2004, the author conducted case study observations among 3 TEISMEs based on the current problems encoun-tered as a result of reliance on TEI. The abstract to the case study observation are detailed below.

2.4.1   Case Study Observation (CSO A)

Business type:	Medium enterprises
Region:	South East
Sector:	Service industry
Staff level:	100
Annual income:	£15million
Business:	Processes marketing
Justifications:	Improve efficiency, maximise marketing, reduce costs
Technologies:	CD-ROM, electronic payments, online order processing, website

The CSO A has experience of working in the classical music sector as crea-tors, performers, promoters and fund-raisers. Since the business' formation in 2000, COS A, has utilised that experience to serve clients ranging from individual artists to orchestras, classical music agencies and trade associations as well as being a source of information for international enterprises such as

Microsoft Encarta. The business concept, developed by two people, revolved around making their combined expertise, information, ideas and contacts gained in extensive careers in the music profession accessible to the public and interested parties. The company provides advice, information, and action on all elements of professional music-making including new technologies; copyright; promotion and publicity; recording and programme research; concert planning and production; project management and fund-raising.

The CSO A classical music website embraces a community of some 400 composers, performers, independent publishers and record labels seeking to attract audiences and stimulate productivity within the (mainly) classical sector. The website also has one of the largest portals serving classical music interests with over 1,000 links from within the UK and worldwide. Clients include the Royal College of Music, the British Music Information Centre, the Incorporated Society of Musicians, the British Red Cross, Southampton University Hospitals Trust, King Alfred's College Winchester and Barnardos. The website provides personalised pages for performers and composers together with entries for record labels and affiliated organisations. They also hold classical music tracks with copyright protection in the digital domain. Resources that are provided online include educational materials, management and services, musicians well being, an on-line music library and 'digital jukebox'. And not just classical music buffs can enjoy the website as it also caters for Jazz, folk, world and easy listening music.

The CSO A was launched in 2001, selling a range of niche classical music, promoting and distributing through world-wide sales the creative products of British artists. This retail arm trades CDs, sheet music, books about music and musical accessories that can be purchased by secure credit-card transaction on-line. The website also provides real audio files and score pages as PDF files so that customers can listen to tracks and view a sample page of music before buying on-line.

In keeping with the basic principles of a successful web presence, CSO A have ensured that their website has been registered with all the major search engines, and that they are prominently located at or near the top of searches relating to their business—something that they check on a regular basis. In order to ensure that the company does not lose out on potential European export orders, they have translated their keywords, page titles, and page descriptions (essential for helping Web surfers to locate their site) into a number of European languages for the Google search engine, where users prefer to search in their own language. The CSO A implemented their e-catalogue in May 2001, the development having been driven forward by the inconvenience of dealing with e-mail orders from the website, and also as a result of the major security concerns from customers in making orders in this fashion. Although CSO A admitted there were teething problems with the e-catalogue, they have been quick to reap the rewards from the facility and believe that their Internet re-lated sales (i.e. all sales originating from viewing the Internet site) have tripled since implementation. Over 20% of total sales now originate from the shopping basket, with approximately 70% of these sales to date being from new custom-ers from around the world. The CSO A, have also been quickly to recognise the value of e-mail as a highly efficient and effective tool for communicating with customers. Every customer inputted into their Sage Accounting System, is subjected to regular targeted information on products of interest by way of e-mail shots and e-newsletters. This not only keeps the customer interested and informed of developments but often results in significant extra orders and helps explain why over 60% of sales are repeat business. CSO A's achieve-ments in gaining maximum value from Internet-eC have been officially recog-nised, as they were recently one of the nominees for the Internet-eC awards. However, they have further ambitious plans for the company, including de-veloping a 'One Stop Music' portal, i.e. a strong on-line presence, offering a virtual outlet for other kind of music. The business ISP has been improved to secure payment processing for the CSO A website and advised on VAT vari-ables for sales outside the European Union. In addition to this ICT help, the business also provided a formal situation analysis and goals for the company, reviewed the business processes and highlighted opportunities for the business to promote through pay-per-click and other internet marketing tools with the aim of improving product indexing on search engines and customer reach.

2.4.2   Case Study Observation B (CSO B)

Business type:	Small enterprises
Region:	North
Sector:	Manufacturing/service industry
Staff level:	18
Annual income:	£5 million
Business:	Processes marketing
Justifications:	Improve efficiency, maximise marketing, reduce costs
Technologies:	CD-ROM, electronic payments, online order processing, website
Risk assessment:	None, but logged all identified risks in the logbook

The idea for CSO B came about when proprietor (Director) was buying gifts for friends' babies. Not knowing quite where to start, she realised the middle to top-end of the baby accessory market was largely untapped. Combining her experience in the fashion industry with hard work, the Director, at the ripe old age of 22 – seized upon the opportunities of the Internet age and set up CSO B is a e-tailing business specialising in the sale of items for mothers, new-born to four-year old children, from traditional toys to luxurious clothing. CSO B evolved from a traditional 'bricks-and-mortar' maternity wear company to a truly 'clicks-and-mortar' online business catering for discerning mothers-to-be. The website offers product catalogues, pregnancy-related information, and an online ordering facility – all backed up with efficient customer service and care. The website was initially used as a marketing tool to promote the printed CSO B catalogue, the first of which was launched in October of 1999. Initially COS B used a simple website to complement the catalogue however it soon became apparent that customers wanted to place orders and deal with the company through the site. CSO B then decided to upgrade it to register customer preferences and expectations; because they planned to cater for a niche market, and felt it was important to get a real understanding of their customer base. In early 2001, further changes were made to create the current interactive site and CSO B is already seeing the results. The benefits of a fully functional, Internet-eC site include reaching a larger audience – almost all overseas orders are driven by the website while the cost of international transactions has been reduced. CSO B provides an additional channel to tap into and make purchases outside of traditional office hours. CSO B's glossy catalogues reflect the high quality of their extensive product range and dispatch to the business' mailing list of over 10,000. While the catalogue is still available on request, overseas customers are encouraged to use the website. It also massively reduces the time spent on the telephone, taking orders and completing complicated credit card transactions. The flexibility of a website means that the company can keep customers up to date, advising them of new additions to the range, sales promotions or when a particular item has been discontinued. If a product is out of stock it can be easily removed from the online catalogue, an amendment that can be made in-house.

While Internet-eC has been essential to expanding CSO B's core customer base and building a strong brand through web-presence, maintaining a personal feel was a priority for Director. CSO B specialises in the sale of traditional mothers, and children's items, because CSO B do cater for the middle to top-end of the market, their customers tend to be the lucky tot's family or close-friends who are looking for high-quality and individual pieces. CSO B range does include essentials but customers are usually looking for gifts or have a special occasion in mind, a Christening, for example. Interaction with customers through the website is actively encouraged through feedback and personalised services such as the Godparent and Grandparent Reminder Service. Customers registering for this service receive birthday reminders 21 days in advance. Customer convenience is emphasised on the website too and CSO B's extensive range is show-cased in five accessible categories: Christening, clothes, nursery, sales items and toys. The company opted for Shop Assistant software, which is both user-friendly and secure although they arrived at this option through trial and error. Initially CSO B used a less flexible piece of software for online transactions which was incompatible with the particular needs of the business. Small businesses have very specific needs in terms of IT and Internet-eC so it is an imperative to partner with a provider who fully understands the business' goals and what to be achieved through e-enabling your business. CSO B quickly realised that setting up an Internet-eC site would be an effective and economical way to break down geographical barriers, and therefore reach a wider audience. Operating an online business would encourage international opportunities that would have the potential to lead to wholesale developments. By promoting the website in all relevant publications, people would be encouraged to visit the site, and offered various methods of purchasing and communication. The use of Internet-eC has helped reduce costs and time consuming in administrative processes, which means CSO B can commit energies to creating extensive, high quality catalogues. It's also allowed COS B to go that extra mile in terms of customer service: by ensuring communication on a personal level, and keeping customers happy. COS B website is Internet-eC enabled for secure online ordering and online catalogue requests, using 128-bit encryption. Online tracking of parcels is used to enable CSO B to meet delivery commitments. The customer database that has been compiled is used for intelligent marketing, allowing the company to implement an Internet marketing strategy through targeted e-mails, and newsletters.

The fact that there are few websites available with pregnancy products makes the CSO B site something of a novelty. The company experienced a 200% increase in sales in the first six months since launch of the site. This increase has led to the design and manufacturing of own-label clothing, increasing product quality, prices and profits. There are numerous expansion opportunities open to CSO B, and the key is to be selective. Without any specific international marketing effort, more hits have been received from Europe and the US than from the UK. Although capabilities were not set up initially to service customers outside the UK, these opportunities will be exploited in the very near future. International enquiries have been received via the website from people wishing to stock or act as distributors for the CSO B label.

2.4.3   Case Study Observation C (CSO C)

Business type: Medium enterprises
Region: Midwest
Sector: Service industry
Staff level: 200
Annual income: £35m
Business: Processes marketing
Justifications: Improve efficiency, maximise marketing, reduce costs
Technologies: Electronic payments, online order processing, website

The CSO C owes its existence to the development of 'open skies' in Europe. Before 1987 European air travel was effectively carved up by the national flag-carriers, which considered the air routes between the major European cities to be their own permanent fiefdoms. Under the old regime flying schedules, fares and even the amount of passengers that each national airline could carry were negotiated between governments in hugely uncompetitive 'bilateral' agreements. Competition from other airlines was almost unheard of. It is no coincidence that the concept of air travels as the preserve of the rich and famous is a hangover partly from this era. That was all changed when the European Commission - in the face of huge opposition from a number of EU Member States wanting to protect their own state-owned airlines from competition - introduced its three-phase ten-year reform process in 1987. Today any airline holding a valid Air Operators Certificate in the EU cannot be prevented from operating on any route within the European Union, including flights wholly within another country. CSO C currently has operating bases throughout the UK and mainland Europe. It is a truly European operation and was one of the few airlines to take advantage of the reforms offered by the single European aviation market.

The CSO C is one of Europe's leading low-cost airline, and keeps costs low by eliminating the unnecessary costs and 'frills', which characterise 'traditional' airlines. Use of the Internet to reduce distribution costs CSO C was one of the first airlines to embrace the opportunity of the Internet when it sold its first seat online in Sept 1999. All seats are sold over the Internet, making CSO C one of the biggest Internet air travel ticket retailer in UK. Passengers receive an e-mail containing their travel details and booking reference when they book online. This helps to reduce significantly the cost of issuing, distributing, processing and reconciling millions of tickets each year. Eliminating free catering on-board reduces cost and unnecessary bureaucracy and management. It is also an important differentiator between CSO C and other airlines and a potent reflection of other low-cost approach. Passengers can purchase food on-board. The concept of a 'simple service model' also reflects a more general point about eliminating other unnecessary, complex-to-manage and costly services, such as pre-assigned seats; interline connections with other airlines and cargo/freight carriage. CSO C flies to main destination airports throughout Europe, but gains efficiencies through rapid turn around times, and progressive landing charges agreements with the airports. By reducing turnarounds to 30 minutes and below, CSO C can achieve extra rotations on the high-frequency routes, thereby maximising utilisation rates of its aircraft.

Since its launch CSO C has simplified its working practices by embracing the concept of the paperless office. The management and administration of the company is undertaken entirely on IT systems which can be accessed through secure servers from anywhere in the world enabling huge flexibility in the running of the airline. The CSO C is one of the successes of the European Internet. From small beginnings CSO C was born out of the Internet boom of the late 1990s but its origins stretch back much further. The Internet plays a vital part in the CSO C business plan, and is critical to its ongoing success. As a low-cost operation, controlling the cost of doing business is crucial to the airline's ability to offer low fares. Because the Internet provides the most cost-effective distribution channel, CSO C has aggressively pursued its strategy of encouraging passengers to book their seats online. Here are some examples of the ways in which COS C give incentives to people to book via the Internet: Passengers booking online receive a discount of £5.00 for each leg of a journey. CSO C first pioneered the concept of offering a discount to Internet customers, an initiative that has been widely copied by competitors. The CSO C promotions are exclusive to the Internet, so that customers must get online if they wish to take advantage of discounted fares. If customers wish to book seats more than two weeks in advance of the departure date of the flight, they can only do so by booking online. As fares generally increase, as the departure dates gets closer, this means that the best fares are first available to those who book via the Internet. Since business started selling seats via the Internet in Sept 1999, the airline has enjoyed dramatic growth in its online sales. The airline reached the one million seat mark in March 2000, and celebrated this important landmark by giving that lucky passenger unlimited free flights for a whole year. Five months later in Oct 2001, CSO C reached one million seats, and it only took another three months after that to reach the two million seats mark, indicating a huge acceleration in the growth of online sales. CSO C has now sold many millions of seats online.

Using credit card to make purchases via the website is a secure way to pay for the flights—as safe as booking through the telephone reservations centre. Millions of seats have been booked successfully online with CSO C. CSO C have put a number of security steps in place to give customers, total confidence when purchasing flights ticket online: All sensitive information, including personal details as well as credit card information, is kept confidential through the use of the secure server software (SSL). This means that information can only be exchanged between the online customer and CSO C, and that no third party can access this data. The padlock symbol on the browser shows which pages are covered by this security system. All historical information regarding credit card, name, and address details is held on a secure computer. CSO C did not retained live records of customer personal details or credit card information on their web servers after the transaction has been completed (customer will need to enter their details each time they book over the Internet).

The analysis of risk incurred that are generated from all the above case study observations were presented in Table 5–15, 5–16, and 5–17. The identified risks are later use to calculate total cost of identified vulnerability (TCIV) (see chapter 5 for detailed analysis).

3.   SHONIREGUN RISK ASSESSMENT MODEL

The literature in 'Risk', 'Risk exposure', and 'Risk Assessment Model' that is available in the field of computing and information systems, most especial those risks that are related to TEISMEs business operations, was reviewed. This has enabled the author to have ground knowledge of what other research has been done in this area and also the starting point of the proposed 'Shoniregun TEISME Risk Assessment Model' (see Figure 4–1, Eq. (4.1)). The weaknesses found in the existing security risk assessment approaches have been reviewed: the model relies on the assessor to formulate the chain of events that describe each of the threats currently facing TEISME business operations. The model presents an investigation of combinatorial explosion of calculation, analysis of the effectiveness of each countermeasure against each threat/vulnerability pair, and spotlights the specific area of improvement needed when new threats are deemed too high risk.

3.1   Addressing Weaknesses Found in the Selected Models

The weaknesses of the selected models that are presented in Table 3–2 are discussed as follows:

Annualised Loss Expectancy (ALE): ALE model weaknesses identified have been applied as follows:
   - A clear and visible understanding of all the elements in both Phases 1 and 2, and with logical steps have been presented in Figures 4–1 and 4–2. The Phase 1 Level 1 'New and Existing TEISME' not only specified who can use the model but also showed that the model is fit for

purpose by giving clarity of business context (the TEISME must state what technology in use, their industrial sector, and business classification). In Phase 2 Level 1 'Risk Estimation' and 'Risk Evaluation', further emphasis was made to show that the model is specifically developed to be used by TEISME, not for any other purposes.

- The rolls-up have been applied to the proposed model in Phase 2 Level 1 'Risk Estimation'. The roll-ups were addressed by proposing a formula which is based on 365 days (see Eq. (4.1) for further details).
- In reality, all security breaches cannot carry the same cost implications. The Shoniregun's TEISME Risk Assessment Model has addressed the weaknesses in Phase 1 Level 1 'Risk Reduction Actions' and Phase 2 Level 1 'Risk Identify' to show that each individual risk has different cost implications, which has been proved by using the 'Risk Estimation', 'Risk Evaluation' and 'Simulation' (see chapter 5 for further discussion).

Illinois method: In Illinois method, minor variations in the values selected can contribute significantly to the time required to carry out the risk assessment.

- In the proposed model the minor variation can only occur when a threat of the same type becomes a perpetual occurrence. This will not create a significant time difference required to carry out risk assessment. Phase 2 Level 1 'Risk Directing' has addressed the latter identified weaknesses by large the proposed model is based on a continuous assessment of TEISME business operations.
- Illinois method averaging can cause countercyclical assessment behaviour resulting in rising values when income is declining or vice versa. There is no need to incorporate the latter weakness into the proposed model, since averaging is not a requirement.
- The actual farm-level data used to estimate residual net income in Illinois method is not required in the proposed model. However, all the data generated within the proposed model are based on actual occurrences of threats/vulnerabilities encountered by TEISME.
- The problem of lack of detailed data needed to arrive at accurate income estimates has been addressed in Phase 2 Level 1 'Risk Directing', where risk log or risk register are compiled for use by 'Risk Identify'. The 'Risk Identify' can either pass the identified risk to the 'Risk Reduction Action' for immediate action and/or to the 'Risk Estimation' for calculating the risk occurrence using the Shoniregun TEISME risk assessment model calculation formula.

Courtney method: The Courtney method has no risk reducing measure.

- The Shoniregun's TEISME Risk Assessment Model has incorporated the weaknesses into the Phase 1 Level 1 'Risk Reduction', Phase 2 Level 1 'Risk Directing' and 'Risk Identify'. The 'Risk Reduction' in the model is an iterative process between Phases 1 and 2. In Phase 1Level 1 'Risk Reduction' iterates between Phase 2 Level 1'Risk Directing', and 'Risk Identify'. The validity of the iterative process is to build a risk logbook or risk register and also identify risk which of the risk requires immediate solution, not to compromise the legitimacy of existing risk reduction action.
- The corresponding effect of risk reduction on annual loss expectancy has been applied to the proposed model and also addressed the factors that need to be considered in the Phase 1 Level 1 'Risk Reduction'. The Phase 2 Level 1 'Risk Estimation' also used the Shoniregun TEISME Risk Assessment Calculation formula to show clarity of applicability (see Eq. (4.1) and chapter 5 for further discussion).

COBRA: The COBRA asset valuation can proceed in advance of final development, but threat/vulnerability assessment cannot because of the need to evaluate the risk occurrences.
- Given an estimated figure for TEISME business operational threat that has not been experienced, may lead to either under or over estimation, when the actual threat really occurred. This weakness is addressed in Phase 2 Level 1 'Risk Evaluation', of the proposed model (see chapter 5 for further discussion).

CRAMM: The CRAMM valued data asset according to enterprise's perception of the likely damage to the enterprise.
- This weakness has been addressed in Phase 2 Level 1 'Risk Directing', where each business transaction might carries different risks, which are address by building a risk log to identify the risk before estimating the damage to TEISME.
- CRAMM recognises only 32 threat types. The proposed model has addressed this problem in Phase 2 Level 1 using the 'Risk Directing' and 'Risk Identify'.

SSESRA: implies that a threat does not change without direct intervention, and time is not a factor.
- With regards to the proposed model these weaknesses have been addressed in Phase 1 Level 2 'Risk Reducing Actions', which shows that threats can change without intervention. These threats are monitor by the 'Risk Monitoring'.

- In the proposed model, time is a factor that has been addressed in Phase 2 Level 1 'Risk Directing', which requires all risk to be logged or registered.

- SSESRA does not take into account dates, durations and cost of security breach occurrences. The proposed model has addressed this weakness in Phase 2 Level 1 'Risk Estimation', by introducing the Shoniregun TEISME risk assessment model calculation formula (see Eqs. (4.1, 4.2), and chapter 5 for further detail).

- SSESRA does not address the issue of where more than one threat is actively attempting to breach the system. It was possible to incorporate the latter weakness into the proposed model in Phase 2 Level 1 'Risk Identify'. The identified risks are immediately response to by using appropriate cause of action from the 'Risk Reduction Action', which roll-up to see if any similar risks has been log or registered against an action or in president of an action. The Shoniregun Risk Assessment Model is multi-tasking and involves continues risk assessment of both single and multi-threat activities.

- SSESRA does not take into account any sensitive information that is stored in the system. This weakness has been addressed in Phase 1 Level 2 'Risk Reduction Actions' using iterative process between .Phase 2 Level 1'Risk Directing', and 'Risk Identify'. The damages to information stored on the service provider servers or in the TEISME systems either in active or sleeping state is very crucial to the total risk assessment of the vulnerability.

3.2   Implementation of Shoniregun Risk Assessment Model

The Shoniregun Risk Assessment Model has been implemented, which consists of two phases. Phase 1 identifies the 'New and Existing TEISME' and 'Risk Reduction Actions', while Phase 2 presents the 'Risk Directing', 'Risk Identify', 'Risk Estimation', and 'Simulation', which are iterative. Phase 1: Risk Reduction Actions interfaced Phase 2: Risk Directing, and Risk Identify to form a loop, which helps to estimates, evaluate and simulates the data that are presented. The Phases involved in Shoniregun Risk Assessment Model are discusses below (see Figure 4–2, Eq. (4.1), and Eq. (4.2)).

Software process models possess more expressive power than representations that underlay traditional risk assessment techniques. Therefore, one might assume that approaches for software process model analysis can be used to identify and analyse TEISME business operational risks. According to Boehm (1989), the goal of risk assessment is to identify risks and to analyse each identified risk in terms of loss magnitude and loss probability. Therefore,

Phase 1   Phase 2

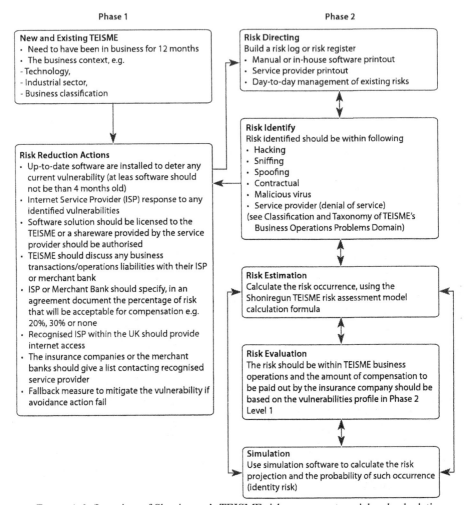

Figure 4–1. Overview of Shoniregun's TEISME risk assessment model and calculation

risk assessment requires the ability to obtain results concerning quantitative outcomes such as time or effort and their occurrence probabilities. The author adopted Boeham's 'Risk Engineering Task Breakdown' for the initial preparation of the 'Shoniregun TEISME Risk Assessment Model'. There are other potential risks identified in the research which are not within TEISME business operations, such as:

- Software installation errors
- Software developer errors
- Social engineering
- Data entry error from end users
- Computer hardware and software failure from end users

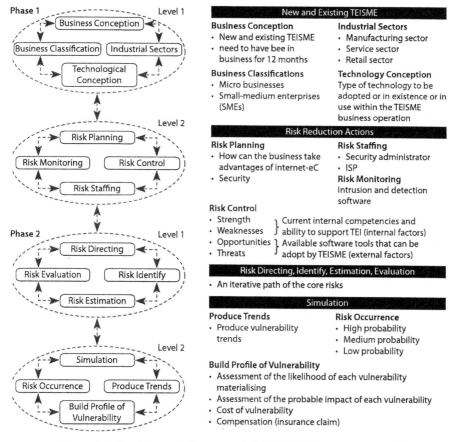

Figure 4–2. Breakdown of Shoniregun's TEISME risk assessment model

- Software package error (seek compensation from provider e.g. Microsoft, Sun Oracle etc.)
- End user's negligence (using unlicensed software, computer games, using CD or diskette that might have virus)

It is clear from the above list that there are a lot of areas in which risk could arise, so it is equally important that all of the possible risks within TEISME business operations are properly identified. However, all known risks must be identified and highlighted, even if some of them are unpopular or unable to compromise to cause any damage and loss of profits or denial of services. All the TEISMEs that participated in the questionnaire survey, structured interview, laboratory experiment and case study observation have been in business for at least 12 months or more in order to gather data and generate trends of vulnerability occurrence. The vulnerability and trends can be used in projecting the future occurrences of similar identified vulnerability and also as a critical guideline for insurance company in calculating the estimated cost of claim by TEISME. To achieve the success in implementing this model, it is necessary to iterate between the phases and levels. This model consists of two phases, and within each phase are two other detailed levels: Phase 1 looks at the TEISME business set up and the 'Risk Management/Requirements'.

The Shoniregun TEISME Risk Assessment Calculation Formula for calculating the Identified Vulnerability is shown below:

$$
\begin{aligned}
\frac{Total\ cost\ of}{identified\ vulnarability} &= \frac{Annual\ sales}{365} \times \underset{occurrence}{Risk} \times \underset{coefficient}{Customer} - \\
&- \underset{inflation\ rate}{Current} \times \underset{agreed\ compensation}{Service\ provider}
\end{aligned} \tag{4.1}
$$

- It is expected that the time of any occurrences should be checked against the past 12 months to calculate the total amount of profit on the specified day of the vulnerability with specific reference to time (Jan Mon 2:00 to 4:00 profit 2,000; in other to calculate total sales, it is necessary to check the TEISME's account records for all profit made between 2:00 to 4:00 for 365 days).
- Risk occurrence is the number of times the specified vulnerability has occurred over the last 12 months.
- The author introduces the Customer coefficient as a result of being able to measure an average loss of customers due to vulnerabilities.
- The Annual Sales excludes tax because the TEISME operates in a tax-free environment.
- The figure 100 used in dividing Denial of Service, corresponds to the fact that 100% security is unattainable on TEISME business operations.

The Shoniregun TEISME Risk Assessment Calculation Formula for Compensation (Insurance Claim) is shown below (cost of software is a single or combined software solution that detects the specific vulnerability):

$$
Compensation = \frac{Current\ cost}{of\ software} \times \frac{Last\ year\ inflation\ rate}{Current\ inflation\ rate} + \underset{vulnarability}{\underset{identified}{Total\ cost\ of}} \tag{4.2}
$$

4.   ANALYSIS OF SHONIREGUN'S RISK ASSESSMENT MODEL IMPLEMENTATION

The two levels within Phase 1 depend on each other and can take an iterative approach:

Phase 1, Level 1.

The phase involves two questionnaire surveys and a structured interview:

i. *New and existing TEISME:*
   - The *first questionnaire survey* started by trying to identify the types of TEISMEs, how long they had been in business, and under what classification would they be associated (see Table 5–5). To achieve this, the first questionnaire survey was performed among 1800 TEISMEs within the co.uk service provider (with 500 responses this feedback was more than the expected outcome).

ii. *Risk reduction action:*
   - The *second questionnaire survey* was performed to find out the current state of the TEISME business operations with regards to impacts and risk assessment of TEISME business operations. The questionnaire survey was based on 400 TEISMEs in UK, broken down into 4 regions (see Table 5–5).
   - The *structured interview* was the section 1 of the second questionnaire survey, which addressed the general information of TEISME business, this part was further enhanced by a follow-up structured interview of 6 TEISMEs directors and managing directors (see chapter 5).

The detailed analysis of Phase 1 Level 1 involved business conception, industrial sectors, technological conception, and business classification (see Figure 4–2).

Phase 1, Level 2.

This phase is within the 'Risk Reduction Actions' presented in Figure 4–1, but in the model breakdown in Figure 4–2. It involves logical steps, in order to identify the required risk planning, risk control, risk staffing and risk management. This Phase 1 Level 2 relates to section 2 of the second questionnaire survey and the responses to the structured interview questions 6 to 11. This phase take a closer look at what is in place for reducing current TEISME business operation risks.

The two levels within Phase 2 are also dependent on each other and can take an iterative approach within and outside the level:

Phase 2, Level 1.

The Phase 2 Level 1 has been and the structured interview.

i. *Risk directing and identifying:* The implementation was further enhanced by 3 case studies observation, which enabled us to build a risk log/risk register 'Risk Directing'. A combination of methodologies was used to identify the current risk facing TEISMEs business operations. Therefore, the author was able to rank the risks identified within TEISME business operations, which are detailed in Tables 5–8, 5–15, 5–16, and 5–17.

ii. *Risk estimation and evaluation:* The data presented in Tables 5–15, 5–16, and 5–17 were used in the 'Risk Estimation' to calculate the risk occurrences. The results of the calculation were used in the 'Risk Evaluation'. The 'Risk Evaluation' outcomes depend on both Risk Identified and Risk Estimation, which will lead to compilation of the vulnerabilities profile. The compilation of the vulnerabilities profile is based on 12 months TEISME business operations. It is valuable to obtain both quantitative and qualitative measures of risk likelihood and impacts, because risk estimation is difficult, subjective, costly, and time consuming.

Phase 2, Level 2.

This is the final stage of the model, which involves simulation tool to process the data generated, and to produce trends that are used to build a profile of different vulnerabilities identified. This vulnerabilities profile and the probabilities of risk occurrence can be relied upon or use as guidelines by TEISME, Insurance companies or Insurance Brokers in the UK to project the future occurrences of TEISME business operational vulnerabilities (see Figures 5–25, 5–26, 5–27, and 5–28).

Each of the questionnaire surveys involved different TEISMEs, to avoid errors or any ambiguity in the analysis of the feedback.

5.   SUMMARY OF CHAPTER FOUR

The available evidence suggests that there is no one best strategy for undertaking research, just as there is no one best method of collecting data or determining the sample size or questionnaire design. Much depends on the situation and the nature of research being undertaken. The questionnaire survey, laboratory experiment, structured interview, and case study observations, are the preferred research methods because of the added advantages of incorporating elements of theory, and implementation. The combination of these methods satisfies the need for methodological pluralism and falls into both quantitative and qualitative research methods. It places the research within the context of existing knowledge and allows building new knowledge. As Oppenheim (1966) suggests the combinatory methodology operates as a healthy check, since fatal ambiguities may lurk in the most unexpected quarters. However, since most of the current risk assessment model did not take into account all the identified weaknesses found within the 6 models reviewed (see chapter 3). The Shoniregun Risk Assessment model has been proposed and implemented within 3 TEISMEs. This model is an improvement on the other models idenified, with some emphases on hidden impacts of TEI on TEISME. The next chapter focuses on the results of the research findings.

REFERENCES

Benbasat, I., Goldstein, D. K., and Mead, M., 1987, 'The case research strategy in studies of information systems', *MIS Quarterly*, September, pp. 369–386.

Boehm, B. W., 1989, *Software Risk Management*, Washington, DC, IEEE Computer Society Press.

Galliers, R. D., 1992, 'Information systems planning in the United Kingdom and Australia: a comparison of current practice', *Oxford Surveys in Information Technology*.

Kane Eileen and O'reilly-de Brun, 2001, *Doing Your Own Research*, Marion Boyars Publishers.

Oppenheim, A. N., 1966, *Questionnaire Design and Attitude Measurement*, Heinemann Educational Books Ltd, London.

Rubin, H. and Rubin, I., 1995, *Qualitative Interviewing The Art Of Hearing Data*, Sage Publications.

Yin, R., 1994, *Case Study Research, Design and Method*, London: Sage.

Zikmund, 1997, Business Research Methods, 5th ed., Sydney: The Dryden Press.

Chapter 5

ANALYSIS OF RESULTS

1.   INTRODUCTION

This study has derived a wealth of data that may be used to understand the impacts of TEI on TEISME's business operations, and the technologies for Internet security.

> 'And it has produce a society that is the image of its own alienation and impoverishment'
> —Charles A. Reich, (1970) The Greening of America.

This chapter presents the results of the questionnaire surveys, laboratory experiment, case studies, structured interviews and the implementation of 'Shoniregun TEISME Risk Assessment Model'. Each question from the questionnaire is reviewed systematically and response rates are measured using percentages and frequencies.

2.   ANALYSIS OF 500 TEISMEs BASED ON CO.UK SERVICE PROVIDER

A preliminary online questionnaire survey of 1800 TEISMEs was conducted within the co.uk service provider, yielding 500 responses. This survey was used to identify the types of TEISME's business operations. The research has acknowledged two types of TEISME, firstly, the businesses that embrace Internet-eC to supplement their traditional business models and secondly, those that conduct their entire business operations online. However, as already established in chapter 1, in order to accept or reject the Hypothesis 1, consideration must be given to the hypothetical statement to re-enforce the research focus:

Hypothesis 1:

- Null hypothesis $(\mathcal{H}_0{}^1)$: As a result of the investigation whether TEISME is complementary to, but not in direct competition with SME;
- Alternative $(\mathcal{H}_A{}^1)$: As a result of the investigation whether TEISME is complementary to and in direct competition with SME.

The preliminary survey findings of the comparison between SME and TEISME are detailed in Table 5–1. The three types of TEISMEs were identified, which are classified as Open TEISMEs, Inter-lock TEISMEs, and Close-in TEISMEs (see Table 5–2).

2.1 Classifications and taxonomy of TEISMEs

The classifications and taxonomy of TEISMEs are based on existing paradigm. Over the past few years, we have seen evidence of an increasing number of people beginning to understand the concept and the importance of Internet-eC. As a result TEI businesses have evolved, taking advantage of these technologies. The wider markets were opened to SMEs, for an even wider range

Table 5–1. Comparison between Traditional SMEs and TEISMEs

Factors	Traditional SMEs	TEISMEs
Start up	• Needs high capital financing • Requires location and equipment to set up Businesses	• Requires very little capital as compared to that for setting up a traditional SMEs • No specific location is a must, can trade any where at any time with a connection to the Internet browser • By uniting buyers and sellers worldwide, online marketplaces cutback on surplus business equipment
Markets	• Region, national, culture	• Globalisation
Knowledge	• Static core competency	• Dynamic core competency
On-going cost	• Reasonable but can be expensive	• Very cheap in relation to business operations
Marketing	• Narrow • Face-to-face buying and selling • Marketing mechanism	• Wider • Internet-eC • Greater competitive advantages
Business Strategy	• Common: reduce cost and increase volume	• No Universal strategy • Fill in a niche new market community

of businesses. This continuous transformation of SMEs' value chain systems has led to the following classification of Internet-eC transactions (Shoniregun *et al.*, 2004):

- *Business-to-business (B2B):* Most of the Internet-eC today is of this type, electronic market transactions between businesses.
- *Business-to-consumer (B2C):* This is retailing transactions with individual shoppers.
- *Consumer-to-consumer (C2C):* This category of consumer sells directly to consumers, which include people to people (P-to-P), e.g. individuals selling in classified ads and selling residential property, cars, etc.
- *Consumer-to-business (C2B):* The category includes individuals who sell products or services to organisations, as well as individuals who seek sellers, interact with them, and conclude a transaction.
- *Non-business eC (NbeC):* The category includes non-business institutions such as academic institutions, not-for-profit organisations, religious organisations, social organisations, and government agencies. The non-business institutions use various types of Internet-eC to reduce their expenses and improve their operations and customer service.
- *Intrabusiness eC (organisational eC):* All the internal organisational activities usually performed on intranets that involve exchange of goods, services, or information. These activities can range from selling corporate products to employees to online training and cost-reduction activities.

The classification and taxonomy of TEISMEs by their nature of business operations are explicitly illustrated in Table 5–2, which is based on the above classification of Internet-eC transactions. It also describes the relationship between existing Internet-eC (rows) and the notion of TEISME's business operations (columns).

Table 5–2. Classification and Taxonomy of TEISMEs business operations

Existing Internet-eC	TEISMEs		
	Open TEISME	Inter-Lock TEISME	Close-in TEISME
B 2 B	✓	✓	✓
B 2 C	✓	✓	✓
C 2 B	✓	✓	✓
C 2 C	×	×	✓
IntrabuseC	×	×	✓
N BeC	✓	×	×

- ✓ (Do Exist)
- × (Do Not Exist)

- *Open TEISME:* SME that can buy or sell to or from any other businesses in the Internet marketplace, this includes: Business-to-Business (B2B), Business-to-consumer (B-to-C), Consumer-to-business (C2B), and Non-business eC (N-BeC)
- *Inter-lock TEISME:* SME that provide niche services or products to the businesses or consumers, within the Internet marketplace this includes the following: Business-to-Business (B2B), and Business-to-consumer (B-to-C)
- *Close-in TEISME:* SME that initiate buying or selling to a specific businesses—members only (can either be businesses or consumers), within the Internet marketplace this includes the following: Consumer-to-business (C2B), Consumer-to-consumer (C2C), and Intrabusiness eC (Organisational eC)

Innovative business professionals have discovered that the Internet can be exploited to offer a number of services both for their customers and for their strategic partners. The outcomes of the 500 TEISMEs that participated in the online questionnaire survey are presented in Table 5–3.

The TEISMEs were also identified by their industrial sector e.g. music, travel and tourism, auctions, training and development, children and adult clothing. The questionnaire responses are as follows; 270 (54%) are Open TEISME, 150 (30%) Inter-Lock TEISME, and 80 (16%) Close-in TEISME (see Table 5–3). The critical argument with this study is that the survey only targeted the co.uk service provider, which can be further question by conducting a large-scale survey that will comprise all service providers in the UK based on the same criteria used within the co.uk service provider.

Outcome of Hypothesis 1

- $(\mathcal{H}_A{}^1)$ is rejected therefore reject $(\mathcal{H}_A{}^1)$ in favour of $(\mathcal{H}_0{}^1)$

Table 5–3. Types of TEISMEs identified within co.uk service provider

Industrial Sector	TEISMEs		
	Open TEISME	Inter-lock TEISME	Close-in TEISME
Music	58	32	20
Travel and Tourism	106	72	20
Auctions	54	24	15
Training and Development	30	13	17
Children and Adults clothing	22	9	8
Total number of questionnaire	500		

- As a result of the investigation TEISME is complementary to but not in direct competition with SME.

The detailed statement of Hypothesis 1 was tested, and the results that led to $(\mathcal{H}_A{}^1)$ rejection are presented in Table 5–19.

3. LABORATORY EXPERIMENTS

Laboratory experiments were performed to test the reliability of TEISME business operations using sniffer packet (see Figures 5–1, 5–2, 5–3, and 5–4). The test carried out was at a random among 50 TEISMEs with prior knowledge of the test, but without specifying when it would be carried out or else the test might create bias (see Table 5–4). The test was performed 5 times on specific TEISMEs. The packet sniffer demonstrated the lack of security that existed in TEISME business operations, which requires an urgent need for reliable risk assessment model. The test also showed the lack of privacy/confidentiality in TEISME business transactions.

The sniffer packet result test shows that 222 (89%) attempts were successful and sniffed into the TEISMEs business operations of those that participated in the experiment and with a lower failure rate of 28 (11%). The failure rate can be explained to be as a result of TEISME's service provider server updates or local web administrative updates. However, in order to accept or reject the Hypothesis 2, consideration must be given to the hypothetical statement to re-enforce the research focus:

Hypothesis 2:

- Null hypothesis $(\mathcal{H}_0{}^2)$: As a result of the laboratory experiment whether absolute security is unattainable on TEISME business operations;
- Alternative $(\mathcal{H}_A{}^2)$: As a result of the laboratory experiment whether absolute security is attainable on TEISME business operations.

Table 5–4. Test log result. Total tests performed 250

Test No	Success	Fail
1	48	2
2	41	9
3	40	10
4	46	4
5	47	3
Total no of tests	222	28

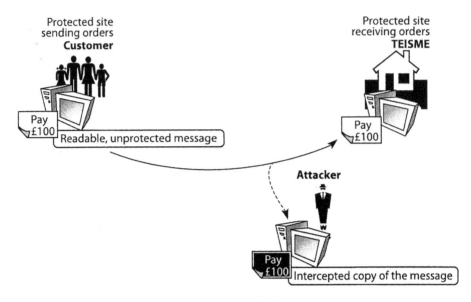

Figure 5–1. Common risk encountered by TEISME within their business operations

The data sniffing on the Internet is achieved whenever a user sends important information over the Internet to TEISME (see Figure 5–1). The information stopped by third party (attacker) before it reaches the destination. Then again it is sent back to the desired destination, so that no one knows that the third party has already seen it. The details copied, without making any changes, so that no one knows that the attacker copied the customer's details, this is referred to as sniffing. With respect to TEISME business operations, transactions can be any form of communication between TEISME and online shoppers, whether it is buying, selling, negotiating, e-mailing or anything that requires sending data. The transactions in Figure 5–2 provide reason for concern as they can be intercepted at any time by a hacker. The activity of interception can be attributed solely to hackers, intercepted copied and then sent on to their destination without the receiver or the sender of the transaction ever knowing the sequence of events that took place in between. The concerns in this type of situation are obvious as the content of these transactions could contain personal, valuable or sensitive information that the online shopper or TEISME would not otherwise want others to see.

The replay attack occurs because of incomplete or erroneous specifications. However, even correct specifications do not necessarily guarantee the correctness of a given implementation. In the Figure 5–2, the attacker could replay a message and the message may look completely legitimate similar to Cipher text. But TCP/IP has the capability to detect accidental replay but not always, however TCP/IP cannot detect malicious replay.

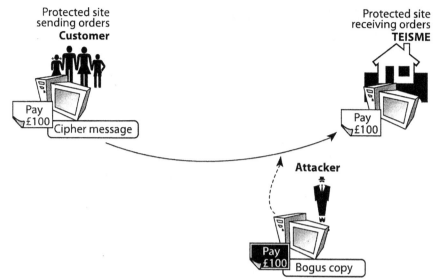

Figure 5–2. Replay Attack

However, this laboratory experiment was performed to show the weaknesses in both hardware and software. So if this risk facing TEISMEs business operations are ongoing, then there is an urgent need for more flexible risk assessment model that can ease the financial risks that might be incurred. The laboratory experiment shows that password sniffer works passively, does not generate any network traffic, and it is very hard to be detected by other users. No additional software is required. The password sniffer runs on the TEISMEs gateway or proxy server, which gets all other network traffic (see Figures 5–3 and 5–4).

Furthermore, TEISMEs are not alone; the failure of many financial institution websites has been proved for lack of information security e.g. Abbey National Bank, Nationwide Bank, Citi Bank, and Barclays Bank have been victims of sniffering, where all customers private account details were displayed online without the consent.

Outcome of Hypothesis 2

- $(\mathcal{H}_{A}^{2})$ is rejected therefore reject $(\mathcal{H}_{A}^{2})$ in favour of $(\mathcal{H}_{0}^{2})$
- As a result of the laboratory experiments and all the detailed weaknesses found in the technologies for Internet security, so absolute security is unattainable on TEISME business operations. The result of the test has proved that 89% of TEISMEs business operation websites are vulnerable to sniffing.

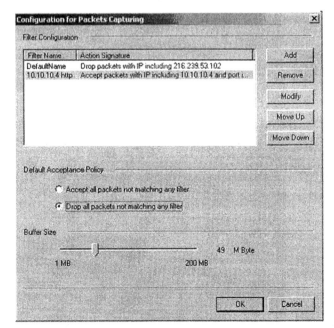

Figure 5–3. Screenshot 1. Display Configuration for packets captured

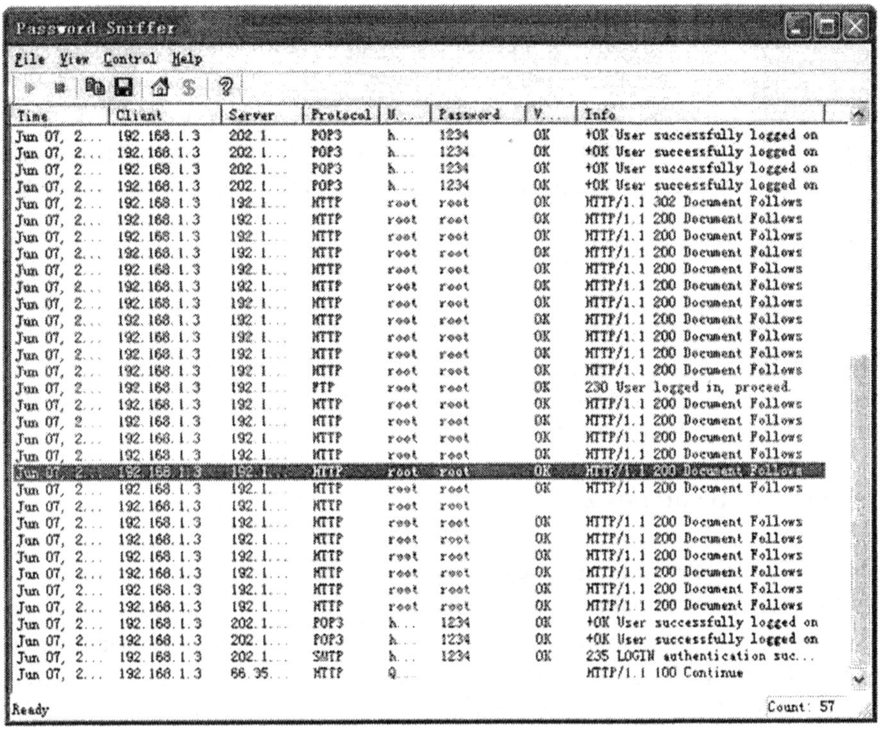

Figure 5–4. Screenshot 2. Display detail information of users

The detailed statement of Hypothesis 2 was tested, and the results that led to $(\mathcal{H}_{\mathcal{A}}^{2})$ rejection are presented in Table 5–19.

4. ANALYSIS OF 400 TEISMEs QUESTIONNAIRE SURVEY

The questionnaire survey was used to find out the impacts and risk assessment of TEISME business operations. Therefore, in order to accept or reject the Hypothesis 3, consideration must be given to the hypothetical statement to re-enforce the research focus:

Hypothesis 3:

- Null hypothesis $(\mathcal{H}_{0}^{3})$: As a result of investigation whether risk assessment is unattainable on TEISME business operations;
- Alternative $(\mathcal{H}_{\mathcal{A}}^{3})$: As a result of investigation whether risk assessment is attainable on TEISME business operations.

The questions in the questionnaire survey are analysed one after the other and the raw data are presented both in a table format, and some are illustrated graphically, which include pie charts, where appropriate.

The Tables 5–5, and 5–6, presents the break down of the TEISMEs questionnaire survey distribution frequency, which was segmented into 5 regions. This distribution coverage has enabled the geographical boundary of the UK to be covered. However, it could be argued that the total numbers of questionnaire survey distribution frequency per city within the regions are low, the total percentage on the 400 questionnaires distributed, shows that 70% did not respond, but with the responses of 118 survey generated 30%, which can be use as a valid research outcome taking into account the combinatory nature

Table 5–5. TEISMEs Questionnaire survey distribution frequency

UK Regions and the Local Authorities	Questionnaire Survey Distribution Frequency	Response Frequency	Relative Regional Response Rate	Relative Rate
Northern England	90	30	33%	
Bolton	10	3	3%	10%
Chester	10	3	3%	10%
Harrogate	10	4	4%	13%
Liverpool	10	2	3%	7%
Manchester	10	4	4%	13%
Total Questionnaire Survey	400	118	30%	23%

UK Regions and the Local Authorities	Questionnaire Survey Distribution Frequency	Response Frequency	Relative Regional Response Rate	Relative Rate
Newcastle upon Tyne	10	5	6%	17%
Sheffield	10	3	3%	10%
Wigan	10	2	3%	7%
York	10	4	4%	13%
Midlands and East Anglia	110	32	29%	
Bedford	10	2	1%	6%
Birmingham	10	3	3%	9%
Cambridge	10	3	3%	9%
Harlow/Stansted	10	2	1%	6%
Northampton	10	4	4%	13%
Nottingham	10	4	4%	13%
Oxford	10	3	3%	9%
Peterborough	10	3	3%	9%
Solihull	10	3	3%	9%
Stoke-on-Trent	10	3	3%	9%
Stratford-upon-Avon/Telford	10	2	1%	6%
London and Home Counties	100	28	28%	
Dartford/Thurrock	10	4	4%	14%
Elstree	10	2	2%	7%
Gatwick	10	3	3%	11%
London	10	3	3%	11%
Reading	10	2	2%	7%
St Albans	10	3	3%	11%
Shepperton	10	2	2%	7%
Watford	10	3	3%	11%
Windsor	10	3	3%	11%
Colchester	10	3	3%	11%
Southern England	60	16	27%	
Bristol	10	2	3%	11%
Cardiff	10	3	5%	19%
Cheltenham/Gloucester	10	3	5%	19%
Exeter	10	2	3%	11%
Plymouth	10	4	8%	30%
Winchester	10	2	3%	11%
Scotland	40	12	30%	
Edinburgh	10	4	10%	33%
Glasgow	10	3	8%	27%
Aberdeen	10	3	7%	23%
Inverness	10	2	5%	17%
Total Questionnaire Survey	400	118	30%	23%

of the research methods. The analysis of the questionnaire survey give a clear understanding of the following:

- Types of TEI used by TEISMEs for transacting businesses
- The risks to which TEISMEs are exposed, how to minimise and managed.
- Types of security control measures adopted by TEISMEs as well as which of these control measures are more frequently used to minimise risk exposure

Table 5–6. Absolute and relative frequency of questionnaire feedback

	Variable	Values	Absolute frequency	Relative frequency (%)
1	**General information on TEISME**			
1.1	TEISME annual sales	£3m	53	45%
		£4m	35	30%
		£5m	12	10%
		£7m	9	8%
		£8m	6	5%
		£9m	3	3%
1.2	Number of employee	4 staff	4	3%
		6 staff	52	44%
		8 staff	16	14%
		14 staff	25	21%
		21 staff	17	14%
		24 staff	4	3%
1.3	Industrial sector	Music	30	25%
		Travel and Tourism	44	37%
		Art and Culture	4	3%
		Training and Dev	10	8%
		Books	20	17%
		Advertising	6	5%
1.4	Industrial classification	e-Service	110	93%
		e-Manufacturing	8	7%
2	**Impacts of TEI on business operations**			
2.1	Type of TEI	a) E-mail	118	100%
		b) Voice Mail	83	70%
		c) Scanner	101	86%
		d) Facsimile Application	21	18%
		e) Facsimile machines (FAX)	33	28%
		f) Teleconferencing	8	7%
		g) Data Conferencing	96	81%
		h) Video Conferencing	8	7%

	Variable	Values	Absolute frequency	Relative frequency (%)
		i) Electronic Data Interchange (EDI)	118	100%
		j) Telephone	41	35%
2.2	Impact of TEI	a) Increasing speed with which supplies can be obtained	118	100%
		b) Increasing speed with which goods can be dispatched	118	100%
		c) Reducing sales and purchasing costs	97	82%
		d) Reduced operating costs	118	100%
		e) 24 hours a day, 7 days a week availability	118	100%
		f) Unlimited shelf-space	88	75%
		g) Access to search and retrieval of systems that ease the customer's job search.	118	100%
		h) Global accessibility from all over the world.	118	100%
		i) Promote products to suit each individual customer	106	90%
		j) Payment Method Negotiation	114	97%
2.3	Internet safety of business operations	Yes	10	8%
		No	108	92%
3	**Risk assessment model**			
3.1	Type of business transactions media	a) Internet-eC	118	100%
		b) Mobile commerce	73	62%
		c) Both Bricks and Mortar and Electronic commerce	0	0%
		d) None of the above	0	0%
3.2	Critical risk exposure	Yes	18	15%
		No	20	17%
		None/Never	80	68%
3.3	Type of risk exposure	a) Malicious damage (e.g. corruption of data and software)	114	97%
		b) Unauthorised access (e.g. unauthorised viewing)	118	100%
		c) Accidental error/human carelessness (e.g. computer operator error)	99	84%
		d) Mechanical failure (e.g. hardware/software error damages file)	81	69%

	Variable	Values	Absolute frequency	Relative frequency (%)
		e) Online Fraud	118	100%
		f) Invasion or loss of privacy/ confidentiality	118	100%
3.4	Risk assessment framework	Yes	111	94%
		No	7	6%
3.5	Risk management process	Yes	111	94%
		No	7	6%
3.6	Risk monitoring	a) Seek opinion of those already in the business	110	93%
		b) Seek the services of a risk consultant	7	6%
		c) Carefully analyse precedents to improve forecasting	13	11%
		d) Look at all of the things that could go wrong and develop a contingency plan in case they do	51	43%
		e) Read newspapers, trade journals, regulations etc to help you make an informed decision	46	39%
3.7	Risk improvement measures	Yes	7	6%
		No	111	94%
3.8	System for identifying risk	Yes	7	6%
		No	111	94%
3.9	Risks quantification	Yes	69	58%
		No	49	42%
3.10	Methods for managing the risk	a) Take out an insurance policy	0	0%
		b) Absorb risk	7	6%
		c) Forecast and plan ahead	7	6%
		d) Agree a fixed fee with a risk management company	7	6%
		e) Make a contingency plan	7	6%
		f) Use experienced and reliable dealers	87	74%
		g) Line up a secondary source of supply	0	0%
		h) Identify and value all assets at risk	50	42%
		i) Put safeguards and controls (e.g. policies, procedures etc) in place	114	97%

	Variable	Values	Absolute frequency	Relative frequency (%)
		j) Assess risk periodically	118	100%
4	**Security issue**			
4.1	Internet business	Yes	118	100%
		No	0	0%
4.2	Unauthorised access	Yes	110	93%
		No	8	7%
4.3	Remote users authentication	Yes	118	100%
		No	0	0%
4.4	Security policy	Yes	19	16%
		No	99	84%
4.5	Security control measures	a) Public key encryption	98	83%
		b) Firewall	82	69%
		c) Digital signature	7	6%
		d) Password	118	100%
		e) Keystroke	5	4%
		f) Email sniffing	21	18%
		g) Personal Identity (ID)	118	100%
4.6	Security/privacy policy	Yes	118	100%
		No	0	0%
4.7	Business operations insurance	Yes	0	0%
		No	118	100%
4.8	Insurance term	a) Less than a 1 year	0	0%
		b) 1 year	0	0%
		c) 2 years	0	0%
		d) More than 3 years	0	0%
		e) None	118	100%
4.9	Compensation claimed	Yes	0	0%
		No	118	100%
4.10	Absolute security unattainable	Yes	97	82%
		No	21	18%

The responses to question 1.5 are not included in the above table.

Figure 5–6. Number of staff employed

4. 1   Section 1 of the Questionnaire Survey: General Information of TEISME's Business

The section 1 of the questionnaire is based on the 'General information on TEISME' consisting of five separate questions, which are interrelated. This section helps to give an overview of the business profiles, and how it fits into the definition of TEISMEs (see chapter 1).

The *question 1.1 'What are your business's annual sales?'* presents the TEISMEs annual sales, which differ from one sector/industry to the other e.g. TEISME's who have annual sales of £3m (million) represents 53 (44%), 35 (30%) with £4m, 12 (10%) with £5m, 6 (5%) with £8m, 3 (3%) with £9m, and 9 (8%) with £7m. This result shows that the largest number of TEISMEs have an annual sales of £3m (see Figure 5-5). The annual sale per TEISME is used to determine if a particular TEISME is within the existing SME definition proposed by both the Bolton Committee (1971) and the DTI (2002). However, the total annual sales of all TEISMEs that participated in the survey are £497m. This total annual sales figure is very high for insurance companies in the UK to overlook in terms of business creation i.e. insuring the TEISMEs business operations.

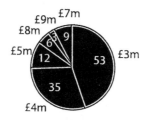

Figure 5–5. TEISMEs annual sales

For TEISME's to ignore the impact of not having any insurance policy against their business operations is an alarming issue, which could lead to bankruptcy in the current climate.

The *question 1.2 'How many people does your business employ?'*—this is a follow up question from 1.1 and a checkpoint on the elements that constitute SME and TEISME. The results are compared to the number of staff employed from the 118-questionnaire feedback shown in Figure 5-6. Since the definition used in this study of TEISMEs falls into the existing SME definition proposed by both the Bolton committee (1971) and the DTI (2002), it is necessary to determine whether all the TEISMEs that participated in the questionnaire survey are actually within the adopted definition framework (see chapter 1). The findings shows that 52 (45%) TEISMEs employed 6 staff, 25 (21%) with 14 staff, 17 (14%) with 21 staff, 4 (3%) with 4 staff, 16 (14%) with 8 staff, and 4 (3%) with 24 staff. However, the annual sales figure in questions 1 is not a reflection on the amount of staff employed.

The *question 1.3 'What industry is your business in?'*—the Figure 5–7 shows the population of TEISMEs can be grouped according to the types of industrial sectors. The largest industrial sector of TEISMEs are from Travel and Tourism which accounts for 44 (38%) of the questionnaire survey, followed by Music 30 (26%), Books 20 (18%), Training and Development 10 (9%), Advertising 6 (5%), Art and Culture 4 (4%). There is no doubt about the continuous increase of new entrants to the Travel and Tourism business, the major airlines have given consent to all their ticket agents, which include the TEISMEs to issue electronic ticket on their behalf.

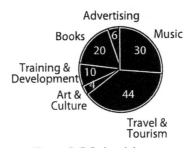

Figure 5–7. Industrial sector

The electronic ticket will soon be the norm and the future of travelling industry. This is a foreseeable impact of TEI, in the way tickets are sold and issued online. Other TEISME's showing increasing sign of growth are the Music and Book sectors. However, it is fair to say that the TEISMEs are well represented in the above distribution, given that the average response rate is 19.7%. It is not uncommon to have under-represented categories with small samples such as Art and Culture, Advertising and Training and Development.

The *question 1.4 'What is your industrial standard classification?'*—The industrial standard classification shows that the e-Service industry, with 110 (93%) responses, takes the largest market share of the Internet-eC, while 8 (7%) are from e-Manufacturing.

e-Manufacturing

Figure 5–8. Industrial classification

However, as mentioned above the Travel and Tourism, Music and Book sectors are growing faster than ever, which are in the e-Services industrial standard classification. The result in Figure 5–8 is an evidence that on-line shopping seems attractive to some sectors of the society than others, because all the downsides of traditional store shopping have been removed with likely efficient ordering, payments, and delivery systems, which are back up by the remote operations.

The *question 1.5 'Position of the person completing this questionnaire'*— the participants in the questionnaire were Directors and Managing Directors. The Figure 5–9 presents the responses from the 37 Directors and 81 Managing Directors who participated. The author opted for this type of participant because they are in a position to reflect thoroughly on the information sought. The reliability, and validity of the source of the information are reflected in the findings.

Figure 5–9. Survey questionnaire participants

The follow-up questions required higher level staff with technical competence, that have the knowledge and understanding of the past and current state of affairs of the business, which is unlikely to be known by a junior members of staff.

4.2 Section 2 of the Questionnaire Survey: Impacts of TEI on TEISME

The *question 2.1 'What types of TEI do you use within your business operations/transactions?'*—the responses to what types of TEI the TEISMEs that

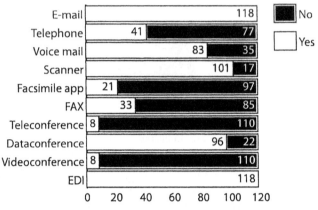

Figure 5–10. Types of TEI use by TEISMEs

participate use for their business operations were not surprising (see Figure 5–10). Unsurprisingly the findings show that all the respondents use Telephone and e-mail. The questionnaire results established that E-mail, and Telephone have 118 (100%) responses with 'Yes' and 0 (0%), 3 'No'. Voice mail with 41 (35%) Yes and 77 (65%) 'No'. Scanner with 83 (70%) Yes and 35 (30%) 'No'. Facsimile Application with 101 (86%) Yes and 35(14%), 6. Facsimile machines with (FAX) 21 (18%) Yes and 97 (82%) 'No'. Teleconferencing with 33 (28%) Yes and 85 (72%) No, 8. Data Conferencing with 8 (7%) Yes and 110 (93%) 'No'. Video Conferencing with 96 (81%) Yes and 22 (19%) 'No'. Electronic Data Interchange (EDI) with 8 (7%) Yes and 110 (93%) 'No'. All the TEI listed within this question are both software and hardware. The interdependence of both the software and hardware are inseparable due to the technological architecture of most TEI even though there are many versions of applications and technological up grading the relationship is so close.

The *question 2.2 'What are the impacts of TEI on your business operations?'*—when cross-examining the responses of the impacts of TEI on TEISMEs business operations the results were within the expectations (see Figure 5–11). The feedback to the questions is as follows: 1. Increasing speed with which supplies can be obtained 118 (100%) 'Yes' with 0 (0%) 'No'. Increasing speed with which goods can be dispatched 118 (100%) tick 'Yes' with 0 (0%) 'No'. Reducing sales and purchasing costs 97 (82%) 'Yes' with 21 (18%) 'No'. Reduced operating costs 118 (100%) 'Yes' with 0 (0%) 'No'. Open 24 hours a day 7 days a week availability 118 (100%) 'Yes' with 0 (0%) 'No'. Unlimited shelf-space 88 (75%) 'Yes' with 30 (25%) 'No'. Access to search and retrieval of systems that ease the customer's job search 118 (100%) 'Yes' with 0 (0%) 8. 'No', Global accessibility from all over the world 118 (100%) 'Yes' with 0 (0%) 'No'. Promote products to suit each individual customer 106 (98%) 'Yes' with 2 (2%) 'No'. Payment Method Negotiation 114

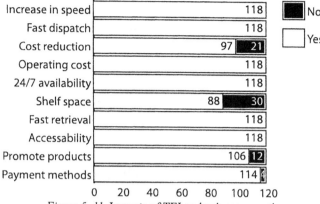

Figure 5–11. Impacts of TEI on business operation

(97%) 'Yes' with 4 (3%) 'No'. It is evident that this question did not establish the criteria for having an expert, or intermediate knowledge in TEI, therefore the responses here are based on the past and current business operational experiences of the Directors and/or Managing Directors.

The *question 2.3 'Do you consider the Internet to be safe for your business operations?'*—the feedback from this question contradicted the responses from question 1.1 (high annual sales), and question 1.3 (increasing growth rate in Travel and Tourism, Music, and Books). If 80 (92%) of TEISMEs Directors and/or Managing Directors agreed that the Internet is not safe to transact business operations, then the question that this result posed is, why are the TEISMEs still doing business on the Internet (see Figure 5–12).

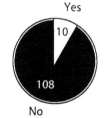

Figure 5–12. Internet safety

The answers to this question seem very obvious, that is, it is easy to set-up a TEISME (see chapter 1 and Table 5–1), and the ability to make abnormal profit coupled with the availability of TEI, has made the majority of TEISMEs fail to think of the immediate cost and the assessment of any vulnerability.

4.3   Section 3 of the Questionnaire Survey: Risk Facing TEISME Business Operations

The *question 3.1 'Which of the following do you use for your business transactions?'*—it was not surprising that all the respondents use Internet-eC 118 (100%) 'Yes' with 0 (0%) 'No' (see Figure 5–13).

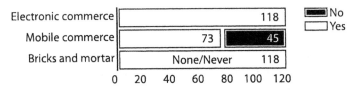

Figure 5–13. Type of TEI used in business transactions

More interesting, the feedback has diversified opinion with mobile commerce usage with, 73 (62%) say 'Yes' and 45 (38%) 'No'.

The *question 3.2 'Do you identify critical risk exposures?'*—the responses to this question open up many debates on how to identify critical risk, which has helped in repositioning Shoniregun Risk Assessment Model (see Figure 5–14).

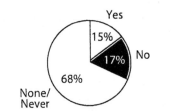

Figure 5–14. Identify critical risk exposures

The feedback from this question definitely calls for attention, with only 15% say 'Yes', 17% 'No' and 68% 'None/Never'. This result is also in line with the outcome of question 2.4 where 80 (92%) of TEISMEs Directors and/ or Managing Directors agreed that the Internet is not safe to transact their business operations.

The *question 3.3 'Which of the following risks is your business exposed to?'*—This question throws a different light and also supports the argument for a dynamic risk assessment model that incorporates any unforeseen vulnerabilities that might be encountered by TEISMEs, due to dependence on TEI (see Table 5–7).

The result of this finding does not come as a surprise; with all the publicity from both the news and literature reviews about the Internet-eC security, virus-

Table 5–7. Unforeseen vulnerabilities encountered by TEISME

	Malicious damage (1)	Unauthorised access (2)	Accidental error/human carelessness (3)	Mechanical failure (4)	Online Fraud (5)	Invasion or loss of privacy /confidentiality (6)
Yes	114	118	99	81	118	118
No	4	0	19	37	0	0
None/Never	0	0	0	0	0	0

es and unsolicited e-mail have created awareness of the gravity of the possible vulnerabilities. The feedback of security risks, which the TEISMEs business operations were exposed to are detailed as follows; 1. Malicious damage 114 (97%) tick 'Yes' with 4 (3%) 'No'. Unauthorised access 118 (0%) tick 'Yes' with 0 (0%) 'No'. Accidental error/human carelessness 99 (84%) 'Yes' with 16 (%) 'No'. Mechanical failure 81 (69%) 'Yes' with 37 (31%) 'No'. Online Fraud 118 (0%) tick 'Yes' with 0 (0%) 'No'. Invasion or loss of privacy/confidentiality 118 (0%) tick 'Yes' with 0 (0%) 'No'. There were no feedback suggestions for further comments.

The *question 3.4 'Do you have a risk assessment framework for your Internet-eC?'*—due to no established standard, TEISMEs business operational risks will be difficult to manage if not impossible; this has been proved by the responses to this question (see Figure 5–15).

No

7

111

Yes

Figure 5–15. Risk assessment framework

The responses to this question were alarming, with the increasing rates at which TEISMEs are being set-up it would be an assumption to say that there is no appropriate mechanism in place that gives guidelines on how best to quantify and assess the risks, which TEISMEs face by reliance on TEI (see chapter 3 for further discussion).

The *question 3.5 'Do you have a risk management process in place?'*—this question is directly related to the development of the risk assessment model, 7 (7%) of the participants have a risk management in place while 111 (93%) have no such mechanism (see Figure 5–16). The outcome of this finding has helped in integrating the risk process to Shoniregun Risk Assessment model (see chapter 4 for further details).

No

Yes

Figure 5–16. Risk improvement process

The *question 3.6 'How do you monitor your business risks?'*—this question seeks the participants' understanding and experiences of how the risks encountered are monitored (in relation to the possible risk that the TEISMEs might have encountered in the last 3 years with regards to their reliance on TEI). The percentages of the feedback in Figure 5–17 are as follows: 1. Seek opinion of those already in the business 110 (93%) 'Yes' with 8 (7%) 'No', 2. Seek the services of a risk consultant 7 (6%) 'Yes' with 111 (94%) 'No'. Carefully analyse precedents to improve forecasting 13 (11%) 'Yes' with 105 (89%) 'No'. Look at all of the things that could go wrong and develop a contingency plan in case they do 51 (43%) 'Yes' with 67 (57%) 'No'. Read newspapers, trade journals, regulations etc. to help you make an informed decision 46 (39%) 'Yes' with 72 (61%) 'No'. No feedback suggestions for further comments. The survey results above indicate that TEISMEs use a verity of ways to find information on how to monitor their risks.

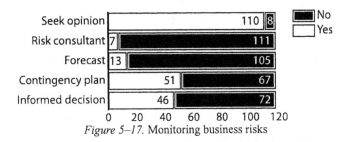

Figure 5–17. Monitoring business risks

The *question 3.7 'Are there any risk improvement measures in place?'*—this question shows an extended outcome to the findings in question 3.4 to 3.6. The participants' feedback is also in line with the hypothesis $(\mathcal{H}_{\mathcal{A}}^3)$, with 7 (7%) 'Yes' and 111 (93%) 'No' (see Figure 5–18). This outcome has enabled the integration of continuous improvements to the Shoniregun Risk Assessment model.

Figure 5–18. Risk improvement

The *question 3.8 'Is there any system for identifying new and emerging risks?'*—it seems obvious when this question was first incorporated into the survey questionnaire to address the problem of identifying new and emerging risk. This question has produced the same responses as question 3.7. It has thrown a light of rejection to any claim that might have previous been published: Only 7 (7%) TEISMEs agreed that they have a system for identifying new and emerging risk, while 111 (93%) showed no such system for identifying new and emerging risk currently facing TEISMEs business operations (see Figure 5–19).

Figure 5–19. Identifying new risks

The *question 3.9 'Do you quantify risks in terms of their monetary impact?'*—this was an expected feedback due to responses from question 3.4 and 3.5, 69 (58%) say 'Yes' while 49 (42%) 'No'. It is now obvious from the responses in Figure 5–20 that TEISMEs can quantify their business operational risk, but what is certain is that none of the TEISMEs claim any sort of compensation.

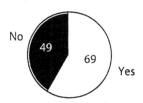

Figure 5–20. Quantifying risks

The *question 3.10 'Which of the following methods are used for managing the Internet-eC risks within your business?'*—this question has drawn attention to the variety of methods used by TEISMEs for managing their Internet-eC (see Figure 5–21). The responses to this question established strong support for the outcome of the case study observations and the structured interview that was conducted as part of the ongoing research.

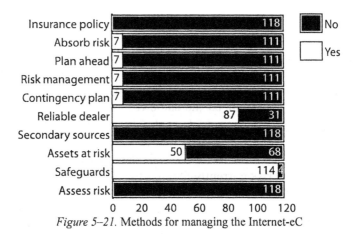

Figure 5–21. Methods for managing the Internet-eC

The results are as follows: 1. Take out an insurance policy 0 (0%) 'Yes' and 118 (100%) 'No'. Absorb risk 7 (7%) 'Yes' and 111 (93%) 'No'. Forecast and plan ahead 7 (7%) 'Yes' and 111 (93%) 'No'. Agree a fixed fee with a risk management company 7 (7%) 'Yes' and 111 (93%) 'No'. Make a contingency plan 7 (7%) 'Yes' and 111 (93%) 'No'. Use experienced and reliable dealers 87 (74%) 'Yes' and 31 (26%) 'No'. Line up a secondary source of supply 0 (0%) 'Yes' and 118 (100%) 'No'. Identify and value all assets at risk 50 (42%) 'Yes' and 68 (58%) 'No'. Put safeguards and controls 114 (97%) 'Yes' and 4 (3%) 'No'. Assess risk periodically 0 (0%) 'Yes' and 118 (100%) 'No'. No feedback suggestions for further comments.

4.4 Section 4 of the Questionnaire Survey: Security of Business Operations

The questions 4.1 to 4.4 present most of the issues and difficulties regarding security of TEISMEs' business operations. The presented the outcomes to *Question 4.1 'Is security an issue for your business operations on the Internet?'*, *Question 4.2 'Are all your IT equipment and terminals protected from unauthorised access?'*, *Question 4.3 'Are remote users authenticated before being allowed to connect to internal networks and systems?'*, and *Ques-*

tion 4.4 'Do you have security policy with regards to your online business operations?' in Figure 5–22.

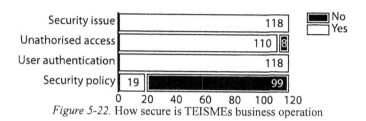

Figure 5-22. How secure is TEISMEs business operation

The questions 4.1 and 4.3 show 118 (100%) 'Yes', the question 4.2 with 110 (93%) 'Yes' and 8 (7%) 'No' while the question 4.4 have 19 (16%) 'Yes' and 99 (84%) 'No'. The responses to all the above questions show the magnitude of the impacts of security issues on TEISMEs business operations.

The *question 4.5 'Which of the following security control measures does your business adopt?'*—the survey revealed that the types of security control measures adopted by TEISMEs in Table 5-3. The survey result shows that Password and personal identity accounts for 118 (100%) of the most common security control measure adopted while the use of Public key encryption shows 98 (83%) 'Yes', with 20 (17%) 'No'; firewall 82 (69%) 'Yes', with 36 'No', Digital signature 7 (6%) 'Yes', with 111 (96%) 'No', Keystroke 5 (4%) 'Yes', with 113 (96%) 'No', and e-mail sniffing 21 (18%) 'Yes', with 97 (82%) 'No'.

However, the analysis presented in Table 5–8 shows that TEISMEs needs to use a combination of security measures to protect their business operations. This view is supported by Huston (2002) who claims that security in the modern world relies completely on layers of defence referred to in the military world, as 'defence in depth'. The defence in depth goes beyond platforms, products, and patches and the protection of assets can no longer be left to simple single-point solutions. He considered the firewall security systems as nothing more than a little speed bump unless it forms an integral part of an overall security solution integrated with components that enhance and support its position. He suggested the use of Network intrusion sensors, host-based hardening and monitoring, network access lists on perimeter devices, and log watching accessories all combined with hardware tokens, honey pots, and a

Table 5–8. Security control measures

	Public key encryption	Firewall	Digital signature	Password	Keystroke	Email sniffing	Personal Identity (ID)
Yes	98	82	7	118	5	21	118
No	20	36	111	0	113	97	0

myriad of other devices, products, and strategies to create an effective technical security bastion. Huston's view strongly supports the hypothesis that 'absolute security is unattainable'.

The response to the *question 4.8 'How long have your company been insured
with this company?'* is negative with all 118 TEISME answered 'None'.

The responses to *question 4.6 'Is your business security/privacy policy
available to the general public'*, *question 4.7 'Is your Internet-eC business
operations insured?'*, *question 4.9 'Have you ever claimed any compensation due to any fraudulent act on your Internet-eC business transactions?'*,
and *Question 4.10 'It is often said that absolute security is unattainable. To
what extent do you agree with this statement?'* are presented in Figure 5–23,
which has shown an indication of the laxity in TEISMEs business operational
security.

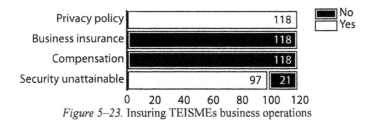

Figure 5–23. Insuring TEISMEs business operations

The question 4.6 has a feedback of 118 (100%) 'Yes' and 0 (0%) 'No',
while questions 4.7 to 4.9 with 0 (0%) 'Yes' and 118 (100%) 'No'. This latter
response is evidence that can be use to support the literature review, the case
study observations and the structured interview outcomes, which suggested
that 'No TEISMEs business operations are currently insured' to be direct 'No
insurance company in the UK are in a position to insure TEISMEs business operations liabilities. The question 4.10 shows a diversify opinion with 97 (82%)
'Yes' and 21 (18%) 'No'. The suggested comment from the 21 responses was
that TEISMEs need to have a continuous security improvement i.e. constantly
updating their security software as and when it is required.

4.5   Section 5 of the Questionnaire Survey: Survey Summary

This section of the questionnaire was based on the overall summary of the
findings, and also asked for general comments on the survey questionnaires
and what the respondent thought should be done to solve this problem:

The *question 5.1* is open-ended, stating that the buying public are increasingly losing confidence in Internet-eC because of lack of guarantee against any
invasion of privacy/confidentiality. *'What is your opinion'*, and *'what would*

you suggest should be done to solve this problem?' Out of 99 participants, 84% did not give any comment; only 19 (16%) offered various suggestions as to possible solutions to TEISMEs business operations and how to boost low customer confidence. The suggestions given are presented in Table 5–9. The Internet-eC has continued to grow rapidly and this survey shows that TEISMEs are worried about the lack of security, most especially the lack of a standardised and flexible risk assessment model.

Table 5–9. Suggestions for possible solutions to TEISMEs' business operations

Suggestions
'More people are buying over the Internet, but growth is perhaps not as steep as would be desired'.
'To add extra level of security and introduce more standardised and flexible risk assessment model'.
'I do not agree that confidence levels are diminishing. A regulatory body to approve Internet-eC processes would help, however'.
'Change perception of public. It is easier to find out more about a customer using their rubbish bins than any amount of information on the Internet/computer systems. '
'Deal with a reputable firm, with honest person at the head'.
'There are a few badly written/managed sizes which give all the rest a bad name'.
'Positive instead of negative press reporting'.
'Identify against loss as standard'.
'Acceleration of PW/Digital Signature Technology and Chip Card production to standardise security across key e/m commerce links'.
'Third party accreditation for traders – not to disclose security measures taken from/ to strangers. Some may lose confidentiality. An awful lot more appear to be gaining confidence'.
'Further development on security control as well as credit security required'.
'Disagree with this statement. Journalists love to say this, but the spending figure proves this to be a huge overstatement. The issues here are not significantly greater than, say, booking a flight over the phone or handing over your credit card to a stranger (waiter) in the restaurant. So over time people will become more accustomed to this method of transaction. Also the companies involved need to take security as serious, and take the necessary security steps (like we do) to avoid needless mistakes'
'Improvement in software design'
'I don't agree with the statement'.
'Educating the public that providing they use sites showing the padlock, that this is probably more secure than giving the credit card to a waiter in a restaurant'
'Increase visibility of secure site policy on Internet-eC sites'.
'Align sites with best practice Internet-eC partner'.
'Sorry. I disagree with your statement. Internet-eC is growing rapidly and most surveys show the public are not unduly worried. In addition, all our Internet-eC is B2B not B2C'.
'I don't agree with the statement, nor is it borne out by figures which show more and more Internet-eC being transacted year after year'.
'Proven track record will help to improve confidence. Remote billing or operating via TWS 200 and 320 Perotios'.

Note: Responses from 19 TEISMEs.

The *question 5.2* asked the participants to specify any problems they might have faced, not covered in section 3 above. Such questions might be related to not having a suitable security or risk assessment procedure in relation to their Internet-eC business operations. Unfortunately, none of the participant gave any comments or suggestions to this question. However, through the analysis of the whole questionnaire it became apparent that the scope of the information was limited and in some areas resulted in restricted information e.g. question 5.1, and 5.2, where participant were given the option to write their comments. The survey results on the impacts and risk assessment of TEISMEs' business operations has proved that:

- 111 of the 118 TEISMEs that participated are not using any risk assessment model.
- All the 118 (100%) TEISMEs that participated are not insured against any of their business operational risks
- 108 (92%) of the 118 TEISMEs that participated believed that security is a problem with 10 (8%) rejected the claim.

5. CORRELATION BETWEEN ANNUAL SALES AND VULNERABILITY

The Pearson's correlation coefficient is the most widely used measure of association for examining relationships between interval variables and focuses specifically on linear relationships. The data in Tables 5–10, 5–11, and 5–12 are used to:

- Assess the degree of correlation between the variable by means of a correlation coefficient,

Table 5–10. Sales figure and vulnerabilities encountered

Average annual sales	£3m	£4m	£5m	£7m	£8m	£9m	Total
No of TEISMEs	53	35	12	9	6	3	118
Total annual sales per category	£159m	£140m	£60m	£63m	£48m	£27m	
Malicious damage	51	34	12	9	6	3	114
Unauthorised access	53	35	12	9	6	3	118
Accidental error	44	29	10	8	5	3	99
Mechanic failure	36	24	8	6	4	2	81
Online fraud	53	35	12	9	6	3	118
Invasion or loss of privacy	53	35	12	9	6	3	118
Total no of vulnerabilities	291	192	66	49	33	16	

Table 5–11. Vulnerability coefficient (vulnerabilities per £1m)

Type of vulnerability	Annual Sales (£m)					
	3	4	5	7	8	9
Malicious damage	0.32	0.24	0.19	0.14	0.12	0.11
Unauthorised access	0.33	0.25	0.20	0.14	0.13	0.11
Accidental error	0.28	0.21	0.17	0.12	0.10	0.09
Mechanic failure	0.23	0.17	0.14	0.10	0.09	0.08
Online fraud	0.33	0.25	0.20	0.14	0.13	0.11
Invasion or loss of privacy	0.33	0.25	0.20	0.14	0.13	0.11
Total	1.83	1.37	1.10	0.78	0.69	0.61

- Express the quantitative relationship between the variables by using linear regression.

The Pearson's correlation coefficient was use to present the 'annual sales and vulnerabilities correlation coefficient': The annual sales figures and vulnerabilities encountered in the last 12 months are based on the questionnaire survey. The TEISMEs annual sales are the dependent variable and the vulnerabilities are the independent variable.

The vulnerability coefficient represents the number of vulnerabilities per million pounds of the annual sales. The coefficient allows the comparison of TEISMEs with different annual sales. The higher the coefficient, the more the TEISME is exposed to vulnerability.

Example

TEISME A has annual sales of £5m and encounters 3 vulnerabilities, the coefficient is equal to 0.60 (vulnerabilities per £1m)

TEISME B has annual sales of £3m and encounters 2 vulnerabilities, the coefficient is equal to 0.67 (vulnerabilities per £1m)

Therefore, TEISME B is more exposed to vulnerabilities than TEISME A (0.67 > 0.6).

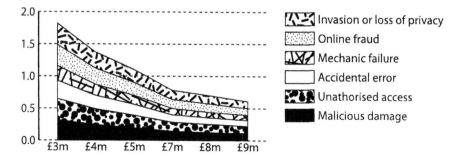

Figure 5–24. Total vulnerability coefficient

Table 5–12. Correlation between annual sales and vulnerability coefficient

Average annual sales (£m)	3	4	5	7	8	9
Total annual sales	159	140	60	63	48	27
Vulnerability coefficient	1.83	1.37	1.10	0.78	0.69	0.61
Correlation coefficient	0.98					

It is assumed that each type of vulnerability is equal to others by its impact. This enables us to find total vulnerabilities (see Figure 5–24).

Hence, there is an apparently high degree of positive correlation between total annual sales of TEISMEs within the same category, and vulnerabilities encountered, in that as total sales goes up, so do vulnerabilities encountered by a similar proportion. Nevertheless, the correlation between average annual sales and vulnerabilities is negative, that means smaller TEISMEs are more vulnerable to financial losses.

Outcome of Hypothesis 3

- $(\mathcal{H}_0^3)$ is rejected, therefore reject $(\mathcal{H}_0^3)$ in favour of $(\mathcal{H}_A^3)$
- As a result of the case study observation, questionnaire survey and Shonire-gun's Risk Assessment Model implementation, the risk assessment is attainable on TEISME business operations.
- The detailed statement of Hypothesis 3 was tested, and the results that led to $(\mathcal{H}_0^3)$ rejection are presented in Table 5–19.

Table 5–13. Identified problems domain of TEISME's business operations

Interviewed Questions that generated responses from TEISME business operations problem domain	Problems Cause by TEISME reliance on TEI
What are the major issues/difficulties that are currently affecting your business operations in relation to Internet-eC? What are the current risks, which your business is vulnerable to and how does your company minimise the risk exposures?	Lack of secured Payment methods Unsecured transaction Stolen credit card (Credit card fraud and Duplication of payment), Hacking, Virus attacked, Data corruption Vandalised the business website (Defamation/ duplication of the websites/website sabotage), Unidentified domain name addresses Denial of services Website imposers Sniffing Contractual liability

6. ANALYSIS OF TEISMEs INTERVIEWED

The 6 TEISMEs that were interviewed consists of 3 small enterprises and the other 3 were from medium enterprises (see Table 5–14). The definition of SMEs has been adopted in selecting the TEISMEs interviewed: based on size, annual sales, and industrial sector classification (see chapter 1).

The Table 5–13 is based on the interviewed responses from 6 TEISMEs business operational problems domain. The types of risk assessment identified do not measure changes that might cause by vulnerabilities/variances. Also the financial loss caused by fraud in relation to the TEISMEs' reliance on TEI within their business operation over the last 3 years, are identified and quantified in value. It has also been established from the interviews, that none of the TEISMEs business transactions are currently insured and the security control measures in place cannot guarantee 100% safety of all business transactions (Shoniregun, 2003).

Table 5–14. The breakdown of 6 TEISMEs interviewed responses

№	Interview Questions	TEISME A	TEISME B	TEISME C	TEISME D	TEISME E	TEISME F
1	What are your company's annual sales?	£5.5 million	£5.2 million	£2.5 million	£13.4 million	£18.2 million	£16.5 million
2	How many people does your company employ?	23 full-time staff	15 full-time staff	15 full-time, 3 part-time	55 staff in total	51 full-time staff	55 full-time staff
3	What industry is your company in?	Music	Travel and tourism	Art and Culture	Children and adults clothing	Training and development	Fashion
4	What is your standard industrial classification?	Service Industry	Service Industry	Manu-facturer /Service Industry	Fashion /Service Industry	Service Industry	Manu-facturer /Service Industry
5	What type of Internet-eC used within your business operations?	B2B and B2C	B2B and B2B	B2B, B2C and C2C	B2B), and B2C	B2B, and B2C	B2C
6	What are the major issues/ difficulties that are currently affecting your business operations in relation to Internet-eC?	Secure transactions, stolen credit card, hacking, virus and data corruption.	Hacking and viruses	Payment methods, secure transaction and quality of art work	Hacking virus, defamation/duplication of the websites in other unidentified domain name addresses	Secure transactions and data corruption	Hacking, credit card fraud, impostors, virus, data corruption

№	Interview Questions	TEISME A	TEISME B	TEISME C	TEISME D	TEISME E	TEISME F
7	How many times has your business experienced denial of service or any internal or external cyber threats within the last 3 years?	20.3 per month	11 per month	11 per month	13.3 per month	22.1 per month	110.9 per month
8	What types of threats are they?	Deformation of business website, impostors	Deformation of business website, impostors	Dummy website, stolen credit cards, website deformation, and viruses	Viruses, defamation, impostors	Business interruptions/denial of service, data corruption, deformation of business website, impostors and duplication of payment	Hackers, virus, data corruption, deformation of business website, and impostors
9	How do you customers pay for their shopping online?	Credit cards and PayPal	Credit cards, PayPal and Advance cheque payment	Credit cards and PayPal	Credit cards and PayPal	Credit cards, PayPal and Cheque guarantee cards	Credit cards and PayPal, e-cash, e-wallet
10	How is the item delivered to the customer i. e. special courier service or by ordinary post?	Ordinary post and special delivery	Ordinary post	Special courier services (DHL, UPS)	In-house delivery and recorded delivery via the post office	Provide the all services online recorded delivery (training CD)	In-house delivery services, courier services and ordinary post
11	Who is responsible for insuring your Internet-eC business operation?	Not insured (the business is responsible for all the loses incurred)	Not insured (the business is responsible for all the loses incurred)	Not insured (the business is responsible for all the loses incurred)	Not insured (the business is responsible for all the loses incurred)	Not insured (the business is responsible for all the loses incurred)	Not insured (the business is responsible for all the loses incurred)
12	How much has your business lost as a result of using TEI?	£38,000	£40,000	£28,000	£25,000–£35,000	£40,000	£91,000

№	Interview Questions	TEISME A	TEISME B	TEISME C	TEISME D	TEISME E	TEISME F
13	What security control measures adopted by your business in relation TEI?	Web administrator and the service provider, provides the security control measures.	Passwords and Daily systems backup	Service provider enforces the security control measures	Service provider provides both security control and web administration	Web administrators and frequently update of security software from the service provider	Web administrator and the service provider, provides the security control measures.
14	What are the current risks, which your business is vulnerable to and how does your company minimise the risk exposures?	Viruses, Denial of services, website imposers and sniffing. Services provider provides update on how to minimise the risk exposures	Hacking Customers data, Viruses, Denial of services, Imposers and contractual liability. Service providers provides updates and the in-house web administrator constantly up grade the security solutions	Hacking, Virus attacked, Denial of service, and website imposers, and contractual liability. Service provider provides update solutions that are installed to minimise the business operations risk exposures	Website sabotage, Data corruptions, and virus attack. Services provider provides update on how to minimise the risk exposures	Business interruptions/denial of service, Data corruption, Vandalised the business website, Imposers and Duplication of payment Service provider provides update on how to minimise the risk exposures	Unsecured transaction, Credit cards fraud, Virus, Data corruption, vandalised business websites, and Impostors Service providers provides updates and the in-house web administrator constantly up grade the security solutions
15	Is your business operation insured? Please can you specify insurance company's name and from when... i.e. 1year 2years... or... more	No!	No!	No!	No!	No!	No!
16	How much has your business claimed from your insurance company over the last 3 years and for what types of business operations.	Not insured	Not insured	Not insured	Not insured	Not insured	Not insured

Outcome of structured interview

- The responses to questions 6, 7, 8, 12, 13 and 14 are in favour of hypothesis $(\mathcal{H}_0^2)$
- The responses to questions 5, 9 and 10 are in favour of hypothesis $(\mathcal{H}_A^1)$
- The responses to questions 1, 7, and 12 are in favour of hypothesis $(\mathcal{H}_A^3)$

It is an established fact that the insurance companies and brokers in the UK are not willing to insure TEISME business operations, and the evidence to substantiate this claim is the responses to questions 15 and 16.

7.   ANALYSIS OF CASE STUDY OBSERVATIONS

The case study observations of CSO A, CSO B, and CSO C have enabled the compilation of the risk incurred by these TEISMEs, and the results are presented in Tables 5–15, 5–16, and 5–17. The abstract to the case study observation are detailed in chapter 4. It can be seen from the three case studies observations that none of the TEISMEs has a risk assessment in place that can be applied to the risk incurred during their Internet-eC business operations, but they only relied on the web administrator and the service provider to rectified any identified risks and update the business on the possible solutions to be provided. The Table 5–18 shows a comprehensive list of classifications of TEISMEs' business operations problem domains identified from the combinations of research carried. The 'Identified Code' (IC) is the total number of each type of TEISMEs' business operations problem domains that was input into the simulation software to generate the probabilities of all identified risk assessment occurrences in the future.

8.   SHONIREGUN TEISME RISK ASSESSMENT CALCULATION

For the purpose of the observation, it is necessary therefore, to multiply the number of risk occurrences. The figure '0' in the divisor represents no compensation agreed with the service provider; therefore no figure is added to the UK current inflation rate.

8.1   Calculation for the CSO A

Calculating the total costs of identified vulnerability (TCIV) and compensation (COMP) of vulnerabilities:

Table 5–15. Risks incurred by CSO A

Risk identified in CSO A	No of Risk Occurrences
Hacking	48
Jamming	20
Malicious Software	49
Sniffing	89
Spoofing	31
Business interruptions/Denial of Service	55
Fraud	
—Corruption of electronic ordering	41
—Duplication of payment	60
—Falsely declaring that a payment was made	80

Table 5–16. Risks incurred by CSO B

Risk identified in CSO B	No of Risk Occurrences
Hacking	71
Jamming	13
Malicious Software	36
Sniffing	18
Spoofing	13
Business interruptions/Denial of Service	19
Fraud	
—Corruption of the electronic ordering	36
—Duplication of payment	43
—Falsely declaring that a payment was made	60

Table 5–17. Risks incurred by CSO C

Risk identified in CSO C	No of Risk Occurrences
Hacking	87
Jamming	42
Malicious Software	76
Sniffing	71
Spoofing	45
Business interruptions/Denial of Service	44
Fraud	
—Corruption of the electronic ordering	63
—Duplication of payment	81
—Falsely declaring that a payment was made	96

Table 5–18. Classifications of TEISMEs business operations problem domains

Types of TEISMEs Business Operations Problems Domain	Transactions/operations problem domains identified
Hacking	Data corruption Website sabotage
Jamming	Vandalised the business website (Defamation/ duplication of our websites) Denial of services
Malicious software	Virus attacked Corruption of electronic ordering
Sniffing	Lack of secured Payment methods Unsecured transaction Stolen credit card (Credit card fraud) Falsely declaring that a payment was made
Spoofing	Duplication of payment Website imposers Unidentified domain name addresses Business interruptions/Denial of Service
Contractual liability	Sales of goods/services Contract
Phishing	Replicating TEISME website and re-directing all transactions to an unauthorised domain name
Spyware	Installs on computer without th user's knowledge Secretly gathers information
Malware	Installs software that makes the computer redundant Crashes system Erases data Sends confidential documents fo customers to unathorised viewers

i. Calculating TCIV and COMP of hacking:

$$TCIV_{hacking} = \frac{£1500000}{365} \times (48 \times 2) \times 0.1 - 3.0 \times £0 = £39\,452.05$$

$$COMP_{hacking} = £100 \times 3.1/3.0 + £39\,452.05 = £39\,555.39$$

ii. Calculating TCIV and COMP of jamming:

$$TCIV_{jamming} = \frac{£1500000}{365} \times (20 \times 2) \times 0.1 - 3.0 \times £0 = £16\,438.36$$

$$COMP_{jamming} = £100 \times 3.1/3.0 + £16\,438.36 = £16\,541.69$$

iii. Calculating TCIV and COMP of malicious software:

$$TCIV_{malicious\,software} = \frac{\pounds1500000}{365} \times (49 \times 2) \times 0.1 - 3.0 \times \pounds0 = \pounds40\,273.97$$
$$COMP_{malicious\,software} = \pounds100 \times 3.1/3.0 + \pounds40\,273.97 = \pounds40\,377.31$$

iv. Calculating TCIV and COMP of sniffing:

$$TCIV_{sniffing} = \frac{\pounds1500000}{365} \times (89 \times 2) \times 0.1 - 3.0 \times \pounds0 = \pounds73\,150.68$$
$$COMP_{sniffing} = \pounds100 \times 3.1/3.0 + \pounds73\,150.68 = \pounds73\,254.02$$

v. Calculating TCIV and COMP of spoofing:

$$TCIV_{spoofing} = \frac{\pounds1500000}{365} \times (31 \times 2) \times 0.1 - 3.0 \times \pounds0 = \pounds25\,479.45$$
$$COMP_{spoofing} = \pounds100 \times 3.1/3.0 + \pounds25\,479.45 = \pounds25\,582.79$$

vi. Calculating TCIV and COMP of denial of service:

$$TCIV_{denial\,of\,service} = \frac{\pounds1500000}{365} \times (55 \times 2) \times 0.1 - 3.0 \times \pounds0 = \pounds45\,205.48$$

$$COMP_{denial\,of\,service} = \pounds100 \times 3.1/3.0 + \pounds45\,205.48 = \pounds45\,308.81$$

vii. Calculating TCIV and COMP of fraud:

$$TCIV_{fraud} = \frac{\pounds1500000}{365} \times (181 \times 2) \times 0.1 - 3.0 \times \pounds0 = \pounds148\,767.12$$
$$COMP_{fraud} = \pounds100 \times 3.1/3.0 + \pounds148\,767.12 = \pounds148\,870.46$$

The total cost of identified vulnerabilities and amount of compensation within CSO A is:

$$TCIV = \pounds388\,767.12$$
$$COMP = \pounds389\,490.46$$

Result

The Figure 5–25 shows comparative impacts of different types of vulnerabilities encountered by the CSO A.

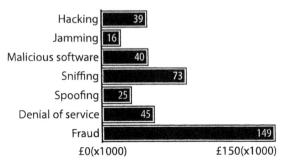

Figure 5–25. Cost of vulnerabilities encountered by CSO A

The amount of total cost of identified vulnerabilities within CSO A constitutes 26% of the annual sales, which means that CSO A has lost 21% (see estimation below).

$$£388\,767.12\,/\,(£388\,767.12 + £1\,500\,000) \times 100\% = 21\%$$

8.2   Calculation for the CSO B

Calculating the total costs of identified vulnerability (TCIV) and compensation (COMP) of vulnerabilities:

i. Calculating TCIV and COMP of hacking:

$$TCIV_{hacking} = \frac{£5000000}{365} \times (71 \times 2) \times 0.1 - 3.0 \times £0 = £194\,520.55$$
$$COMP_{hacking} = £100 \times 3.1\,/3.0 + £194\,520.55 = £194\,623.88$$

ii. Calculating TCIV and COMP of jamming:

$$TCIV_{jamming} = \frac{£5000000}{365} \times (13 \times 2) \times 0.1 - 3.0 \times £0 = £35\,616.44$$
$$COMP_{jamming} = £100 \times 3.1\,/3.0 + £35\,616.44 = £35\,719.77$$

iii. Calculating TCIV and COMP of malicious software:

$$TCIV_{malicious\,software} = \frac{£5000000}{365} \times (36 \times 2) \times 0.1 - 3.0 \times £0 = £98\,630.14$$
$$COMP_{malicious\,software} = £100 \times 3.1\,/3.0 + £98\,630.14 = £98\,733.47$$

iv. Calculating TCIV and COMP of sniffing:

$$TCIV_{sniffing} = \frac{£5000000}{365} \times (18 \times 2) \times 0.1 - 3.0 \times £0 = £49\,315.07$$
$$COMP_{sniffing} = £100 \times 3.1\,/3.0 + £49\,315.07 = £49\,418.40$$

v. Calculating TCIV and COMP of spoofing:

$$TCIV_{spoofing} = \frac{£5000000}{365} \times (13 \times 2) \times 0.1 - 3.0 \times £0 = £35\,616.44$$

$$COMP_{spoofing} = £100 \times 3.1/3.0 + £35\,616.44 = £35\,719.77$$

vi. Calculating TCIV and COMP of denial of service:

$$TCIV_{denial\ of\ service} = \frac{£5000000}{365} \times (19 \times 2) \times 0.1 - 3.0 \times £0 = £52\,054.79$$

$$COMP_{denial\ of\ service} = £100 \times 3.1/3.0 + £52\,054.79 = £52\,158.13$$

vii. Calculating TCIV and COMP of fraud:

$$TCIV_{fraud} = \frac{£5000000}{365} \times (139 \times 2) \times 0.1 - 3.0 \times £0 = £380\,821.92$$
$$COMP_{fraud} = £100 \times 3.1/3.0 + £380\,821.92 = £380\,925.25$$

The total cost of identified vulnerabilities and amount of compensation within CSO A is:

$$TCIV = £846\,575.34$$

$$COMP = £847\,298.68$$

Result

The Figure 5–26 shows comparative impacts of different types of vulnerabilities encountered by the CSO B.

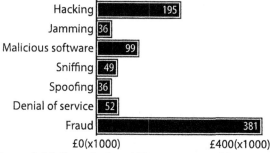

Figure 5–26. Cost of vulnerabilities encountered by CSO B

The amount of total cost of identified vulnerabilities within CSO B constitutes 17% of the annual sales, which means that CSO A has lost 14% (see estimation below).

$$£846\,575.34 \,/\, (£846\,575.34 + £5\,000\,000) \times 100\% = 14\%$$

8.3   Calculation for the CSO C

Calculating the total costs of identified vulnerability (TCIV) and compensation (COMP) of vulnerabilities:

i.   Calculating TCIV and COMP of hacking:

$$TCIV_{hacking} = \frac{£3500000}{365} \times (87 \times 2) \times 0.1 - 3.0 \times £0 = £133\,479.45$$

$$COMP_{hacking} = £100 \times 3.1\,/3.0 + £133\,479.45 = £133\,582.79$$

ii. Calculating TCIV and COMP of jamming:

$$TCIV_{jamming} = \frac{£3500000}{365} \times (42 \times 2) \times 0.1 - 3.0 \times £0 = £64\,438.36$$

$$COMP_{jamming} = £100 \times 3.1\,/3.0 + £64\,438.36 = £16\,541.69$$

iii. Calculating TCIV and COMP of malicious software:

$$TCIV_{malicious\,software} = \frac{£3500000}{365} \times (76 \times 2) \times 0.1 - 3.0 \times £0 = £116\,602.74$$

$$COMP_{malicious\,software} = £100 \times 3.1\,/3.0 + £116\,602.74 = £116\,706.07$$

iv. Calculating TCIV and COMP of sniffing:

$$TCIV_{sniffing} = \frac{£3500000}{365} \times (71 \times 2) \times 0.1 - 3.0 \times £0 = £108\,931.51$$

$$COMP_{sniffing} = £100 \times 3.1\,/3.0 + £108\,931.51 = £109\,034.84$$

v.   Calculating TCIV and COMP of spoofing:

$$TCIV_{spoofing} = \frac{£3500000}{365} \times (45 \times 2) \times 0.1 - 3.0 \times £0 = £69\,041.10$$

$$COMP_{spoofing} = £100 \times 3.1\,/3.0 + £69\,041.10 = £69\,144.43$$

vi. Calculating TCIV and COMP of denial of service:

$$TCIV_{denial\,of\,service} = \frac{£3500000}{365} \times (44 \times 2) \times 0.1 - 3.0 \times £0 = £67\,506.85$$

$$COMP_{denial\,of\,service} = £100 \times 3.1\,/3.0 + £67\,506.85 = £67\,610.18$$

vii. Calculating TCIV and COMP of fraud:

$$TCIV_{fraud} = \frac{£3500000}{365} \times (240 \times 2) \times 0.1 - 3.0 \times £0 = £368\,219.18$$

$$COMP_{fraud} = £100 \times 3.1/3.0 + £368\,219.18 = £368\,322.51$$

The total cost of identified vulnerabilities and amount of compensation within CSO A is:

$$TCIV = £928\,219.18$$

$$COMP = £928\,942.51$$

Result

The Figure 5–27 shows comparative impacts of different types of vulnerabilities encountered by the CSO C.

The amount of total cost of identified vulnerabilities within CSO C constitutes 27% of the annual sales, which means that CSO C has lost 21% (see estimation below).

$$£928\,219.18 / (£928\,219.18 + £3\,500\,000) \times 100\% = 21\%$$

8.4   Comparative Analysis of CSOs Vulnerabilities

The Figure 5–28 shows comparative vulnerability analysis of the three CSO.

Although it is arguable that the trend could have been more significant if a larger-scale observation had been carried out on 50 to 100 CSOs, but there is still evidence of justification from the results of this research.

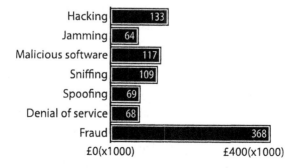

Figure 5–27. Cost of vulnerabilities encountered by CSO C

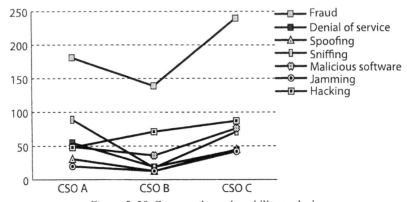

Figure 5–28. Comparative vulnerability analysis

9.   RESULT SUMMARY OF HYPOTHESES TEST

The survey questionnaire, case study observations, laboratory experiments and structured interviews (combinatory research methodology) have been carried out in an attempt to prove or reject the hypotheses stated in chapter 1. The total outcome includes other elements that have led the author to prove or reject the three hypotheses (see Table 5–19).

10.   SUMMARY OF CHAPTER FIVE

There is clear evidence from the questionnaire survey feedback, structured interviews and case study observations that security is unattainable on TEISME's business operations. The TEISMEs are exposed to several risks in their everyday business operations and thus use a combination of security control measures to minimise their risk exposure. Furthermore, an effective security cannot be achieved by the use of one form of security measure, but by layers upon layers of security measures, which will also require a flexible risk assessment model for continuous assessment of the security measure. The combinatory methodology adopted in this research has enabled us to develop a comprehensive classification of the types of vulnerabilities facing TEISMEs business operations (see Table 5–18) and also open windows of opportunities to stimulate the identified vulnerabilities. The author has produced important analysis, which will aid in recommendations of adopting 'Shoniregun Risk Assessment Model'. The 'Shoniregun Risk Assessment Model' was developed based on the problem regime compiled as a result of the 400 questionnaire survey, 6 TEISMEs interviewed and 3 case study observations, and also taking into consideration the weaknesses that has been identified from both the exist-

Table 5–19. Summary of hypotheses tested and results

Hypothesis tested	Reason in favour
Hypothesis 1	$(\mathcal{H}_0{}^1)$ Accepted. Reason for acceptance of $(\mathcal{H}_0{}^1)$ All TEISME customers are online $(\mathcal{H}_A{}^1)$ (see chapter 1) Not all goods or services can be sold online (see chapter 7)
Hypothesis 2	$(\mathcal{H}_0{}^2)$ Accepted. Reason for acceptance of $(\mathcal{H}_0{}^2)$ As a result of the laboratory experiments, absolute security is unattainable on TEISME business operations. The result of the test has proved that 89% of TEISMEs business operation websites are vulnerable to sniffing. The generic weaknesses of hardware and software (see chapter 2) for problem with network protocol layers and application security $(\mathcal{H}_0{}^2)$ The results of section 4 of the second questionnaire survey show a total rejection for $(\mathcal{H}_A{}^2)$ Weaknesses in the existing risk assessment model, $(\mathcal{H}_0{}^2)$ (see chapter 3) 108 (92%) of the TEISMEs that participated it the Impacts And Risk Assessment Of TEISME Business Operations agreed that the security is a problem $(\mathcal{H}_0{}^2)$ 111 (94%) of the TEISMEs that participated are not using any risk assessment model, this might be associated with the weaknesses identified from the study $(\mathcal{H}_0{}^2)$ Total cost of identified vulnerability (TCIV) is very high e.g. CSO A lost 21%, CSO B lost 14%, and CSO C lost 21 %. These figures represent the total losses incurred by CSOs as a result of customers who are unable to buy goods or services through their website.
Hypothesis 3	$(\mathcal{H}_A{}^3)$ Accepted. Reason for acceptance of $(\mathcal{H}_A{}^3)$ As a result of the case study observation, questionnaire survey and Shoniregun Risk Assessment Model implementation, the risk assessment is attainable on TEISME business operations. Calculation of the correlation coefficient between total annual sales and vulnerability coefficient which give us 0.98; The calculated cost of each identified vulnerabilities for CSO A, CSO B and CSO C and their total costs of identified vulnerabilities are calculated below: CSO A: $TCIV = £388\,767.12$; CSO B: $TCIV = £846\,575.34$; CSO C: $TCIV = £928\,219.18$; The comparative vulnerability analysis of the three CSOs presented in Figure 5–28.

ing risk assessments and the technologies for Internet security.

It is evident from the findings that a staggering number of TEISMEs agreed that absolute security is unattainable on their business operations. Similarly, TEISME is complementary to, but not in direct competition with SME (see section 2). It is also evident in the results of this study that TEISMEs are exposed to a plethora of risks in their day-to-day business operations and that they use a combination of security control measures for minimising risks which are not and currently can not be insured by any UK based insurance company (see Table 5–8).

Indeed, there is no one best security control measure and effective risk assessment model. The believed that the adoption of Shoniregun Risk Assessment model would be a way forward to compromise the weaknesses found in the literature review, the questionnaire survey, structured interviews and case study observations.

However, the next chapter critically evaluates the issues relating to this study.

REFERENCES

Bolton, J., 1971, Small firms report of the committee of inquiry on small firms, London, HMSO.

Department of Trade and Industry (DTI), 2002, 'Information Security Breaches Survey', p. 20; ukonlineforbusiness.gov.uk/cms/template/infor-security.jsp?id=213097 (January 8, 2003).

Huston. B, 2002, 'A Higher view of Defense in Depth'; www.itworld.comh/nl/securitys-trat/02202002/ (February 20, 2002).

Shoniregun, C. A., Chochliouros, I. P., Laperche, B., Logvynovskiy, O., and Spiliopoulou-Chochliouros, A., 2004, Questioning the Boundary Issues of Internet Security, e-Centre for Infonomics: London.

Shoniregun, C. A., 2003, 'Are existing Internet security measures guaranteed to protect user identity in the financial services industry?', International Journal of Services, Technology and Management (IJSTM), Volume 4, pp. 194–215.

Chapter 6

CRITICAL EVALUATION AND DISCUSSION

1. INTRODUCTION

The past decade has witnessed dramatic changes in business processes. The number of businesses that store and access confidential and business-critical data in digital form on computer networks or over the Internet has increased dramatically. The importance of Internet security has, therefore, become an important aspect as the threat-level of Internet-eC crime increases. Although, current literature acknowledges the specific issues that many Internet-eC encountered in order to survive in this dynamic, high risk and competitive business environment, but the questions regarding risk liability of TEISMEs business operations remain un-answered and the available risk assessments lack accuracy and justification for their use. This chapter critically evaluates the issues relating to this study.

2. CHALLENGES OF TEI ON INFORMATION SECURITY

The emergence of the Internet is attracting a plethora of TEISMEs aiming to exploit the potential benefits from trading digitally and the TEISME business operations has gained numerous benefits from using TEI; the TEI have at the same time made TEISMEs more vulnerable to breaches in their business operations and their information security is definitely an issue. *How and where do we draw the line and how do we ensure that what is behind the line is safe?* That kind of technological breakthrough is going to be needed to really make advance, or to have a risk assessment that will give an accurate projection where others have failed (Bond, 2000). Traditionally, security was used by businesses to protect property of a physical nature, by the use of a security guard or an alarm system. In today's world the security guard and an alarm system still serve as an effective deterrent to the common thief. They do nothing however to protect TEISMEs against the unauthorised access and deprivation of information by hackers (cyber terrorists) via the Internet, which happens under their very noses. A study by the Department of Trade and Industry (DTI) (2002) has concluded that, nearly two thirds of small businesses with crucial or sensitive information have suffered serious breaches of security. These studies and the statistics highlight the very real risk of an attack on a website and the scale of the problem, which unfortunately seems to be spiralling out of control. The computers and service providers are seen to be targets that can be attacked ('do to'), or tools that can be used (do… with, on, or from). From this perspective, computer security is distinguished from information security. Cheswick *et al.* (2003) defined computer security as 'keeping anyone from doing things you do not want them to do to, with, on or from your computers or any peripheral devices.' A report published by the DTI in April 2002, found that computer hacking, cyber fraud, and software bugs are costing Britain up to £10 billion a year. According to the DTI, 50% of all businesses were victims of such attacks compared with 25% in 2000 and less than 1 in 5 in 1998. The report found that attacks by hackers on SMEs more than tripled in the past years and 4 out of 5 the businesses have been victim of virus or fraud in 2001. The average cost of each security lapse is £30,000, and fraud and hacking had cost well over £500,000 (see Figure 6–1) (Fraud Advisory Panel, 2003). In relation to a security of TEISME networks there is little data available on this understandably confidential subject. One of the few is the number of SSL servers. The OECD found that, on a per-capita basis, the USA had six times as secure servers as the EU. The Figure 6–2 below shows that the percentages of credit cards abused has been relatively low compare to virus attacks on businesses among the 16 countries survey by Netcraft and Eurobarometer in 2000.

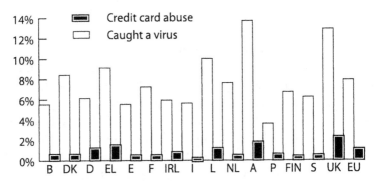

Figure 6–1. Security problems of credit cards and viruses (% Internet users)

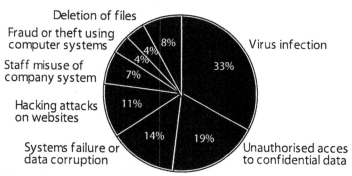

Figure 6–2. DTI Information security breaches survey 2002

Furthermore, due to all the fraudulent acts that have taken place, businesses are trying to make their TEI more secured, but the root problem is that the majority of Internet business users does not possess technical knowledge and lack the know-how on security for their systems. The Netcraft and Eurobarometer (2000) results presented in Figure 6–1 shows similar outcomes to the survey conducted by the DTI 'Information Security Breaches Survey 2002', with an estimated 33% viruses, indeed, viruses are still the most profound security breaches reported so far (see Figure 6–2) (DTI, 2002a).

The unprotected systems are fair game for hackers who would use them as attack platforms in order to promote their own goals. The increasing numbers of TEISME who do not take the necessary steps to protect their own systems are further compounds with unprotected system problems. However, even though orders are sent through secure applications, many businesses still print out orders on paper, which could be stolen or copied easily. Unless businesses streamline their order and payment processes and connect back office applications, the security of front end might not lead to fully secure transactions. The various concerns of TEISME with regards to TEI will now be looked at. The risk of a computer virus attack is increasing at an alarming level. E-mail service provider MessageLabs saw the number of hostile e-mail attachments triple between 2001 and 2002. In the early months of 2001, MessageLabs found that 1 in every 1053 e-mails coming through their company's gateway had a malicious attachment (DTI, 2002a).

3. SHARED THREATS

Horton *et al.* (2000) state that there are risks involved in sharing information and also no aspect of Internet-eC is independent of other critical factors, and that a massive amount of information is transmitted continuously to help maintain vital services and economic well-being. TEISMEs needs to identify what Horton *et al.*, called 'a complete threat population' when assessing threats of information security. However, this study has identified eight key risks, which can threaten TEISME business operations. These eight key risks are discussed below:

3.1   Fraud

Fraud has a worldwide impact and is highly publicised in many Internet-eC research reports. In the third quarter of 2000, and again in the third quarter of 2001, Gartner surveyed online retailers with the largest transaction volumes across several industries regarding electronic payment issues, including the issue of online fraud. Online fraud rates have held steady since 2000, despite significant efforts by merchants, card issuers and law enforcement to curb fraud. In 2000, online fraud losses were 1.13% of $44.2 billion in annual online sales. In 2001, some $700 million was lost, representing 1.14% of $61.8 billion in online sales (Kerr and Litan, 2002). These figures are presented in Figure 6–3, which does not includes additional labour and fees spent on fraud investigations or merchant fines that are sometimes imposed by credit card companies for high levels of charge-back, which include outright fraud and other disputes Is Internet transaction fraud increasing or decreasing?

Although the nature of fraud in questioned, it can be committed by a member of staff or by people outside the TEISME business operations (they may be parties in a foreign country) using the website as a tool. The following fraudulent activities are most commonly encountered by TEISMEs:

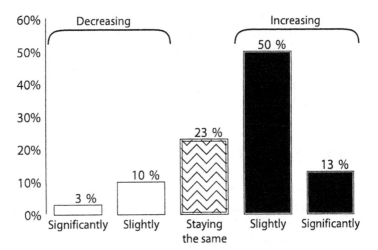

Figure 6–3. Merchants' view of online fraud trends

- Unauthorised movement of money (making payment to fictitious suppliers located in areas (safe havens) where recovery of money is difficult (Switzerland)
- Misrepresentation of company tenderers
- Corruption of the electronic ordering or invoicing
- Duplication of payment
- Denying an order was placed/received
- Denying receipt of goods
- Denying that payment was received or falsely declaring that a payment was made.

The fact that some of the TEISME's employee themselves, and many handsomely paid, are largely involved in fraud, the author strongly suggests that TEISME's business operational security is unattainable. According to Smith (1998) total security can never be guaranteed either in the physical world or the virtual universe of open networks, so companies looking at Internet-eC need to evaluate the level of fraud that they can expect, bearing in mind that the risk of fraud losses on commercial transactions is comparatively small. This raises the question of the security of the Internet-eC. There are many types of fraud, the most significant of which has been seen by the introduction of credit and debit cards to our society, which has seen the crime of Internet fraud. Fraud can take place at a retail outlet when an unauthorised user (a person whose name is not specified on the card, but pretends to be that person whose name is specified) of a credit or debit card uses it to purchase goods or service. In much the same way, fraud can take place on the Internet, and this is what is known as Internet Fraud.

'Internet crime is the most significant problem Visa is dealing with in Europe'
— John Prideau (Visa: Executive Vice President, 2000)

The situation has also been made worse by the fact that when ordering goods by credit card, they can be delivered to an alternative address or addresses, whereas before, when paying for goods using this method, any goods ordered had to be delivered to the card holders address.

3.2 Loss of Privacy/Confidentiality

The success of TEISMEs business operations largely depends on information on the Internet. But customers are increasingly concerned about the amount of information required and the degree of security the TEISMEs and their service provider applies to the information. The result is that if people who provide the information are less confident that the information they provide is not adequately protected, then they may not be willing to provide it next time they visit the TEISME's website. The information at risk includes the customer's name, contact details, previous purchases, services provided, and criminal or medical records.

According to Shoniregun (2005) keynote speech in Trento, Italy, states that when engaging in transactions or simply communicating over the Internet, most people naively assume that their message remains private. In fact, it is quite easy for an interested party to eavesdrop on other people's Internet conversations. While the electronic age has made communication arguably easier, it has made intercepting communications easier for unknown third parties. The TEI introduces technology that poses new challenges to TEISMEs business operations. On-line activities can be recorded to track, which files or websites one has visited. Both TEISMEs and their Internet service provider collect such information. The e-mail addresses can be collected for 'spamming' —the practice of sending unsolicited e-mail and other electronic communication to TEISMEs and their customers, which leads to many hours of filtering these unwanted messages, which is not cost effective on the long run.

> 'The right to privacy is the right of the individual to decide for himself how much he/she will share with others his/her thoughts, feelings, and the facts of his/her personal life. ... Actually what is private varies from day to day and setting to setting.'
> —Off of Sci & Tech of the Exe Off of the US President (1999)

Globally speaking, not all countries see information as the property of the collector. In 1995, the European Parliament announced a directive stipulating that individuals on whom information is collected be made aware of the users of the information, the purpose for the collection, to whom the information may be disclosed, right of access, and correction. On-line businesses constantly gather and use demographic information from users who are afraid that their personal data, including credit card numbers or their behaviour on the Net, many be sold, used, or revealed in an inappropriate manner. Such fears keep many consumers from shopping on-line (Haag *et al.*, 2000; Turban *et al.*, 2002).

3.3   Lack of Authentication

Lack of authentication refers to a transaction without being authorised to do so. Because of the sheer mass of information being circulated during TEISMEs business operations and the concerns over the amount of information required and the degree of security applied to the information, it becomes important to provide adequate authority to customers who are involved business transactions. However, once a transaction has been accepted over the network, it becomes legally binding and liability is created for a party involved in the transaction. The risk here is that because 'the paper-based controls are limited to allow reconciliation, the authentication process may well accept the unauthorised party indefinitely and go undetected'. The risks may result from corruption of a list of signatories, creation of fictitious supplies (masquerade), unauthorised ordering or approving a transaction etc.

> 'Security analysts agree that most computer fraud is accomplished by traditional methods, involving physical access to sensitive data. Nonetheless the public perception of data networks is of an electronic world plagued by swarms of ingenious hackers.'
> —ISOCOR (1999) Marking the Commercial Superhighway Happen',
> January.

Authentication is proving that 'you are who you say you are'. This is a concern for both TEISMEs and their consumers. The pure number of virtual retail outlets offering goods at discounted prices is like a paradise for bargain hunters everywhere. Some of the websites advertising these goods or service have never been heard of before and are not established retailers. A few cases have been reported where virtual shops have been created, that are remarkably similar to well-known companies, tricking the customer in believing that they are an established retailer and accept payments for goods or services that they never intend to deliver or where the description of an item is significantly different to that advertised (also an aspect of fraud). The subject of authenticity also arises in e-mail spoofing, when a user receives an e-mail that appears to have originated from one person, but is actually sent from another person trying to impersonate a third individual. The goal of e-mail spoofing is to trick the user into divulging information or replying with information that is confidential.

3.4   Repudiation

In certain circumstances, the TEISME transaction conducted over the network system indicates that buying and selling have taken place, but one of the parties repudiates or denies it. This can result in invalid contracts, TEISME not being paid for goods and services delivered, or customers not receiving services/goods already paid for. In turn, this can create liabilities that can result in a company going out of business.

3.5   Corruption of Data

This is the violation of data integrity. According to Gosh and Swaminatha (2001), the data integrity attacks are not often discussed in the context of Internet, they are nevertheless of concern to the Internet-eC community as it impacts upon TEISME business operations transactions. The violations in the information sent over networks are often incidental and unintentional, but the potential to maliciously alter the information in order to affect some outcome do exist in different ways. This argument has been supported by Martin (2000), that the commonly held view is that risks involve activities that can be performed remotely through web resources; the reality, however, is that almost all corruptions are conducted within the system. Examples of malicious damage that can be done by hackers, staff, clients or suppliers range from amending catalogue without authorisation, destruction of audit trail through tampering with the ordering process, to disrupting online tendering, or posting inaccurate information online (e.g. stock information). This suggests that corrupt data may render TEISMEs business contract invalid.

3.6   Business Operation Interruptions/Denial of Service

The TEISMEs' business operations interruptions are considered as a key risk because they are tantamount to a denial of service (i.e. making services unavailable), the ultimate Internet security nemesis. The business interruption or denial of service can lead to financial crisis and lawsuits. For example, Internet providers that depend on BT communication system may be denied services to their clients if there is a major breakdown in the BT communication system. Thus the major risks to be considered by TEISMEs include the following: denial of security tools, infrastructure failure (due to lack of resources), how to assess the claim and who will pay compensation.

3.7   Inadequate Funding

Inadequate funding is classified as a risk element for TEISMEs' business operations, because both the software or hardware that make up TEI are regularly changing which means that TEISMEs will need to be kept up to date with the advancement in TEI which eventually will cause TEISMEs to continuously upgrade their TEI. This demands substantial investment as well as the business process being re-engineered.

3.8 Social Engineering

Social engineering is defined as an outsider trying to trick legitimate personnel into disclosing information or granting inappropriate access (Gragg, 2003). An attacker use social engineering to collect information that might be of interest: the network layout, names and/or IP addresses of important servers, version numbers of operating systems and software, and internal security tools of the system. In reality, social engineering is not limited to phone calls (Farrow, 2005). In reality, social engineering is not limited to phone calls. TEISME can teach employees on how to recognise a possible social engineering attack. Condition specific to a practical TEISME must be considered. However, as the entire Paradigm around security has shifted from one issue to the other, the technology for Internet security becomes the daily concern for TEISME business operations.

Social engineering is one of the hardest attacks to stop and is an inevitable risk for all TEISMEs and their customers. It takes advantage of the weakest element in the security chain—people. Why attempt to hack into a system, when one can probably get the information such as a log-in password from the help desk or the service provider's staff?

Social engineering can be divided into two main categories: computer and human-based. The computer-based social engineering takes the high-tech route. Examples of computer-based social engineering include pop up boxes that inform the user of a problem, and ask the user to enter his or her password to rectify a problem. Once the user enters the password, it would then be transmuted to be attack. The human based social engineering adopts the low-tech approach. An example of human-based social engineering is when a hacker phones up a help desk to gain vital information from the technical support staff. This is surprisingly easy to do since most people are inherently trusting and would disclose sensitive information to their friend(s) unknowingly. There is a misplace if trust that free discussion at lunch time or at dinner even among friends in a social gathering can led to information which provides clues to some vital security breaches. So the argument that arises here is that how do TEISMEs employees know when there is a breach of security.

4. TEISMEs BUSINESS OPERATIONS ARE NOT IMMUNE TO INTERNET ATTACKS

According to Horton *et al.*, (2000), thousands of unauthorised attempts are made to intrude into systems that control key information resources and infrastructure components, including power grids, communication networks, banks, transportation systems, and defence facilities. All the businesses that

Table 6–1. Average cost of worst security incident

Security incident	Overall	Large businesses
Disruption to business	£5,000–£10,000	£50,000–£150,000
	Over 1–2 days	Over 1–3 days
Time spent responding to incident	£500–£1,000	£3,000–£6,000
	Over 2–4 man days	Over 10–20 man days
Direct cash spent responding to incident	£1,000–£2,000	£5,000–£10,000
Direct financial loss (e.g. loss of assets, fines etc.)	£200–£500	£2,000–£4,000
Damage to reputation	£100–£300	£5,000–£20,000
Total cost of worst incident on average	£7,000–£14,000	£65,000–£190,000

use the Internet or other shared networks or depends on other infrastructure components are immune to any attacks. But some TEISMEs enable intruders to gain 'system administrator status', download sensitive files such as passwords, implant 'sniffers' (what is dubbed here as Internet dogs or spy-ware) to copy transactions, insert 'trap doors' to permit easy return, or implant programs that can be activated later for a variety of purposes. The Hackers have been around for approximately twenty years, shortly before the more commercial use of the Internet began. They are comparable to modern day burglar, except with one significant difference, a hacker does not have to be physically present at the scene of a crime. All that is required for any intrusion to take place is the use of a computer terminal that has an Internet connection, location of where the unauthorised entry or appropriation of property or information is to take place and the appropriate software and techniques of accessing internal networks and personal computers. The hackers continue to develop new software and various techniques for accessing internal networks and personal computers. The website www.alt2600.com provides information on the latest sites attacked by hackers and the links to tools that they use. More hacking software is now readily available on the Internet for free. For example, Portscan 1.2 is a utility, which allows the user to scan ports on any target system. The user specifies the target IP address. The program then scans all ports between 1 – 65536. The resulting information can then be used to find loopholes in a security set-up. Another tool similar to this is IP-Prober; it allows open ports to be scanned in order to gain entrance to a network. Password cracking represents another method hackers use to enter networks. Again several tools for cracking passwords and codes can be found throughout the Internet. The majority of these tools work by generating potential password combinations including both letter and number codes. The majority of these software tools can repeat this process, millions of times. As a consequence, the number of UK businesses that suffered a security breach continues to rise. The Table 6–1 (PricewaterhouseCoopers, 2004) shows the average cost of worst security incident and the ranges are quoted because of the inherent uncertainty involved in extrapolation.

However, the analysis of the second questionnaire survey shows that TEISMEs used a combination of security measures to protect their business operations. This view is supported by Huston (2002) who claims that security in modern world relies completely on layers of defence referred to in the military world, as 'defence in depth'. The defence in depth goes beyond platforms, products, and patches and the protection of assets can no longer be left to simple single-point solutions. He considered the firewall security systems as nothing more than a little speed bump unless it forms an integral part of an overall security solution integrated with components that enhance and support its position. The network intrusion sensors, host-based hardening and monitoring, network access lists on perimeter devices, and log watching accessories all combined with hardware tokens, honey pots, and a myriad of other devices, products, and strategies that can be use to create an effective technical security bastion. Huston's view strongly supports the hypothesis that 'absolute security is unattainable'. The number of attacks from outside crackers is catching up to the frequency of unauthorised access from insiders. Insider attacks also rose for the third straight year, with 55% of the respondents reporting incidents, a 10% increase from last year (BMRB, 2000). Indeed, many companies have opened themselves to attack by installing a firewall without dedicating resources to manage it effectively. Effective security requires an adequate budget, staff training, and management support. A firewall is not a one-time silver bullet. The most recent security lapse has been exposed, the potential risk to TEISME business operations and merchants who share web servers with other businesses, is that, it is possible to locate and compromise a private key that is encrypted and buried in the disc storage of a web server. This discovery offers the possibility that a hacker with access to TEISME business's server or their merchants server could locate cryptographic key that would allow access to secure credit card numbers.

5.   RISKS AND TRUST

As the Internet-eC becomes the *de facto* platform for doing business, it remains a vast frontier of 'untamed and uncontrolled' networks. However, no one can afford to ignore the presence of Internet-eC or the future potential growth. Analysts suggest that there is no way of making the Internet '100% safe', therefore, organisations and governments are forced to implement security policies, technological software and regulations in order to control unauthorised intrusion into business networks (Shoniregun, 2003). Safety of TEISME business operations becomes an essential component of risk and trust, but it is unclear whether risk is an antecedent of trust, or is an outcome of trust. Risk-taking behaviour and trust behaviour are really different sides of the coin; what really matters is that the connection between risk and trust depends on the situation and the context of a specific, identifiable relationship such as the impacts TEI on TEISMEs and risks assessment of their business operations.

Risk-taking takes into account the profitability of the occurrence of an event between parties and the difference in the anticipated ratio. The anticipated ratios can be either positive or negative emotional consequences to the parties. The probability of negative consequences will depend on how risky the situation is and the existence of security measures that can avoid the risk occurring. However, organisations and individuals vary considerably from one another in the degree of assurance they require before they will act in a situation that has the potentiality of dangerous or negative consequences. The following are the most common security risks on Internet transactions:

- *Spoofing:* Because of the low cost involved in website creation and ease of duplication, illegitimate sites are created and appear to be normal
- *Unauthorised disclosure:* Hackers can intercept data during transmission to get sensitive information
- *Unauthorised action:* Competitors or even unhappy customers can vandalise and alter websites making them malfunction or become incorrect. This has become apparent for small and medium sized businesses because they cannot afford sophisticated security software
- *Data alteration:* Contents of transactions can be changed whilst in transit e.g. user names, bank/card details are most vulnerable (BT Trust Wise, 2001).

As commercial activities on the Internet increase, consumers and businesses will expect that their use of network services is secure and reliable, that their transactions are safe, and that they will be able to verify important information about transactions and transacting parties. Many things people take for granted in normal buying and selling of goods and services, in the real world cannot be taken for granted in cyberspace. In order for the Internet to be accepted as a viable platform for Internet-eC it is necessary to establish a foundation of trust (Inada, 2000; Katsuno, 1998). All of the above security risks of Internet transactions are burning issues of concern in the global platform. In October 1996 two 'consortiums': the Internet Law and Policy Forum (ILPF) and TRUSTe, were formed to help address the Internet's 'no rule' state. Whereas, ILPF focuses on Internet law, the nucleus of the TRUSTe consortium is to increase the level of trust between sellers and buyers in electronic/digital communications, particularly Internet shopping upon which both e-com and m-com businesses are largely based. The TRUSTe was founded on the belief that 'the greater the level of trust among the participants in a transaction, the lower the transaction costs'. The author also believes that the greater the level of trust amongst the parties involved, the more confidence there will be in e-com/m-com business, and the more willing people may be to shop on the Internet and, possibly, the less risk there will be in conducting Internet–eC. The main principles governing the TRUSTe include:

- Informed consent: consumers have the right to be informed about the privacy and security consequences of an online transaction before entering into it
- No privacy without appropriate security: an inextricable link exists between the privacy and security of an online transaction. Privacy is impossible without appropriate security
- Privacy standards vary according to use context: no single privacy standard is adequate for all situations. Any standard to be considered should be in the context of 'the best business practice'. This appears to complicate the situation as best business practice varies from industry to industry and from country to country. What is more, corporate clients may not perceive it as the best business practice.

One question comes to mind. 'Do TEISMEs inform their customers about the privacy and security risks consequences of an online/real-time transaction before selling to them?' The answer is negative. The new challenges are how to assess risks and manage trust in an electronic environment. The building of trust models is hindered by the unfriendly nature of security technology (Shoniregun, *et al.,* 2004). Dean Adams, a trust consultant and member of ECAF (European Certificate Authority Forum) states that the banks were the first to recognise that while one may see pounds and pence or dollars and cents on the computer screen, what one is really dealing in is trust, if one loses the trust, he/she has lost the business, potentially irrevocably. The global nature of the Internet as a public network means that trust has even greater importance in the virtual world, than in traditional commerce. In an information technology age anything and everything seems possible. Cases of Internet crime and abuse are becoming part of our daily life. The following are some notably public cases:

- *Case 1:* Masters of Deception (Hackers): A network of 1000 hackers who call themselves Masters of Deception (MoD) were indicted by the US Federal grand jury for committing what was described as one of the largest thefts of computer information and services in history. The hackers were severally charged with computer tampering, Internet fraud, illegal wiretapping, and conspiracy. The MoD broke into over 25 of the largest corporate computer systems in the USA, including Equifax, Inc. (a credit reporting firm with 170 million records), South-western Bell Corporation, New York

Telephone, and Pacific Bell. All the hackers (under 22 years of age) pleaded guilty and were convicted and imprisoned (Keen *et al.*, 1998).
Similarly, Fortuna Alliance Company took $6m from thousands of people by deception, by placing advertisements at several websites and inviting thousands of customers on the web to invest as illustrated in Case 2:

- *Case 2:* Fortuna Alliance Company: Fortuna Alliance of Billingham, Washington, took $6m from thousands of people in an illegal investors' pyramid scheme advertised on the Internet. Fortuna placed adverts at several websites inviting thousands of customers on the web to invest $250–$1750 with the promise of earning, at least, $5000 per month if they could persuade others to invest. The fraud was discovered and in May 1996, the Federal Trade Commission obtained a court order to freeze the assets of the Fortuna Alliance Company (Business Week, 2001).
The case of abuse (the commission of acts involving a computer that may not be illegal but are considered as unethical) was also apparent when Timothy Lloyd abused the privilege of his office as the chief computer network administrator at Omega Engineering Inc, as explained in Case 3:
- *Case 3:* Timothy Lloyd's Logic Bomb – the case of a malicious damage, Timothy Lloyd, a former chief computer network administrator at Omega Engineering Inc, planted a 'logic bomb' that deleted the company's software programs, worth $10m. Logic bomb is a malicious program that is set to trigger at a specified time. Timothy was charged with malicious damage and stealing $50,000 of computer equipment, which included a backup tape that could have allowed Omega to recover its lost files. Found guilty, Timothy was dismissed (Keen *et al.*, 1998).

It is not only a question of whether a site is technologically safe from fraudsters, but also whether it is trustworthy. Egg.com ran into trouble in April 1999 when accounts holders found they could look at others confidential details; a similar problem hit Halifax's online share-dealing service. These are examples where the internal organisation is at fault because of inappropriate privacy precautions. These are the kind of incidents that shatter customer confidence. The risks to which the TEISMEs are exposed, is detailed in Table 5–8.

Online purchases are dominated by credit cards. According to a study by the Activmedia consultancy, credit-card payment is used in 98.5% of Internet transactions worldwide. In the USA, credit-card transactions over the telephone and web accounted for US$90 billion in 2000 with an average transaction of US$80 (Rodriguez, 2001). Europay, the European arm of card network MasterCard, advised that 6% of all fraud in the Continent is Internet-related. Credit-card losses on the Internet rose by £2 million to £7 million in 2000. Organised crime is the main issue to face organisations. Credit-card companies and banks are spending large sums to counter the perceived risks of Internet scams, which in turn continue to be one of the biggest worries for online shoppers. John Briggs, Head of Banking Alliances at Earthport, (providers of secure online payment software) states that the perception is still there in consumers' minds that it is not safe to buy or sell on the Internet. The 4th May 2002 marks the second anniversary of the infamous Love Letter virus out break 'I love you'. This is now marked as the Internet's day of infamy, because the entire world witnessed destruction on a scale never before seen and it turned our attention to the importance of Internet security and the constant battle to keep virus and hacker threats at bay. Since then, there have been viruses aimed at PDA's, the first cross-platform and first peer-to-peer computer viruses. According to Srivats Sampath, the President and CEO of McAfee. com Application Service Provider (ASP) 'this is just a sampling of what we expect to see in the future as we further migrate to a digital society'. The love letter remains among the most prevalent viruses circulating on the Internet today. It took only 6 hours to spread the worm around the world, causing an estimated US$7 billion in damages (McAfee, 2001). The virus clogged business e-mail servers, and caused organisations to shut down their networks to repair the damage and prevent further infection.

6.   TEISME BUSINESS OPERATIONAL RISK LIABILITY

The increase in cyber terrorism is a major concern for TEISMEs business operations and is not restricted by geographical boundaries. Although access violations and other security incidents can have a major impact on an organisation (as recent high-profile 'denial of service' attacks have demonstrated), simple malfunctions such as loss of services, equipment or facilities are the most readily identifiable threats. At the most basic level, almost every human activity carries a measure of risk. Whether it is crossing the road or ordering a meal, people calculate their exposure to danger and adjust their behaviour accordingly. The whole process is usually automatic, except when people suffer a near miss in bad weather, or discover a cockroach in the salad. Then, issues of risk and its twin partner trust come very quickly to the forefront of our minds. Similar issues are starting to arise as the commercial and governmental processes are moved into a more open networked environment. Concepts of trust and risk that developed over hundreds of years – based on traditional paper-based methods of communication or finance, or that relied on computer systems and networks physically closed to the outside world – are now being challenged by the still largely unknown implications of a truly interconnected world. When one mentions the subject of IT or network security to most people in the industry, however, it is likely to get a stock range of responses that rarely consider the broader implications of risk and trust in the networked world. And it is here that some pitfalls lie for network owners and users of all types as they try to exploit the potential of Internet-eC:

- Information security is often seen solely in terms of the basic hardware or software such as firewalls or encryption that can be used to control access or authenticate and protect messages.
- Decisions on information security are usually left to technology staff to make and implement, with senior management rarely being involved in the process.
- Many security problems are caused by all too human misperceptions of where dangers actually lie and the ability of particular measures to avoid them.
- Security is seen as being 'negative', contributing nothing to a company's performance, but interfering instead with a whole range of accepted working practices and creating additional work for already stretched resources.
- Security only needs to be reviewed when there is some major change within the business or when an attack of some kind actually happens.

These viewpoints, while once perhaps having had some validity, are now becoming dangerous assumptions that cannot only increase the vulnerability of an organisation to attack from within or without, but may actually cripple a TEISME without the need for any particular subversive intervention. Products or technologies should only be used within the context of an overall IT security policy, when there is a specific problem that needs addressing and where risk can be quantified, however roughly, to justify the investment or the possible impact on business operations. That information is an organisation's most valuable asset, has become a cliche in recent years. Commitment to the principle – at least where its security is concerned – is often only given lip service by senior executives, despite the legal responsibility that they have to protect their resources to the best of their ability. Also, as electronic exchanges of all types become increasingly common, the ability to trust the integrity of information source, a business partner's IT environment, or even a telecoms operator will have an important impact on that organisation's brand values. In the same way that a value can be assigned to a brand for quality, safety or some other consumer criteria, so too will the worth of trust in TEISME's business operations. However, vulnerabilities must be analysed and monitored in a disciplined way as possible, with the results being made available in forms, graphic or text, that are readily understandable in projecting any future risk occurrences and use decision-making either by TEISME or the insurance companies. Negative perceptions of security must be changed and this is another management job. A culture must be created that sees security as a business enabler, not a hindrance and one that can actually allow innovation, through new processes and new customers, not stifle it. If, by operating safely, TEISME can take more risks, then there is more potential for profit. Casting security policy in stone may have been appropriate in the castles of the 'Middle Ages', but even they had the choice of raising or lowering the drawbridge as conditions changed. Along with cost and ubiquity, one of the main benefits of the newer networking technologies is flexibility, while threat levels can rise and fall even during a single day's operations as a new site comes on line or a new virus gets loose on the Net. Vulnerabilities on a network must be capable of being monitored dynamically and information about new threats or infrastructure weaknesses made readily available as they emerge. An organisation's assets and policy may be static, but threats by their very nature are mobile and mutable. All is fine in theory, but *'how can something so intangible as risk or trust be measured?'* (see chapter 5). Physical assets can be easily counted and their values totalled together and balanced against the cost of countermeasures such as bars, locks, alarms or security patrols. Information and the emerging virtual trading communities seem far more difficult to track. This is where a series of initiatives – some public and some private – have been at work over recent years, usually in low-profile mode, finding ways of measuring risk, defining policies and processes that can help manage risk and security, and developing globally recognised standards of electronic trust (see chapter 3 for further discussion).

The payment protection is only guarantee to the maximum of financial losses on one particular transaction but only pay to the customer by their bank who authorised payment for the fraudulent transactions *'Who will insured TEISME business operations risks or any financial losses incurred during their normal business transactions'*. As with any other area of risk, businesses can choose to accept IT security risks, mitigate them or transfer them using insurance cover. Unfortunately, for all UK businesses, risk transfer is no longer an option. Increasingly insurance companies are tightening their general policies to exclude the rising cost of insurance payouts in the light of high profile IT related incidents. So most UK businesses either are not covered by any insurance policy for damage arising from IT security breaches or do not know whether they are covered. This pattern is similar for all size of UK business. External consultants have also been busy reviewing BS7799 compliance, with almost half of BS7799-compliance organisations having their compliance independently assessed by a third party. Very few of these were formally certified on the BS7799 certificate Register; most have simply had some form of security audit (PWHC and DTI, 2002). The UK government is bringing new legislation to prevent the cyber crimes to prevent the financial frauds online.

However, the cyber laws are confined to the physical boundaries of the countries in which they are made, this again raises the question about risks of TEISMEs business operations, but without a risk assessment measure that can be applied to the vulnerability facing TEISMEs' business operations the future of many TEISMEs are very doubtful without insurance cover. Ever more powerful personal computers, converging technologies and the widespread use of the Internet have replaced what were modest, stand-alone systems in predominantly closed networks. Today, participants are increasingly interconnected and the connections cross national borders. In addition, the Internet supports critical infrastructures such as energy, transportation and finance and plays a major part in how companies do business, how governments provide services to citizens and enterprises and how individual citizens communicate and exchange information. The nature and type of technologies that constitute the communications and information infrastructure also have changed significantly. The number and nature of infrastructure access devices have multiplied to include fixed, wireless and mobile devices and a growing percentage of access is through 'always on' connections. Consequently, the nature, volume and sensitivity of information that is exchanged as expanded substantially (OECD, 2002). The shared secret between two parties conducting business was a worldwide approach. But secret passwords require a great deal of trust between parties sharing the secret. Most computer break-ins today are due to compromise by system users or hackers who use legitimate accounts to gain access to general security. Determining the identity of a person is becoming critical in our vastly connected information society. As a large number of biometrics-based identification systems are being deployed for many civilian and forensic applications, biometrics and its application have evoked considerable interest. No one can afford to ignore the presence of the Internet-eC or its future potential growth. Analysts suggest that there is no way of making the Internet '100 percent safe', this statement has also proved the hypothesis $(\mathcal{H}_0^2)$. Business data are at risk when they are exposed to the Internet. Current technologies provide a number of ways to secure data transmission and storage, but other approaches to Internet security focus on protecting the contents of electronic transmissions and verification of individual users. Secure electronic transmissions are an important condition for conducting business on the Internet.

7.   CURRENT DEVELOPMENTS IN INTERNET SECURITY

Every industry has its own particular needs and requires certain safeguards to protect its data from damage. The public and private sectors have their own strengths and weaknesses on Internet security. Each industry requires certain safeguards to protect its data while in transit. Developing a plan that has proportionately more strength than weakness is always the goal. However, the

Internet is an untamed frontier that is still young and growing. It may take some time to develop stronger methods for data security. Protecting an organisation from the perils of the Internet is similar to the job of a security guard working during the night shift: As long as he stays awake and keeps his eyes open, the chances are that nothing will happen. While companies arm themselves with the latest IDS and virus software, there is still a chance that someone from the outside can get in and wreak havoc on the company's system. Software and hardware configurations keep most of the intruders at bay, but being able to recognise abnormal activity when it occurs seems to be the best method. This requires well-trained IT staff to constantly monitor the network for deviants, using the system software to set up audits in all the right places. As technology continues to evolve and software and hardware improvements are implemented, there may come a time when hackers not only will be forced to stay outside the company walls, but will also be exposed by law enforcement during the process.

The future of Internet security, therefore, resides in human intervention and innovation. Implementing hardware and software solutions, as well as using human intervention to continually monitor the network, are two of the best ways to keep abreast of attacks from the outside. One of the latest technologies in the security market, which was introduced at the NetWorld + Interop trade show in Atlanta, is a technology called adaptive security. This development is a result of Internet Security Systems (ISS) formation of the Adaptive Network Security Alliance (ANSA) around an application program interface for its real secure intrusion detection system (Eschelbeck, 2000). The technology requires the enlistment of major infrastructure vendors, such as 3Com, Lucent, Compaq, Entrust and Checkpoint, to enable their products to talk with ISS's intrusion detection monitors. By communicating between ISS's monitor and the vendor's products, firewalls and switches could be reconfigured in response to perceived break-ins, thereby diminishing the lag time between detection and prevention and ultimately, making the network virtually impossible to penetrate.

In addition, SSL, the standard for secure Internet transmissions used by credit card companies, may get a face-lift in the near future. To improve the security between themselves and their customers, the credit card companies have been developing another standard called the secure electronic transaction (SET) standard, which may have an effect on the security of Internet transaction. The SET focuses on confidentiality and authentication of data/information transfer. SET-compliant software will not only make sure that thieves cannot steal a credit card number, but also keep a merchant from seeing the number while still providing assurances that the card is valid. The transmission will pass through the merchant's hands directly to the credit card user, which will then decrypt it and credit the merchant's account (PC Magazine, 1999).

The possibility of the back-end authentication process (in a networked situation) being compromised by the passing of illegal data may represent a point of vulnerability. The authentication engine and its associated interface could be fooled. It is necessary to suggest a measure of risk to the biometrics system in use, especially when the authentication engine may not be able to verify that it is receiving *bona fide* live transaction data (and not a data stream from another source). Even a highly accurate biometrics system can reject authorised users, fail to identify known users, identify users incorrectly, or allow unauthorised person to verify as known users. In addition, if a third-party network is utilised as part of the overall biometrics system, for example using the Internet to connect remotely to corporate networks, the end-to-end connection between host controller and back-end application server should be carefully considered.

However, in most cases, biometrics systems cannot determine if an individual has established a fraudulent identity, or is posing as another individual during biometrics enrolment process. An individual with a fake passport may be able to use the passport as the basis for enrolment in a biometrics system. The system can only verify that the individual is who he or she claim to be during enrolment, unless a large-scale identification system is built in which all users are matched against all other users to find duplicates or individual attempts to enrol more than once. Although biometrics has been used for years in high-security government and military applications, but the technology is now becoming affordable for use as a network authentication method and general security feature. It is tempting to think of biometrics as being sci-fi futuristic technology that should be used in the near future together with solar-powered cars, food pills, and other fiendish devices. There are many references to individuals being formally identified via unique physiological parameters such as scars, measured physical criteria or a combination of features such as complexion, eye colour and height. The automated biometrics has been in existence for more than 30 years now. The matching fingerprints against criminal records is important for the law enforcers to find the criminal. However, the manual process of matching is very tedious and time-consuming. In 1960s, the Federal Bureau of Investigation (FBI) in U.S. began to automatically check finger images and by 1970s a good number of automatic finger-scanning systems had been installed. Among these systems, Identimat was the first commercial one. The system measured the shape of the hand and looked particularly at finger length (Zhang, 2000). Its use pioneered the application of hand geometry and set a path for biometric technologies as a whole. Internet security methods can work together within a network in various ways. The Figure 6–4 illustrates how common Internet security technologies such as a firewall or Remote Access Service (RAS) server with biometrics user authentication can be used to protect against data intrusion from the outside and within. If a user tries to access this server with combined biometrics and is not authorised to do so,

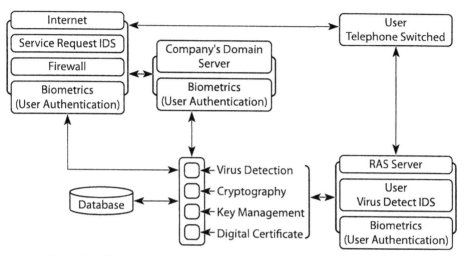

Figure 6–4. Combining common Internet security technologies with biometrics

the IDS will alert IT staff of that entry, even though the user may or may not have the right biometrics user authentication. Since the IDS uses both static and dynamic monitoring systems to monitor direct attacks and abnormal network accesses, the server is dually protected from potential harm. The data encryption is also used throughout the network. Users calling in from a switched telephone network to a RAS server on a Windows NT network can use data encryption via point-to-point tunnelling protocol (PPTP) to exchange data from their laptop or home computer to the Internet through the corporate network and vice versa. When a user connects to the network through a RAS server, the user is given the same access right as any other user in the company. The user can connect to the RAS server and send encrypted data to another computer or server using PPTP. The RAS server also has its own safeguards, such as user callback to a specific phone number to establish a connection and user authentication, encrypted passwords and user permissions. Data encryption can be implemented between a corporate server and a vendor or supplier through an Internet. If data security is imperative on an Internet, both parties could use encryption to ensure privacy and data protection. By incorporating a VPN on an extranet, both the company and its supplier can ensure maximum data security (Shoniregun, 2002)

In addition to Internet and VPN, digital certificates and key management are two other alternatives for data security. If a company has an enterprise network that spans a large geographical area, corporate officials could use this technology to protect sensitive data from unauthorised access. For example, if the human resources and finance departments need to share sensitive data, they could communicate through the corporate intranet and use key management to protect the data and digital certificates to verify the accuracy of transmission.

Even though the VPNs and extranets provide some type of security, key management and digital certificates are simply two more locks and keys that could be set in place for peace of mind. Setting up a secured network is a daunting task. It requires careful thought, adequate planning and the perspectives and recommendations of a team of IT staff. The Internet service provider network should be configured so that it is scalable and flexible to handle additional hardware and software as the network grows with combined Internet security technologies and biometrics.

Indeed, much attention has been paid to biometrics in recent months as a means to increase security for public places and businesses. Biometrics technology is superior to other identification solutions because it verifies a person's identity based on a unique physical attribute rather than some paper or plastic ID card, and as such, the number of biometric implementations is on the rise. Public awareness and acceptance of biometrics is increasing steadily as well. People realise the improved safety this technology offers us collectively as a society. Biometrics will provide greater protection to TEISMEs business operations and their financial assets, which more essential than ever before. Biometrics can better safeguard our most critical data that could cause us the most harm if accessed by the wrong person. With as little as a home address, driver's license number or bank account number, criminals can use the Internet to find out all kinds of personal information about an individual. In some US prisons, visitors to inmates are subject to verification procedures in order that identities are not swapped during the visit. Criminals can obtain the necessary data to get new credit cards issued in your name, print fake checks in your name, obtain bank loans in your name, and perpetrate other creative scams in your name to profit at your expense. By the time one finds out what has happened, serious damage can be done. Victims of identity theft often spend years and thousands of dollars clearing their names and credit reports.

The implementation of payment-processing systems that utilise biometrics with private account management can easily prevent online credit card fraud. Biometrics can be incorporated at the point of sale, thereby enabling consumers to enrol their payment options e.g., checking, credit, debit, loyalty, etc., into a secure electronic account that is protected by, and accessed with, a unique physical attribute such as a fingerprint. Cash, cards or cheques are not needed to make purchases, so there is no need to carry them in a purse or wallet. Not carrying a purse or wallet eliminates the chances of it being stolen or lost while shopping. The biometrics transaction-processing systems will allow both TEISMEs and their consumers to manage point-of-sale payment easily and securely. This solution is particularly well suited for personal check use. Biometrics can also offer increased protection for check-cashing services, whether personal or payroll. By requiring biometric identity verification before allowing a check to be cashed, the possibility of it being presented by anyone other than the intended payee is eliminated. A biometrics verification and identification can ensure that a person is who he or she claims to be, or can identify a person from a database of trusted or suspect individuals. If the identity of a traveller or employee is in question, biometrics can be a highly effective solution. An individual using a forged or stolen badge or ID card, if required to verify biometrically before entering a secure area, would likely be detected if his or her biometric does not matched the biometric on file. An individual claiming a fraudulent ID can be identified from a database of known criminals and linked to biometric identification systems, which may prevent him or her from boarding an airplane.

8.   GOVERNMENT CONCERN OVER SECURITY

The Internet was supposed to be all about freedom, but, given this freedom, people manipulate it for self-gain. Regulation has been brought to the attention of governments and professional bodies all over the world. The Internet is so vast and difficult to control; how can one govern something that goes beyond the geographical boundaries and traditional, territorial-based law? The unrestricted days on the Internet are numbered! Last year saw the start of what is to come in terms of regulating and controlling cyberspace. In the UK, the Regulation of Investigatory Powers Act (RIP Act) allows the police broad access to e-mail and other online communications (The Economist, 2001). Financial fraud has been a serious white-collar crime problem for a very long time, but in the Information Age, it is also computer and Internet crime. In late 1999 and early 2000, a spate of Internet-eC crime made front-page headlines (Power, 2002):

- In late 1999, Visa USA wrote a letter to financial institutions informing them that a hacker had stolen more than 485,000 credit card records from an Internet-eC site and then secretly stashed the database on a US government agency's website.
- In January 2000, a Russian hacker, identified only as Maxim, released as many as 25,000 credit card numbers stolen from CD Universe, an online music retailer. Maxim claims to have stolen 300,000 card numbers from CD Universe and allegedly attempted to extort $100,000 from the company.
- Approximately 2,000 records were stolen from SalesGate, including credit card numbers and other personal information.
- According to Loxly information Service, a leading Thai ISP, a hacker hacked into the ShoppingThailand.com and stole credit card information on 2,000 customers.

The Lloyds bank, Barclays, Natwest, Abbey Nationale, Nationwide, Morgan Stanley, Royal Bank of Scotland, Halifax, HSBC and other international financial institutions have sent series of e-mails and posted letters to inform their customers of scam, such as customer details and credit card frauds, which are still ongoing.

The UK government have pledged to work closely with TEISMEs to help curb high-technology crime. The National High-Tech Crime Unit was launched on the 18th April 2001, which will train up to 80 officers to investigate cyber crime as part of a £25 million government program. In January 2000, Jack Straw announced that he was giving the National Criminal Intelligence Service (NCIS) £337,000 to draw up a detailed plan for a high-tech crime squad (Sommer, 2000). Again, perhaps it could be argued that governments are not necessarily tackling the problem from the right angle. If everyone knew the facts, they might ask why public money was being spent to protect sloppy businesses. The UK Terrorism Act was extended in February 2001, to include 'cyber-terrorist(s)'; the definition now covers London-based terror groups who plan attacks here and abroad (Burns and Eaglesham, 2001; Shrimsley, 2001).

In December 2000, ISO/IEC 17799: 2000 was published as an international standard and the Code of Practise for Information Security Management. The UK Government sponsored the project. It aims to allow compliant companies to publicly demonstrate that they can safeguard the confidentiality, integrity, and availability of their customer's information (Gamma, 2001).

In Europe, most people expect that information they provide to a commercial website will be used only for the purpose for which it was collected. Many European countries have laws that prohibit companies from exchanging consumer data without the express consent of the consumer. In 1998, the European Union adopted a Directive on the Protection of Personal Data. This directive codifies the constitutional rights to privacy that exist in most European countries and applies it to all Internet activities. In addition, it prevents businesses from exporting personal data outside the European Union unless the data will continue to be protected in accordance with the directive. Under new EU Law, European consumers may now sue EU-based Internet sites in their own countries, and the rule may well be extended internationally. The Council of Europe (41 countries) introduced the world's first international treaty on cyber crime. However, the European Internet-eC market should become easier as the European Commission gets ready to eliminate layers of regulation and bureaucracy. As part of the move, e-traders will not have to comply with dozens of consumer protection laws created by member states. The Commission will ask member states to remove all persistent barriers to Europe-wide Internet-eC, as well as changing from a sector by sector approach and transforming to a service by service (Marketwatch, 2001).

The USA, endorsed the gist of the Council of Europe's cyber crime treaty, which aims to harmonise laws against hacking, Internet fraud and child pornography. America favours self-regulation and sector laws. In contrast, the EU relies on comprehensive privacy laws that are enforced by data-protection agencies. Both agree that cyber space must be treated differently and that it needs laws and legal institutions of its own. Technologies to filter information will be introduced and the demands of Internet-eC rather than governments will drive improvements. The EU and USA harmonised a 'safe-harbour' agreement in November 2000, protecting companies from having their data flow severed, as long as their privacy policies comply with certain principles (The Economist, 2001). The US Securities and Exchange Commission (SEC) regulates the US Securities market. In early March they announced the fifth in a series of Internet fraud sweeps. They found perpetrators were using a range of fraudulent online techniques to raise funds for private ventures. The Regulatory arm of the US National Association of Securities Dealers (NASDR) issued new guidelines for online business practices when financial recommendations and advice is given. These will be treated no differently from those operating on the telephone or by mail (Labate, 2001).

An article published in the Guardian, on 20 January 2000 gave quite startling statistics produced from research by consumer organisations worldwide. It was found that whilst cyber shopping accounts for only 2% of credit card transactions, it generates 50% of complaints and when ordering online, one in ten items ordered never arrive. The struggle between freedom and control on the Internet is set to continue for some time. As the Internet becomes the *de facto* platform for doing business, it remains a vast frontier of 'untamed and uncontrolled' networks. Accenture (2001), experts in consultancy and technology predict that the 'Internet-economy will top US$1 trillion by the end of this year'. The prediction is yet to become a reality as a result of the present slow down in the global economy climate caused by September 11 terrorist attack on the USA. Moreover, no one can afford to ignore the presence of the Internet-eC or its future potential growth.

According to Graham Welch, Regional Vice President for RSA Security in the UK, 'e-business can never be 100% safe'. In his opinion people are the main culprits. Financial Institutions are most vulnerable, as they are the easiest targets. Graham reckons that there is no way of overcoming the 'people factor'; security software solutions can only reduce the risks. He recommends continued testing, especially for the financial services industry (White, 2001; Power, 2002). The potential for fraud is much higher in the virtual world, although being able to access information from anywhere in the world at any time is perceived as a major benefit of Internet-eC. The hackers and dishonest employees will continue to manipulate information for self gain, but if Internet-eC is to become the dominant business platform of the 21st century, all the above must operate in a secure way all other things been equal (Schneider, and Perry, 2000; Chaston, 2000; Dutton, 1999).

However, the power of the Internet does not come without its risks. TEISMEs security is still a nightmare threatening to manifest illegal activities. Due to the sheer amount and value of transactions that are involved, to do business on the Internet, customers and businesses need to feel secure and reassured that the TEI environment is private. TEISMEs must consider appropriate action, the cost of securing their networks and to deploy an effective security policy and infrastructure and include; interoperability, scalability, and ease of use and proven solutions (Kelly, 2001; Kare-Silver, 2000).

9.   SUMMARY OF CHAPTER SIX

The Internet security demands attention at multiple levels. Although biometrics is still relatively expensive and immature, but the integrated multiple biometrics features such as fingerprints, palm prints, facial features and voice patterns to authenticate a person's identity and verify his or her eligibility to access the Internet are in the development stage (Shoniregun, 2003). Most of the time when security on the Internet is mentioned, it is assumed that the data is safe from hackers or unauthorised third parties. However, 'what exactly does security on the Internet cover?' and 'Is it just unauthorised access of data or more?', Many researchers have highlighted six criteria that the Internet has to satisfy in order to be considered 'secure' i.e. confidentiality, authenticity, integrity, non-repudiation, access control and availability, but what has not yet been emphasised is that the Internet cannot be 100 per cent secure and the urgent need for risk assessment model for TEISME business operations. However, no insurance companies in the UK are willing to insure TEISMEs business operational risks but to insure the risks that may be encountered electronically will foster trust. The increasing number of private communications over the Web, particularly business transactions, will require a higher level of security. If a problem occurs with a business transaction or a Web company is accused of bad business practices, it may become very difficult to establish liability. Who should be held accountable—the TEISME, the banks or the trust intermediary? The authentication may become an important condition of conducting business electronically. Indeed, TEISMEs cannot ignore the problems of Internet security as this would result in the loss of competitive advantage in the market place. What the future holds for Internet security technology such as biometrics cannot be predicted to the rate technology is advancing but what is certain is to have a more flexible risk assessment model that can be adopted by both TEISMEs and insurance companies. The ethical issues surrounding biometrics technologies are of major concern. The right to privacy is one of our most cherished freedoms. As society grows more complex and people become more interconnected in every way, we must work even harder to respect the privacy, dignity and autonomy of each individual. We must develop new protection for privacy in the face of new technological reality (Clinton, 1997), if not, there should be a simple framework model such as the proposed Shoniregun's Risk Assessment Model that can be adopted by both TEISMEs and insurance brokers to assess any possible risks a TEISME might encountered during business operations. This issue of privacy is central to biometrics. Critics complain that the use of biometrics poses a substantial risk to privacy rights. Evaluating this argument requires a proper understanding of what privacy rights entails. But if biometrics are the way forward in making sure that all TEISME business operations are fully secure then the questions to ask are: *'How much will it cost to implement such security solution(s)?'*, *'Who should be trust with genetics information?'*, and *'How long will it take the expert hacker to decrypt such human genetic codes?'* These are some of the concerns of TEISMEs and online shoppers. Indeed, the human race has not only brought its business to cyberspace, it has brought its exploration of the psyche there, too. In the digital world, just as everywhere else, humanity has encountered its dark side. Information Age business, government, and culture have led to Information Age crime, Information Age war and even Information Age terror (Shoniregun, 2003; Liu, 2001; Timmers, 2000).

REFERENCES

Accenture, 2001, 'Internet-eConomy will top $1 trillion by end of 2001', *Financial Times*, 19 March.

BMRB Research Group, 2000, Internet Monitor, *International Research Report*, October.

Bond, B., 2000, 'The e.volving New e.conomy – A Roundtable with Gartner Analysts, Gartner Special Report', *eAI Journal*, pp. 16–20, October.

BT Trust Wise, 2001, *Securing Your Website for Business – A Step By Step Guide for Secure On-Line E-Commerce*, BT.

Burns, J. and Eaglesham, J., 2001, 'Police in new pledge to help curb cybercrime', *Financial Times*, March 21.

Business Week, 2001, 'Gone but not forgotten E-commerce', *Business Week*, January 22.

Chaston, I., 2000, *E-marketing Strategy*, McGraw Hill.

Cheswick, W.R., Bellovin, S.M., Rubin, A.D., 1994, *Firewalls and Internet Security: Repelling the Wily Hacker*, Addison Wesley Professional Computer Series.

Clinton, W.J., 1997, *Commencement Address*, Morgan State University, Baltimore, MD, May 18; www.epic.org/privacy/laws/clinton_speech_5_18_97.html (February 21, 2005).

Department of Trade and Industry (DTI), 2002, 'RSA Security, Symantec Genuity, Country wide-Porter Novelli and PriceWaterHouseCooper', *Report on Information Systems breaches survey 2002*, London, DTI URN02/319.

Dutton, H., 1999, *Society on the Line, Information Politics in the Digital Age*, Oxford University Press.

Eschelbeck, G., 2000, 'Active Security: A proactive approach for computer security systems', *Network and Computer Application*, 23, pp. 109–130.

Farrow, R., 2005, *'Social Engineering'*; www.watchguard.com/infocenter/editorial/1302.asp (January 25, 2005)

Fraud Advisory Panel (FAP), 2003, 'The fraud Cybercrime advisory, What every SME panel should know', Technical Report, Chartered Accountants Hall.

Gamma, 2001, 'Gamma Security Systems Limited: increasing confidence in information', *IS17799: 2000*; www.gammass1.co.uk.

Ghosh, A. K. and Swaminatha, T. M., 2001, 'Software security and privacy risks in mobile E-Commerce', *Communications of the ACM*, 44(2):51–57.

Gragg, D., 2003, *A Multi-level Defence Against Social Engineering*, SANS Institute.

Haag, S., Cummings, M., Dawkins, J., 2000, *Management Information Systems for the Information Age*, 2nd ed, McGraw-Hill Education.

Horton, T.R., LeGrand, C.H., Murray, W. H., Ozier, W. J. and Parker, D. B., 2000, *'Managing information security risks'*; www.taudit.org/forum/riskmanagement/f319rm.htm (June 22, 2001).

Huston. B, 2002, *'A Higher view of Defense in Depth'*; www.itworld.comh/nl/securitys-trat/02202002/ (February 20, 2002).

Inada, S., 2000, *'Promotion of Intranet commerce through enhanced security, users'*; erols.com/sinada/commerce.html (May 4, 2001).

Kare-Silver, M. D., 2000, *E-shock 2000 – The Electronic Shopping Revolution: Strategies for Retailers and Manufacturers*, Macmillan Business.

Katsuno, M., 1998, *A Borderless World: Realising the Potential of Global Electronic Commerce*, Organisation for Economic Cooperation and Development (OECD), October 7, pp. 4–56.

Keen, P. G. W., Mougayar, W., Torregrossa, T., 1998, *The Business Internet and Intranets: A Management Guide to Key Terms and Concepts*, Harvard Business School Press, USA.

Kelly, R., 2001, 'Secure- procurement', *Finance On Windows*, Spring, pp. 22–27

Kerr, K., and Litan, A., 2002, *'Online Transaction Fraud and Prevention Get More Sophisticated: Companies, Markets, Forces'*, Gartnerg; www.gartnerg2.com/research/rpt-0102–0013.asp (November 6, 2003).

Labate, J., 2001, 'Downgrade deals blow to online brokers', *Financial Times Companies & Finance*, The Americas, 2 March.

Lui, J., and Ye, Y., 2001, *E-Commerce Agents, Marketplace Solutions, Security Issues, and Supply and Demand*, Springer.

Marketwatch, 2001, 'Consortium to address e-business challenges', *Finance On Windows*, Spring pp.42–48.

Martin, C., 2000, 'An International and Strategic Networks: An SME Perspective', Paper presented at the *5th International Manufacturing Research Symposium International and Strategic Network Development*, The Centre for International Manufacturing, Cambridge University September.

McAfee, 2001, *'McAfee. com conmemorates one-year anniversary of the infamous "ILOVEYOU" virus outbreak with free virus scan and protection'*, Internet Wire; www1.Internetwire./release_clickthro ugh?release_id =26442&category=technolog (May 1, 2002).

Netcraft and Eurobarometer, 2001, 'e-Europe 2002 Impacts and Priorities', *140 Final: Communication from the Commission to the Council and the European Parliament*, Commission of the European Communities, Brussels; www.ekt.gr/ncpfp5/ist/info/material/e europe/impact_en. pdf (November 13, 2003).

OECD, 2002, 'Guidelines for the Security of Information Systems and Networks Towards a Culture of Security', *Recommendation of the OECD Council*, 1037th Session, July 25.

PC Magazine, 1999, *The future of Internet security*, March.

Power, R., 2002, *Tangled Web: Tales of Digital Crime from the Shadows of Cyberspace*, QUE.

PricewaterhouseCoopers, 2004, *Information Security Breaches Survey 2004 Technical Report*, in association with Computer Associates, Entrust and Microsoft—DTIrecommendation; www. pwc.com/images/gx/eng/about/svcs/grms/2004TechnicalReport. pdf (March 23, 2004).

PWHC and DTI, 2002, 'Information Security Breaches Survey', *Technical Report for (URN 02/318)*, UK Government DTI, PriceWaterHouseCoopers.

Rodriguez, J. M., 2001, 'Card-carrying catastrophe', *Financial Times – Connectis*, April.

Schneider, P. and Perry, J. T., 2000, *Electronic Commerce*, Thomson Learning.

Shoniregun C. A., 2002, 'The Future of Internet Security', *Communication of The ACM: Ubiquity*, v.3, no.37, p.1, October 29.

Shoniregun, C. A., 2003, 'Are existing Internet security measures guaranteed to protect user identity in the financial services industry?', *International Journal of Services, Technology and Management (IJSTM)*, v.4, pp.194–215.

Shoniregun, C. A., Omoegun, A., Brown-West, P. and Logvynovskiy, O., 2004, 'Can eCRM and trust improve eC customer base?', in the *Proceedings of the IEEE conference on E-Commerce technology*, San Diego, California, USA, pp.303–310.

Shoniregun C., 2005, 'Keynote speech on Security Architecture', *IEEE SAINT Conference 2005*, Session 18, Trento, Italy, February.

Shrimsley, R., 2001, 'Cyber crime – covered by extended law on terrorism', *Financial Times*, February 20.

Smith, A. M., 1998, 'Electronic Commerce', *Institute of Directors*, Directors Publications, p.62.

Sommer, P., 2000, 'Investigating cyberspace', *Computer Weekly*, January 27; www.computer-weekly.com, (December 27, 2001).

The Economist, 2001, 'The Internet and the law', *The Economist*, January 13, pp.25–27.

Timmers, P., 2000, *Electronic commerce: strategies and models for B-to-B trading*, John Wiley.

Turban, E., King, D., Lee, J., Warkentin, M., and Chung, H.M., 2002, *Electronic Commerce: A Managerial Perspective*, Prentice Hall, New Jersey.

White, M., 2001, 'Networking in a networked economy', *Finance on Windows*, Summer, pp.82–83.

Zhang, D. D., 2000, *Automated Biometrics Technology and Systems*, Kluwer Academic.

Chapter 7

CONCLUSION

The chapter 1 has set the background for this research, while chapters 2 and 3 discusses the impacts of TEI on SMEs and the risk assessment of TEI on TEISMEs. These two latter chapters have given the foundation of the study, which are further explored by using the research methods suggested to capture the experiences and the views of TEISMEs in relation to the impacts and risk assessment of TEI on their business operations. The chapter 4 focuses on the techniques of acquiring data and information for the procurement of knowledge. The methods and methodologies adopted aids in studying the subject matter. Both quantitative and qualitative processes of collecting data were employed which encourages a rich mixture of analysis and conclusive findings. In chapter 5, there is a detailed analysis of the results and chapter 6 is a discussion chapter, which critically evaluates the research area. However, this chapter concludes with recommendation, contribution to knowledge and future work.

1. GLOBAL ISSUES AND INTERNET SECURITY FACING TEISMEs

This study has revealed that all the TEISMEs share common operational problems and faces global Internet security risks. Therefore, a risk model must be in place to take into consideration the possible disasters that TEISMEs encounter during their business operations with necessary contingency measures (Shoniregun, 2004b), (see Figures 4–1 and 4–2). Protecting the security and privacy of information exchange on the Internet is absolutely critical to the success of Internet-eC. Other issues of concern to the TEISMEs are as follows:

i. *Lack of single, unified Internet users directory:* The obstacles: Whereas it makes sense to have a unified Internet users directory, so that faceless sellers can be traced. Available evidence dictates that it is not feasible to have a unified Internet users directory because of the nature of the boundaryless Internet-eC. This is compounded by the emergence of mobile commerce, which can be transacted from anywhere, at any time, in the world. The issue of privacy/confidentiality further complicates this. Besides, people with no fixed address are not excluded from making a living on the Internet, and this helps to throw more light into the thorny road to the creation of single, unified Internet users directory.

ii. *The ease with which users change location and work habits:* Kroll (1994) compares an Internet directory to the telephone, and finds out that whereas there is one company responsible for producing and maintaining the phone directory, entering, deleting, and re-entering customer details in the phone directory as they own new phones, change phone numbers, or move places, including the collection of accounts, there is no such a thing on the Internet. In contrast, 'there is no one group on the Internet to deal with, no one has to collect information, and in many cases, no money changes hands'. An account can be set up for anyone by anyone who has a workstation on the network. Thus, since there is no monthly charge for the account, there seems to be no reason to turn your account off if one cannot stop using it 'it just sits there looking like the active account and this illustrates how difficult it is to keep data accurate'. While it may be possible to create an Internet directory by sheer force of law, it will be difficult to get the co-operation of users.

iii. *Lack of standards for directories:* This is another obstacle on the road to achieving a single, unified Internet directory. The author has earlier argued that Internet is a no-man's land and unpoliceable. Similarly, creating a standard is an Achilles' heel. Attempts have been made and are still being made, but little success has been achieved. For example, the International Standards Organisation (ISO) has managed to develop X.500 standard, it took a long time to achieve. However, many organisations had during the period of development, developed their own standards, which are operationally effective, and consequently, refused to change to the ISO's standard. This appears to adopt the Japanese philosophy: 'If it ain't broke, why fix it'. This is not the first time the ISO's standards were ignored or resisted by organisations that felt it was unnecessary to change if their system is functioning properly. The users of the Transmission Control Protocol/Internet Protocol (TCP/IP) resisted change from TCP/IP to the ISO's Open

System Interconnection (OSI) 7-layer model, even though the OSI model was developed by ISO to solve the problems of the TCP/IP model, which has only three out of seven standard layers of the OSI model. Besides, the TCP/IP model only describes the TCP/IP protocol and it is not suitable for describing the non-TCP/IP protocols (see chapter 3 for further discussion on the problem with TCP/IP and the protocol layers).

iv. *Worries about security and privacy:* With a massive array of TEI related data stored in the database/data warehouse about customers and TEISMEs alike, some of data is highly sensitive, there is a need for privacy/confidentiality and security, to protect data being transmitted against being intentionally altered by someone other than the sender. In addition, when organisations go international, there are concerns about security, which, if not checked, might create global risks.

Moreover, security of TEISMEs business operations has posed a serious control problem because the Internet was originally a private network for the military, and later for education and entertainment. Thus, it was not designed as a public network and the designers never anticipated the Internet use as a trading medium. However, extant and empirical findings have demonstrated that their vision was myopic. Often, some organisations refuse to provide any information about users of their system, simply because the e-mail address contains the user's log-on name and one of the common ways through which hackers break in, is to find a valid user name and then try common pass words. Some organisations think that exposing user's names on the Internet is a breach of security and as such, does not release the names of users of their system to the unified directory.

v. *Concern for lack of a unified Internet Law:* There are worries about problems posed by the absence of binding global Internet law, and there is a growing need for an international regulation to be put in place. Keen *et al.* (1998) put forward four reasons why it is necessary to have a regulated Internet:

- The Internet lacks central location or head office
- The Internet is electronic
- Internet is digital
- Internet is global

With all these quantum leaps in technology, TEISMEs have taken the world by storm. Transacting businesses on the Internet with no boundaries, the sky appears to be the limit of their market potential with staggering benefits, but there comes with it great risks. The Internet market on which TEISMEs operate is a 'no man's land'. Thus, with this boundary-less TEI marketplace, combined with the fact that one does not physically see whom he/she is dealing with, and sometimes, one does not know the country from which the seller is operating. There is no single authority controlling the

Internet industry, and no president. The security risk issues such as the invasion of privacy, data integrity, fraud, theft, malicious damage and lack of insurable risks on TEISMEs business operations are causing a great concern to the society. There is no national or global law at present time that can stop anyone from trading on the Internet, and the Internet environment is 'unpoliceable'.

The eSecurity4Britain (ES4B), was organised by a number of small companies who were concerned by the rising numbers of viruses and attacks by cyber-criminals. The ES4B new website acts as a forum for small firms to access expert advice about things like implementing security policies, risk management and virus protection. Visitors will also be able to log on to live discussion events and will have access to a directory of security system providers. According to Gerard Liston, one of the founders of ES4B: dealing with online security is often just one more task that does not receive the priority it deserves. Research by the DTI shows that 44% of businesses are subject to electronic attacks at least once a year. Pricewaterhouse Coopers states that the average cost of an attack is £30,000 (Liston, 2003). The subject has become even more pressing recently as anti-war campaigners target the websites and computer systems of businesses in the UK and the USA. The research has also proved that majority of TEISMEs are not adequately prepared to deal with IT security issues. Most are likely to address the need to prepare and respond only after a breach occurs. The result is that when a breach is detected, many decisions will be made in haste, which in some cases might not be beneficial to the enterprise. Often TEISMEs, with limited IT budgets and expertise, represent 'soft targets' for any vulnerability. Yet TEISMEs are the least able to absorb the damage a random, malevolent vulnerabilities might cause due to lack of insurable policy that can compromise with the changing risks facing TEISMEs business transactions .

Furthermore, the increased complexity and openness of the network thus makes the question of security more complicated than hitherto and necessitates the development of sophisticated security technologies at the interface between network of different security domains, such as between Intranet and Internet or Extranet, and ISP. The limitations of the Internet security tools and the fact that the current Internet security tools are neither the panacea of every vulnerability encountered in TEISMEs business operations, in itself triggers the urgent need for a simple and clearer risk assessment model that can be adopted by TEISMEs, Insurance companies and their brokers, to assess identified risks and keep TEISMEs in business.

It is a well-established fact that the traditional security measures such as password and identification cards cannot satisfy every security requirement. Various physiological and behavioural biometrics for the authentication of individuals have broader applications such as the control of access to personal computers, private files and information repositories, building access control, and many others. Although biometrics is still relatively expensive and immature, integrated multiple biometrics features such as fingerprints, palm prints, facial features and voice patterns to authenticate a person's identity and verify his or her eligibility to access the Internet are in the development stage. The biometrics devices will continue to improve, becoming even more accurate and reliable as Internet technology evolves. As biometrics technology becomes more acceptable, the proliferation of applications should multiply into many phases of our daily activities. The growing interest in combining common Internet security technologies with biometrics will increase the growth and popularity of blended Internet security methods in the future and make TEISMEs business operations just a little safe. Nevertheless, the ethical issues surrounding biometrics remain unanswered; this is definitely outside the scope of this research.

1.1   TEISMEs are facing dramatic changes

The TEI are still relatively new to the SMEs in the UK compared to the United States. The anticipated growth rates for Internet users are driving force for the penetration of TEISMEs. One important reason for this fast market development is the technological evolution: the costs for hardware and software are constantly falling, new web technologies allow an easily implemented networking, open interoperable standards allow to seamlessly integrate Internet-eC and mobile commerce (emC) tools into already existing environment and user interfaces.

The Internet provides ample opportunity for providing the age-old truism, there are many risks that must be addressed. The old Latin expression 'Caveat emptor' (Let the buyer beware) seems quite timely today. Ultimately, it all comes down to 'Sed quis custodiet ipos custodes?' 'But who is watching the watchers' (Neumann, 2003), there are no easy answers to the risks encountered by TEISMEs business operations. Improving risk was, and is, a key issue for TEISMEs, as the need to prove to potential customers that their site is secure. The preliminary research shows that nearly three-quarters of Internet transactions were being abandoned before sales are completed. The problems were abundantly clear, and whilst not easy to immediately correct, should by now have been addressed.

Security experts have long been saying that secure systems, and especially security standards, need to be designed through an open process, allowing review by anyone. Unfortunately, even openly designed standards sometimes result in flawed cryptographic systems. The IEEE 802.11 wireless LAN standard is a good example, in which several serious cryptographic failures hardware devices were sold (Wool, 2000). Security is of particular importance when sensitive information is sent through the Web. Users must rely on the security of the browser's SSL protocol, although the closed padlock icon in a browser window depicts a secure connection. Whenever the padlock is snapped or a security-related message pops up (Levi, 2003), TEISME should be alerted and the security of the connection provides by the ISP scrutinised.

The personal online purchasing is the trend in the future and the safe payment mode is one of the main reasons that affect consumers to accept electronic payment. According to the research reports, paying by credit card is the most popular method of electronic payment. The study of a safe mechanism to use credit cards for the online purchase environment is then important. Since cryptographic technology is applied to deal with the security process in electronic payment and to satisfy the safe and economic affairs, cryptosystems become an important topic in network purchasing. According to the definition of ISO/IEC 7498-2, the information security service has to take into consideration the confidentiality, authentication, integrity, non-repudiation and access control. The goal of secure payment technique is to reach these requirements. Netscape Corporation announced SSL protocol in 1994 before VISA and MasterCard announced SET in 1996 for Internet transaction processes. SET is not popular to success since it is difficult to use while SSL has obvious security leak. Although VISA and MasterCard develop later on their own revised transaction mechanism 3-D Secure and SPA, the shortcomings of these two mechanism makes them not to be accepted well yet.

The hackers and virus writers in particular have used diversity to their advantage; polymorphic viruses are currently in vogue. Such viruses are generally encrypted with a weak cipher, using a new key each time the virus propagates, thus confounding signature-based detection. However, because the decryption routine cannot be encrypted, detection is still possible. Virus writers are on the verge of unleashing so-called metamorphic viruses, where the body of the virus itself changes each time it propagates. This results in viruses that are functionally equivalent, with each instance of the virus containing distinct software. Detection of metamorphic viruses will be extremely challenging (Stamp, 2004). The author also believes that the more advertising of successful hacks leads to better educated companies therefore making hacking into those systems harder the next time around. It has not been possible to determine from the research whether businesses are learning from hackers or if they are just covering their tracks and do not want the bad publicity. So the security evaluation of any electronic payment mechanism shows that the integrity, confidentially, authentication, non-repudiation and concealment to whom with certificates cannot be guarantee.

Following the investigation into the available hacking prevention methods, it was discovered that the IT industry is currently flooded with a number of options, however, TEISMEs are faced with a considerable amount of difficulty when deciding on which methods to adopt within their organisation. Most vendors are only concerned about selling their products, but not actually meeting the requirements of individual businesses. This is why the fact that most businesses have invested so much money into Internet security does not actually protect their system or network. Furthermore, there are also organisations who try to cut corners and costs, but in the long term end up leaving themselves vulnerable to the attacks of hackers.

Lastly, implementing a firewall has so long been seen as the absolute security measure for systems, but in the recent years firewalls have been broken into and the repercussions of such being immense. There are other methods of securing your system, for example, if the firewall is broken into, having simple user authentication mechanisms could prevent the hacker from having direct access to files. Having up to date anti-virus software in place could prevent virus infections by hackers and many more. There is also a virus threat Evolution, which has grown considerably over the years, according to the Network Associates 'The time required for malicious code to spread to a point where it can do serious infrastructure damage halves every 18 months' (LaCroix, 2003).

In the past, there were individuals who hacked software and systems simply for the challenge of doing so. In a few cases, these individuals were subsequently employed by the organisation to test the strength of their systems and help find loopholes in their security. A few actually came up with an improved version of the system. On the other hand, there are individuals whose sole intent is to steal source code or have malicious intent and this is the main disadvantage of hacking. From this research work, it has been observed that hacking has evolved from being termed as a 'practical joke' to being a malicious act. The trend of the evolution of hacking began with individuals who set out to have a 'laugh' by hacking into systems for the fun of it. The trend then continued with individuals who felt they had the skills to improve on what others had implemented and wanted to prove it to the world i.e. the invention of UNIX. However, this trend started to change when individuals discovered they could cause harm to existing systems but using programs like worms and virus to cause harm to organisations. Other individuals use this 'skill' for personal gain by using it to acquire information. Not withstanding, hacking has involved from being termed as a thing of little relevance to being a skill that could be employable.

On a serious note, security will always be an issue, which cannot be solved, and there is no specific solution at present time in making TEISMEs business operations secure, or risk free. But on the other hand, there two possible solutions available to those TEISMEs who want to continue trading regardless of the risk involved:

i. The technological solution to on-line security breaches or possible risks will requires continuous improvement and awareness of new security measures.
ii. TEISMEs needs to build trust on their Internet-eC business transaction by assuring the on-line shoppers that all transactions are insured against any possible risks both to contents transfers /or products which should state clearly the insurance company's name and logo. If need be on-line shoppers can verify from the Insurance company's Website to check what type of risks is the TEISMEs in question insured against but how will this be possible, if the insurance companies in the UK are not willing to insured TEISME's business operations within national boundary to talk less of international boundaries. This act as a catalyst in giving online shoppers the trust and protection that a particular risk and/or risks is/are insured against before purchasing the item(s).

However, based on the research and personal opinion, TEI are definitely here to stay. In support of this argument, Dutton (1999), states how the classic dystopian novel of the twentieth century (George Orwell, 1939), pivoted around the emergence of television and the logic of electronic surveillance. Half a century later, the growing centrality of the Internet has generated updated Orwellian visions, as portrayed in 'The Net' a film produced by Columbia Pictures in 1995, where the heroine's life and identity are transformed, deleted, and restored on-line. Nevertheless, many questions concerning TEI remain unanswered and frequently unasked.

In the Internet world, transactions are often carried out in a 'faceless' environment. The anonymous nature of such transactions means that a person cannot know for sure whom they are dealing with. Information is also often transmitted in the clear over such open networks with few security precautions. This raises concerns especially where the information is of a sensitive nature such as credit card details or personal details. Data sent over an open network is also susceptible to alteration by an unauthorised third party, whether for fraudulent or mischievous purposes. If any component of a transaction is alternated in transit, the transaction will not be processed accurately. There is no perfect payment system around world that satisfies all the requirement of security system. Nine out of ten online credit card frauds in the UK go unpunished, as many Internet retailers do not bother to report cases and police rarely follow up complaints (Husein, 2002). The anonymity of the Internet enables criminals to make cross-border purchases with stolen credit card details at relatively little risk of ever being caught. Many users are wary of the use of credit card online because they have to send their credit card information via a low-security network, to a person they have never met, a store they have never been to or a corporation they have never heard of. If one is an online merchant, sooner or later he/she is going to be stung by credit card fraud. It seems the Internet is fast becoming the first choice for thieves and it is no wonder consumers have reservations about using credit cards online. Thinking specifically about using the Internet as a means to support TEISME business operations, one issue to be addressed is the obvious lack of security in the Internet. Almost all networks are insecure, but it is essential that TEISMEs should have a model that is applicable to assess their business operational risks. The virtual world is an open haven for cyber criminals from countries all over the world. The very nature of Internet with its faceless sellers and buyers makes it an easier target for crimes. There are currently no International laws or regulations governing Internet-eC. This in it self poses a huge transactional risk for both sellers and buyers. The UK government are not putting the required checks and balances in place, to ensure that all TEISMEs with a presence on the Internet meet basic security criteria. During most online payment transactions, credit card companies only verify if credit card number is correct and then match the number against the customers billing address. The whole electronic payment transaction medium is flawed and carries huge risk. Even though technology such as SSL can be used to secure transactions between the web browser and web server there are still risks which has been identified from the reviewed literature, survey, structured interviews, laboratory experiments and case study observations.

2.   RECOMMENDATIONS

This study has revealed that there is an urgent need for a risk assessment model that can be applied to TEISME business operational risks. It was also found that it is necessary for all TEISME to identify the products (goods or services) suitability for Internet-eC. The suitability of any products that needs to be sold on the Internet-eC is just one factor that needs to be taken into account by TEISME that is perhaps given that many TEISMEs launch Internet-eC websites without thinking through what it will take and how the website will impact their business.

Without a solid business plan, regardless of whether the business has an 'e' in front of it or not, the TEISME have already prescribed their own downfall. Nevertheless, a trend is apparently beginning to emerge regarding which commodities sell well electronically and which do not. It appears that the sectors of travel, technology, literature and music are reaping the benefits of online retailing whilst other sectors are missing out. The success of the Internet-eC will also depend on a variety of factors independent of the Predictive Model of Internet-eC suitability, such as security and risk assessment of TEISME business operations (see Eq. 7.1) (Shoniregun and Midwood, 2004).

Table 7–1. Examples of predictive indices

Product	Tactility	Convenience	Price advantage	Suitability index
Groceries	8	7	1.25	18.75
Automobiles	8	9	0.9	15.3
Furniture	8	9	0.75	12.75
Shoes	9	5	0.8	10.4
CDs	2	3	0.8	4.5
Books	2	3	0.7	2.8
Software	1	1	0.8	1.6
Flights	1	1	0.8	1.6

$$\text{Suitability} = \text{Tactility} + \text{Convenience} \times \text{Price advantage} \quad (7.1)$$

The lower the value, the more suitable the goods for Internet-eC.
Whereby:

- Tactility is an integer, between 1 and 10, of the necessity of the product to be physically viewed and/or tested; 1 being the least tactile and 10 the most.
- Convenience is an integer, between 1 and 10, of the ease of delivery of the product in question; 1 being the most convenient and 10 the least.
- Price advantage is the price of the electronically ordered good, in percent, relative to the price of the cheapest same, or similar, good in a bricks-and-mortar enterprise.

A few real-world examples for the predictive model may be considered. Firstly, an online software company, which offers multimedia software to download with a 20% discount when ordered online. The tactility value will be 1; software is the least tactile of all goods, for it cannot be physically inspected. The value for convenience must also be 1; download is surely the easiest method of product delivery. Price advantage of the online items, expressed as a percentage of the bricks-and-mortar shop price, is 80%, or 0.8. The calculation is express as follows:

$$\text{Suitability} = (1 + 1) \times 0.8 = 1.6$$

Since the value is very low, the product is extremely well suited to the electronic medium. Using the example of fresh vegetable and grocery produce, the product has a high tactility index of 8; it ideally needs to be physically tested for ripeness and quality. Its convenience integer is also a high 7; it is a perishable good and needs to be handled with care. Price advantage, if one assumes a £5 surcharge on an order of £20, is 125% or 1.25. Therefore:

$$\text{Suitability} = (8 + 7) \times 1.25 = 18.75$$

The high figures in Table 7–1 column titled 'Suitability index' indicate unsuitability of goods or services for Internet-eC (Shoniregun and Midwood, 2004).

2.1   TEISMES business operational risk

The Predictive Model of Internet-eC suitability does not assess the TEISMEs business operational risks, but it helps TEISME to decide whether the goods or services are suitable for Internet-eC or not. As soon as the visibility of the identified goods or services proved significant to the TEISMEs business operations, the next most important aspect of their business operations is to find a way of assessing any possible vulnerability that might be encountered during their business operations. Risks are inevitable within TEISMEs business operations, but most significantly is to find models that are suitable enough to assess possible risks and to calculate possible claims against the risk occurrences. For this reason the Shoniregun TEISME Risk Assessment Model have been proposed, which includes the calculation formula and the probability simulation of available data (see chapters 4, and 5 for further discussion).

It is not being claimed that Shoniregun TEISME Risk Assessment Model is the perfect solution for assessing TEISME business operational risks, but advantages of the model are that it is very easy and flexible to adopt and also all the weaknesses found from the other 6 models in this study have been integrated. The acceptance of this proposed model will require a further test run among large TEISME participants, which will help in the realisation of how flexible it is to be adopted by both TEISMEs and insurance companies in the UK.

2.2   Contribution to Knowledge

This study has revealed the lack of in-depth research in the TEI impacts on SMEs, classification and taxonomy of TEISMEs, weaknesses of technologies for Internet security, and the risk assessment of TEISMEs business operations. The contribution of this research to knowledge is as follows:

- Classification and taxonomy of TEISMEs business operations.
- Current technologies for Internet security and their weaknesses.

- Shoniregun's TEICME Risk Assessment Model based on the weaknesses from the existing models.
- Classification regime of problems encountered by TEISMEs.
- Framework on how to assess the risks encountered by TEISMEs.
- Implementation of the risk assessment model.

This study will help in addressing the critical issues facing TEISMEs as they endeavour to move into new business environment and it will provide a window on the future understanding of the impacts and the risk assessment of technologies for Internet security. Moreover, the Shoniregun Risk Assessment Model has been designed to provide a one-stop shop reference for a variety of risks to which TEISMEs business operations are exposed. These risks are of great concern to the society, the governments, and businesses. Thus the study of the impacts and the risk assessment of technology for Internet security are not simple but necessary for the TEISMEs business operations, government and the Internet security professionals to control the increasing complexity, scale, changes and to adopt new strategies/systems of how to assess the Internet security risks.

3.   FUTURE WORK

It is noted that many other factors are relevant to the successful utilisation of TEI and the risk assessment of TEISME business operations. The Shoniregun risk assessment model will be developed into a software tool, and also weighting will be assigned to past, current and future identified vulnerabilities, which will incorporate both technical and non-technical factors.

REFERENCES

Dutton, H., 1999, *Society on the Line, Information Politics in the Digital Age*, Oxford University Press.

Husein, F., Gausrab, A., and Bensaci, E., 2002, *'Mobile Commerce-Business model for success'*, University of Ottwa's Excutive MBA, January, p.4; www.cata.ca/china/documents/mobilepresent.pdf (September 23, 2003)

Keen, P., Mougayar, W. and Torregrossa, T., 1998, *The Business Internet and Intranets: Manager's Guide to Key Terms and Concepts*, Boston: Harvard Business School Press, USA.

Kroll, E., 1994, *The Whole Internet: User's Guide and Catalogue*, 2nd ed., O'Reilly & Associates, Inc. USA.

LaCroix, T., and Witty, J., 2003, *'Trends in Information Security: Security Update 2003'*, www.google.com/search?hl=en&ie=UTF-8&oe=UTF8&q=Trends+in+Information+Securi ty%3 A+Security+Update+2003 (February 27, 2004).

Levi, A., 2003, 'How secure is secure Web browsing?', *Communication of the ACM*, July, p.152.

Liston, G., 2003, 'eSecurity4Britain', *Business Europe Newsfeed*, BusinessEurope.com; www. esecurity4britain.org (December 2, 2003).

Neumann, P., 2003, 'Risks in Trusting Untrustworthiness', *Communication of the ACM*, September, p.120.

Orwell, G., 1939, *Coming up for Air*. William Heinemann Ltd.

Shoniregun, C. A., and Midwood, G. P., 2004, 'An Investigation of Inevitable Sectorial Bias In E-Tailing(eT)', in the *Proceedings of Hawaii International Conference on Business, Honolulu*, Hawaii, USA, June, pp. 2657–2663.

Stamp, M., 2004, 'Risks of Manoculture', *Communication of the ACM*, March, p.120.

Wool, A., 2000, 'Why security standards sometimes fail', *Communication of the ACM*, December, p.144.

INDEX

W

X